HEALING HOMOSEXUALITY
Case Stories of Reparative Therapy

Joseph Nicolosi, PH.D.
with the assistance of Lucy Freeman

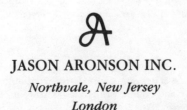

JASON ARONSON INC.

Northvale, New Jersey
London

This book was set in 11 pt. Garamond by Lind Graphics of Upper Saddle River, New Jersey, and printed and bound by Haddon Craftsmen of Scranton, Pennsylvania.

Copyright © 1993 by

10 9 8 7 6 5 4 3 2 1

Library of Congress Cataloging-in-Publication Data

Nicolosi, Joseph.
    Healing homosexuality : Case stories of reparative therapy.
    / by Joseph Nicolosi; with the assistance of Lucy Freeman.
        p. cm.
    Includes bibliographical references.
    ISBN 0-87668-340-5
    1. Gay men—Mental health—Case studies.   2. Psychotherapy—Case
studies.   3. Homosexuality, Male—Case studies.   4. Gender identity
disorders—Case studies.   5. Fathers and sons.   I. Freeman, Lucy.
II. Title.
RC558.N52   1992
616.85'834—dc20   92-16501

Manufactured in the United States of America. Jason Aronson Inc. offers books and cassettes. For information and catalog write to Jason Aronson Inc., 230 Livingston Street, Northvale, New Jersey 07647.

For

FRANK NICOLOSI

A salient father who prepared me for this work—
strong in discipline, and generous with affection.

Contents

Introduction   vii

1. Albert—The Little Boy Within   1

2. Tom—A Married Man   23

3. Father John—The Double Life   45

4. Charlie—The Search for the Masculine Self   65

5. Dan—The Angriest Man   89

6. Steve—The Seeker of Male Symbols   105

7. Edward—Agony of a Youth   119

8. Roger—"Do I Really Want to Be Here?"   145

9. Men Together—How Group Therapy Heals   177

10. How Reparative Therapy Works   211

References   225

Index   227

Introduction

Using actual transcripts from tape-recorded sessions, this book illustrates the basic principles of my previous, more technical work, *Reparative Therapy of Male Homosexuality*. In it you will find clear pictures of the way I work with clients as they face the distortions that obscure their true masculine selves.

Some tightening of verbal expression and simplifying of clinical issues were necessary to highlight the themes of the reparative process. Also, in order to preserve the privacy of the men, each case history has been woven as a composite of several clients with similar issues. No case story fits any particular client in every detail. Any resemblance to any one particular individual is purely coincidental.

At all times, I have tried to stay close to the actual words of the clients, since only they can express the struggle and frustration, the insights and satisfactions of the reparative process. By remaining faithful to my clients' verbal expression, I have attempted to convey the human drama that forms the foundation of reparative theory and therapy.

The Gay Liberation Movement has been very successful through the drama of personal testimony. When all the theoretical arguments were presented to the American Psychiatric Association in 1973, both for and against the idea of homosexuality as pathology, it was the socio-political perspective that had the most influence. Listening to some gay men's personal stories of frustration in treatment, the psychiatric association omitted homosexuality as a diagnostic category.

Now, exactly twenty years later, we are offering the opposite sort of personal testimony, that of homosexual men who have tried to accept a gay identity but were dissatisfied and then benefited from psychotherapy to help free them of the gender identity conflict that lies behind most homosexuality. While each client has his unique story, I have chosen eight men as representative of the personalities I have encountered in the twelve years during which I have treated over 200 homosexual clients. Each one of us possesses aspects of these eight men— such as the frailty of Albert, the integrity of Charlie, the rage of Dan, the narcissism of Steve, and the ambivalence of Roger.

Some readers may be surprised by the directive style of my therapeutic intervention. In part, this impression may be due to the editorial synthesis of the transcript. For brevity and clarity, some of the subtleties may have been compromised.

On the other hand, reparative therapy *does* require a more involved therapist—a "benevolent provocateur" who departs from the tradition of uninvolved, opaque analyst to become a salient male presence. The therapist must balance active challenge with warm encouragement to follow the father–son, mentor–pupil model. This is an essential principle of reparative therapy.

Reparative theory does not explain all forms of homosexuality, but only the predominant syndrome I have found in my practice.

This therapy is not for all homosexuals. Gay Affirmative Therapy may be preferred by some. Many homosexuals prefer to believe "I was born this way," thus avoiding the challenge of addressing the issues we deal with here. However, no conclusive evidence has been found for any such biological basis for homosexuality. Although some men may be temperamentally predisposed to passivity and sensitivity (and therefore the gender identity injury that can lead to homosexuality), it has always seemed to me that "I was born this way" is just another way of saying, "I just don't want to look at developmental issues that made me homosexual."

This book is written at a time of unprecedented public debate on the political, legislative, and psychotherapeutic issues of homosexuality. As we go to print, debates now rage as to gays in the military, gays in the Boy Scouts, and Colorado's and Oregon's gay rights amendments. Within every branch of the mental health professions, attempts are now being made to label reparative therapy illegal and unethical, on the grounds that it produces no change and actually does the client more harm than good.

Any psychotherapy that attempts to treat homosexuality is likely to provoke skepticism. Such a reaction is understandable, given the history of treatment. Past hostilities acted upon the homosexual in the name of treatment include electro-shock therapy, castration, and brain surgery. A great deal of social injustice has been perpetrated upon homosexuals by those who use as justification the fact that homosexuality is a developmental disorder.

It is not our intent to contribute to reactionary hostility. However, there is a distinction between science and politics, and science should not be made to bow to gay political pressure.

The National Association for Research and Therapy of Homosexuality (NARTH) has recently been formed to combat politicization of scientific and treatment issues. NARTH will defend the rights of therapists to treat dissatisfied homosexuals. Just a few months after its inception, over one hundred licensed psychiatrists, psychologists, family counselors, and social workers had already become members of this organization. NARTH will defend the right of therapists to continue to study and refine therapeutic techniques for men and women who are struggling with homosexual thoughts, feelings, and behaviors that they do not want to accept as part of their deepest identities.

I wish to express my appreciation to those earlier psychoanalytic researchers within the preoedipal, reparative drive tradition who informed my understanding of my clients, and especially to Sandor Rado, M.D., Irving Bieber, M.D., and Charles W. Socarides, M.D.

Albert—The Little Boy Within

Albert walked cautiously into my office, looking uncertain, as if he didn't quite know why he had come to see me. He gave me a quick, shy glance, then busied himself with the view of Ventura Boulevard outside the window.

"I'm happy to meet you, Mr. O'Connor." I motioned him to an armchair, and hesitantly he lowered himself into it.

I took the chair opposite Albert and looked into the pale face of a neatly dressed, somewhat plump young man. Albert looked around the room and then commented, "I like your plants. Your office looks like a botanical garden."

I've always favored the color green. On walls of forest green hang classic Italian prints of the high Renaissance era. Over the couch, there's a delicate, soft amber print of da Vinci's *Madonna and Child*. There are lush green plants in Italian terra-cotta pots, which tower over the picture windows up to the ceiling. Two massive arched bookcases of dark walnut dominate opposite walls, heavily laden with books and cascading with potted ferns and ivy. I knew Albert would appreciate the ambience. He had told me on the phone that he worked in a nursery.

His next words were, "This looks like my room at home—all this greenery." He managed a faint smile. "Wherever I am, I always try to surround myself with plants and flowers." Albert spoke in a slightly effeminate tone, with the wistful quality of a lost child.

"An old lady came into the nursery today with a dying fern," he told me. " 'You're not giving it enough light,' I said to her. 'Ferns love lots of light, as long as it's indirect sunlight.' She was so appreciative. I love to help people that way." A satisfied smile crossed his face. "I've often felt like that dying fern—not having been cared for properly."

I sensed a fragility, almost a frailness, in Albert, who seemed to have been left far behind in the dreamy world of childhood. Albert still lived with his parents in the same rambling ranch house in Malibu that he had grown up in. His only sibling, an older half-brother, had long since moved away from home and married.

During his first few sessions Albert was quiet, sometimes staring at me with earnest brown eyes as though he did not know what to say. It wasn't until weeks later that he finally felt comfortable enough to reveal his intense sexual feelings. Albert felt himself to be a little boy trapped in a man's body, torn apart by desires he didn't want to recognize. As he told me his story, the good little boy image broke down and his words became more graphic. Then his voice would become shrill, almost hysterical.

One rainy day Albert started to talk about a common aspect of the homosexual experience, which I call *alienation from the body*. Most homosexuals describe a detached fascination with their bodies, rather than the comfortable familiarity more often seen in straight men. In fact, it is that natural comfort about their bodies that often makes straights appealing to gay men. Albert's own detachment from his body was extreme. He had been raised in a home where the masculine body was considered shameful and dirty.

That day he sat down in his chair almost defiantly, reporting in his boyish voice, "It's been a bad week and I've been having lots of weird feelings. I've hardly been able to deal with them." He added, a tone of guilt in his voice, "I've been feeling horny."

"It's been a bad week because you've been feeling horny?"

"Yes. I haven't been able to sleep. I've been feeling angry without knowing why." He went on, "I realize now that my reaction to any sexual feeling is always fear, then anger."

"Your anger is a defense against the fear, but fear of what? Why do sexual feelings frighten you?"

"I don't know," he answered helplessly. Then, "I've got a lot of conflict—shame—about anything physical about me."

I nodded, listening.

"My mom always made a big deal about anything to do with the body."

"Really?"

"Yeah. When I was little, she would have a heart attack every time I would lose control and wet my bed or something. If I got sick, she would call in all the aunts and uncles and just about have a nervous breakdown. And then—she really went crazy one time when she caught me in some kind of sex play with my cousin."

"What happened?"

"My cousin started it. All those years he did it to me, I never considered sex a molestation. I never realized he was using me. In fact, I thought he was my best friend."

"How old were you when you started?" I asked.

"About 9, and my cousin was 15. He was very aggressive sexually. He always wanted to fool around. I was at that isolated stage where I wasn't connected to anyone. And," he admitted, "I'll have to say I was desperate for love. Now I have to forgive myself for accepting sex as love. I allowed my cousin to do things to me that I felt were wrong and I hated. I was crying inside but I put on this act and allowed him to do whatever the hell he felt like."

I asked, "How often did this happen?"

"Many times. Every time he came to the house over a period of years."

"What about your parents? Weren't they there?"

"I don't know where they were. I have no idea. I just felt helpless the entire time. If I didn't go along with what my cousin wanted, I wouldn't have had him as a friend. He's a born manipulator. Ever since I was little he manipulated me to get what he wanted. For a long time I went along with him externally. But inside I never really wanted it. Even while I thought I was getting love, what he did to me brought out my hatred."

Albert continued, "Finally, my cousin brushed me aside. Once or twice I got into the same kind of sexual stuff with another guy in high school, pleasing him so he'd be my friend. I don't know why I've let men manipulate me. I guess because they seemed adventurous and exciting and we did fun things together afterwards." Albert was talking about that quality of masculine adventurousness and fun missing from the life of the good little boy.

"And what did your mother do when she caught you that time with your cousin?"

"She punished me . . . hit me with a belt and locked me up for a couple of hours in the bathroom. To this day, I think that's why I'm claustrophobic. She said God destroyed a whole city because of people who did things like I did."

Albert continued, "Like I said, I've only had sex a couple of times since those incidents with my cousin. Each time, on the outside I went along with it, but on the inside I hated it. I'd think, 'I don't want it, it hurts.' Then the next moment I'd think, 'Come on, it doesn't hurt. It only hurt when you were molested as a kid.' I still feel like a kid when it comes to sex."

I explained to Albert the theory of reparative drive—that his sex play as a boy was an attempt to explore and secure his own maleness through contact with other males. Like most men who enter reparative therapy, Albert felt relief and reassurance in understanding that his homosexual behavior was an attempt to undo the alienation he felt from his own masculinity.

Albert had described to me a very isolated childhood. He had experienced very little contact with other boys, and no affirmation of his maleness from either mother or father. Feeling inadequate as a male, he had attempted to find attention, affection, and approval (the three A's, as I explained) through homosexual contact. The shame that his mother conveyed to him only deepened his sense of alienation from maleness.

"You need to feel more relaxed and accepting toward your body," I told him.

"I know," Albert said. "I feel like I'm behind the wheel of a big truck, but I don't have a driver's license. I feel like a little boy in a man's body." Then his boyish voice harshened and grew louder. "It really is hard for me, damn hard. I've always felt so goddamn guilty when I can't control myself."

"You've felt your male body was never accepted by your parents."

"I always hated shaving," he said, "and I hated being horny. In fact, I still do."

As if being heard and understood for the first time in his life, Albert freely expressed his deep and long-buried frustrations. "Any bodily function seems like a problem." His words tumbled out in a brittle staccato. "Every single time my body has to do its thing—gets horny—I feel very tense. I know I'm going to lose control and masturbate. Then I get scared someone will find out. I always try to force myself to have an orgasm before I go on a trip. I'm afraid if I stay at a friend's house or go camping with someone, I'll have a wet dream. I'm terrified that someone will see my bed is wet.

"I pray when I have to go to the men's room at the nursery that I'll be alone. Finally I walk into a stall and try to pee."

"You're pee shy," I said.

"What?" He looked at me, surprised.

"It's called 'pee shy' when a man has trouble urinating in a public restroom. It's an assertion issue that is related to being homosexual."

He fell quiet, then said, "I feel terrible that I'm a sexual human being who can feel horny and have an erection. Worse yet, that I think about having sex with men."

Then he asked tremulously, "Why do I deserve this humiliation, Dr. Nicolosi? What crime did I commit?"

"Your 'crime,' " I said, "was possessing a male body."

"I feel humiliated by my sexual feelings," he confessed. Then a wail, "I am totally, totally, totally ashamed of them.

"Masturbation," he said, "is my way of punishing my

parents for not telling me about sex. It's my way of getting back at my mom, my dad, and my church for not letting me be sexual.''

"It's a rebellion against being treated as a neutered being," I pointed out. "Your masturbation is actually an assertion."

"Yeah," Albert said, pride in his voice. "It's basically a 'fuck you' attitude about one of the most painful things in my life. It's been fifteen years that I've been in this battle. It's a way to say to my parents, 'You didn't really know or want the male *me* so I had to find a way to let *me* out.' "

"We know that homosexual men tend to masturbate more often than heterosexual men," I told him. "It's an attempt to make ritual contact with the penis . . . to connect with the lost maleness.''

Albert nodded, considering that. "I have so much fear inside," he confessed. "I'm scared to be masculine, scared to be a man. There's this thought that hounds me, 'Oh, you really can't do it!' "

His shoulders heaved in a deep sigh of discouragement. "What am I telling myself this stuff for?"

"It's a script that you follow," I said.

"Why is sexuality fine for everybody else, but not O.K. for me?" he demanded. "Why can't I grow up like everyone else?"

He answered himself as accurately as I could have, saying, "I still can't relate to my mom and my dad as an adult would. I still feel like a kid around them."

I had heard these words often enough from my homosexual clients. "I can be the good little boy with Mom and Dad, but I don't know how to be a man with them."

As the months proceeded, Albert continued to progress in small but significant ways. He was taking steps in self-assertion and was not torturing himself so much with guilt for his sexual feelings.

The case of Albert is a dramatic example of a man who could not accept his natural masculine strivings. Yet many homosexuals describe a similar background of being treated like the pure, good little boy devoid of sexual feelings. Typically this false identity is given to the boy by the mother. The father—who would be the only valid source of masculine identification—remains emotionally absent, failing to intervene or even notice his wife's excessive influence.

It is quite common to find anxious mothers in the backgrounds of homosexual men. These intrusive, hovering mothers intend the best for their sons, but are unable to recognize and respond to their authentic needs.

"I remember my mother would say positive things to me, but I knew they weren't true. Once my feelings were hurt by some boys playing kickball. I must have been about 8, and I was kind of klutzy. I remember Mom saying, 'Oh, you don't need those boys. You're too good for them anyway.' "

He laughed ruefully. "Her consolation felt good, but even then I suspected that she was lying. I went along with it because it made me feel good."

"And what was the lie?"

"That I was somehow better than those other boys, that I didn't need to play with them."

Although Albert's mother was anxious and overinvolved, she was also, paradoxically, neglectful. Albert told me how as a small child, he had had chronic ear infections. In her anxiety to do the right thing, his mother had overmedicated him with a continual supply of antibiotics. As a result, he developed a severe reaction to penicillin, which still, to this day, causes him problems.

Albert reflected, "I realize how very much my parents have taken away my dignity." He continued in a sad voice, "Only with you do I feel free to let out that ugly side of me." He stopped, then added in a bewildered tone, "It's weird. Recently I've begun to feel more and more distant from my parents. This distancing is very odd. Because in spite of everything, I still do love them."

"No, it's not odd," I reassured him. "You're facing important, long-buried issues. You're finally taking an honest look at your parents and how they affected you. You have to step back to do that."

He sighed, sounding frustrated. "I wish I could see you

every day for a month, so I could get this struggle behind me. I'd like to take a whole month off from my job and get this crap over with.''

"You can't hurry the process of self-acceptance," I told him. "It's not easy to change the way we see ourselves. It takes work, based on a gradual process of small successes."

Albert looked disappointed. "Well, at least I've gained some control over my compulsive masturbation. It's not such a battle as it used to be.

"At one time I actually went for over a year without masturbating. I prayed, I walked for miles, I did whatever I could to get my mind off the demands of my body. I felt the experience to be very humbling. But then I started to lose control again. I was constantly having homosexual fantasies. I was thinking about sex all the time. I sexualized every word that could be sexualized. Like each time I heard the word 'come,' I'd think of an orgasm. I felt very scared, and that's when I came to you."

I interrupted, "Even though you white knuckled it for one year, masturbation still controlled you. If you're going to gain control over this, you're going to have to relax and be more tolerant of yourself."

He resumed his confession. "When I got out of control, I used to talk dirty. I could write the filthiest porn stories you'd ever believe." He giggled. "Total pornography." Then added, "It was a hate response. A rage response. It wasn't me. I was always the pious St. Francis." He smiled cynically. "Caretaker of the trees and flowers."

Clearly Albert suffered from an obsessive-compulsive tendency. Being permitted in therapy to express these anxious "dirty secrets," especially to another man, served to diffuse their intensity.

He said, hysteria again taking over, "How can I change the mixed-up state I'm in, when this feels like the way I'm supposed to be? The good boy is what my parents want. Yet my body drives me in a different direction. This just seems like a built-in contradiction."

"You're certainly living that contradiction," I pointed out. "You're trying to be both the good little boy *and* someone who masturbates compulsively." I added, "And you're trying to cut yourself off from your own gender, as if you were schizophrenic."

Albert said thoughtfully, "I think a lot of my behavior is in response to all the abuse I got as a boy, just for being a boy. I remember thinking, 'Gosh, maybe if I were a girl, my parents would love me.' "

"Why would they have loved you more for being a girl?" I asked.

"I don't know." Puzzlement in his voice. "But my mom certainly couldn't handle my being a boy. As for my father—he couldn't have cared less either way, really. He had very little to do with me. When he *was* involved, he was doing something with David, his kid from his first marriage."

Albert fell silent, then brought up another barrier in his childhood. "My mom ruled the house. She was on top of my father and me all the time. Twenty-four hours a day. My dad, like me, was totally overridden by her domination. I doubt if anything he said could have had an effect on me."

His voice rose once again to the hysterical level as he said, "Why don't I remember things my father and I did together? Why are these memories so buried, so distant?" He answered himself: "Because every memory of Dad is overshadowed by Mother. Everything was dominated by her . . . completely in her power."

Then, almost a scream, "Why do you think I feel so powerless? I still *am* in her power. She stands over me this very day, in command of everything."

"You're absolutely right," I said.

He calmed down somewhat, then went on in a more normal voice, "It's not *my* life, it's *her* life I'm leading. No joke. Every single day something comes up where it's a *Mother thing* I decide I have to do. As I stand in the kitchen and bite into a cracker, I know I'd better not let crumbs fall on the linoleum. 'Crumbs will attract ants, Albert.' The hairs on the bathroom sink need to be wiped up with a tissue. 'Good boys leave the bathroom exactly as they find it, Albert.' These *Mother things* come down on me constantly."

So this was why Albert identified with the plants he cared

for. He was mothering his plants as *he* wished to be mothered—
gently and kindly.

"I realize I have a choice to make," Albert said. "I can
choose to be very nice and shallow while I'm here with you, or
I can be brutally honest and use this time for my recovery."

"That's right," I told him. "The essence of therapy is to
slowly recall the hurt. Then to slowly reclaim the true self that
the hurt has made you detached from."

"Since coming here," Albert said, almost angrily, "I've
been feeling more like a little child, more uncontrolled and
emotional. I've cried more in the last few weeks than in the last
five years."

I explained that therapy brings out buried feelings, and
this is as it should be.

"Lately I've been at the point where I let my emotions take
over . . . thanks to you," Albert said sharply.

I wasn't sure whether I heard sarcasm, but decided not to
question him. "How do you feel when you cry?" I asked him.

"Ashamed, of course. When I was a small boy, I made a
vow not to cry and I'd always stuck to it." His voice sounded
proud. "But this crying comes from really deep inside. It comes
from a real hurt . . . a deep wound, like I was torn away too
early, separated from something for which I still feel a deep
yearning."

"You can still come back to that something for which you
feel a deep yearning," I told him.

"How will I do that?"

"Through insight, then through new relationships."

"New relationships?"

"Yes. Because intellectual understanding alone doesn't
really change people."

"What does?" Albert asked thoughtfully.

"New experiences change people. You are not as yet
experiencing nonsexual intimacy with a man. That's the next
challenge for you to work on."

Albert always appeared regularly for his hour. He was
never even a second late, as though he considered each moment precious. One day he told me—in what was becoming a

firmer, more assertive tone—''I've started making major break-throughs here. Big bolts of lightning, shocks of awareness. I can see that I've been making progress.''

One day he announced something he had not told me about. He said, "It was my mother who really encouraged me to seek therapy. She could see I was lonely and unhappy, so she thought it might help if I spoke to someone. I don't earn much at the nursery, so she and Dad are giving me money to come."

I was surprised. She had not sounded like a woman who wished her son to learn more about his true self. Of course, she didn't know the real issues he was dealing with.

"That was very understanding of both your parents," I said.

"It's really my mom," he corrected. "Dad is just going along with her decision."

Mindful that—as they say in Hollywood—there's no such thing as a free lunch, I asked, "Well, how do you feel about your parents paying for your therapy?" My concern was that Albert might feel compromised by their generosity.

"Fine!" he said emphatically. "They got me into this mess, so they can get me out of it!"

This made sense, given Albert's circumstances. Accepting his answer for the time being, I made a note to be on the lookout for any parental intrusions.

"Recently I've been finding myself looking more at men," Albert told me. "I do a lot of mental window shopping, which only makes me feel worse. I went to the mall last night and I felt attracted to this guy I saw, about my age—but I had both this magnetic pull toward him, and this need to push away from him."

"I think the reason you find yourself looking at other men," I said, "is that you don't yet have a fitting male picture inside you and so you keep searching for that image of maleness on the outside."

Albert nodded. "So much of the attraction feels like curiosity, just wanting to know what guys are like!" There was a sound of desperation in his voice.

"But what part of you felt like pulling away?

"The part that feels a fear of men." I heard Albert's

same-sex ambivalence, so characteristic of the homosexual condition. Even while eroticizing men he felt uncomfortable around them.

Then Albert seemed to feel the need to flee a confrontation with his painful ambivalence. He returned instead to a discussion of his blissful babyhood. I decided to go with it.

"I wish I could forget all the conflicts of sex and adulthood," he was saying. "I wish I could return to the love I felt so freely when I was a baby and happy just existing. Later, the realities of life turned everything into a bad dream."

"Exactly what was it that turned such a happy existence so sour?" I asked.

Following another short silence Albert said, "I think when I lost that deep sense of bonding with my mother, the fear started. When I had outgrown Mother, there was no adult identity that fit me. I had this sense that I was just suspended, abandoned."

"In some ways, you were. At a critical period in your development—the *gender identity phase*—you had to individuate yourself from your mother and develop a masculine identification through your father. It was your father who personified the demands of the outside world. As Freud said, the father personifies The Reality Principle. But you never received the necessary support from him, or any other masculine figure."

Albert suddenly changed the subject, again retreating to the more pleasant subject of his dreamy childhood. "I used to draw a lot. I was a good artist. All the pictures were feminine things—roses, colorful birds, ballerina dancers in tutus. Not soldiers or cars but images of beauty. I never drew men. I didn't have a good picture in my mind of men. I really wasn't sure what a man should look like.

"If I tried to draw the Holy Family the baby would look normal—sort of a generic baby face. But I'd spend the most time creating the Blessed Mother. The folds and creases of her veil, her hair, her nose, her lips. I'd try hard to create the ultimate, most beautiful Madonna. When it came to St. Joseph, I wouldn't have a clue. I simply couldn't draw his face.

"Then when I was 11 or 12 I recall trying to draw pornographic pictures and feeling very unsatisfied because I couldn't capture the male. It disturbed me because I would draw men who looked feminine. I tried to draw a male pornographic picture, but it always ended up looking like the Madonna.''

Feigning a pious tone, I said, ''Certainly the Madonna was more pleasing to God than pornography.''

''Probably.'' Albert laughed. ''But you know, maybe this is why some gay men are into designing women's fashions . . . they still look on their mothers as the Madonna.'' He added, ''My mother always managed to mix me up in my perception of people. You might say she mixed me up in deciding where she ended, and I started.

''Even now, when I'm talking with a woman customer at the nursery and I'm connecting with her . . . I feel like her, the same as her. It feels like two women chatting. And I don't want that. It reminds me of when I was a teenager and I took a girlfriend to Dairy Queen. On the outside it looked just like it was boy friend–girl friend, but on the inside I felt we were the same. Ugh! I hate that! When I think back on it, it feels disgusting!''

I was happy to hear Albert describe his discomfort, knowing his individuation from the feminine was now well underway.

''You know,'' Albert said, ''there are times you want to be by yourself. For your manhood.

''I've been trying to firm up my body, so I've put weights in my garage where I exercise. When I get sweaty, I strip down to my underwear. So then my mother walks into the room and says, 'Oh, great! Let's exercise together!'

''I tell her, 'but I don't want us to exercise together.' There I am sweating and heaving weights in my jockey shorts, but none of that seems to faze her.

''Mom and I both belong to the same health club, and she wants me to go along with her. She grew up in a family that was always together,'' Albert said. ''That's her interpretation of the way things should be—togetherness.''

''Maybe you should explain yourself to her,'' I said. ''She was never a young man. She doesn't know how you feel.''

Albert's complaint about his parents was rather typical of male homosexuals: as a boy, he never got enough of the father, but he had too much of the mother. While he resented father's absence in his life, he resented mother's intrusiveness and interference. Father never empowered, and mother sapped what power he had. I urged him, "Explain to your mother what you're trying to accomplish for yourself."

In a discouraged tone, Albert said, "The trouble is I don't know how to tell her." He sounded puzzled. "I just don't think she hears me. We always end up arguing."

"It takes your energy away," I commented.

"That says it. Nobody can sap my energy like my mom."

I repeated, "Nobody can take your masculine energy away like your mom."

Albert heaved a mighty sigh, sadness on his face as he allowed himself to delve into his hidden thoughts.

I decided to try for an associated idea. "And this is why you're fearful of getting close to women."

"Is it?" The voice of a surprised child.

"Yes. Because you don't trust women. You have platonic girlfriends, but when you start to feel closer to a woman, you fear you'll lose control to her. You fear she'll take away your personal power like your mom."

Then I asked, "Can you talk to your mother and tell her how you feel when you're with her?"

"She doesn't understand me," he said quietly but firmly. "If I try to explain my need for independence she'll feel rejected and insulted."

"Is there anything you feel ready to tell her?"

"About some of the deficits, the needs."

"Fine," I agreed. "That is the essence of the homosexual problem, anyway. Speak to her in terms of wanting to develop a more solid sense of your masculinity."

Albert talked on. "For the past two weeks I have been riding my bike with Jack, a guy I met at my bike club. We do ten miles on the Coast Highway before I go to the nursery."

"Great. This is a guy you enjoy being with?"

"Yeah. I get up in the morning and it's not like this

wimpy, drag-me-out-of-bed feeling. I *like* to get up early, just when it starts getting light and the coast air is still cool.

"Jack and I get along really well, and the great part is that I don't worry what he thinks about me. But I'm always still a bit timid about bike riding. I worry someone else might be watching me and think, 'Oh, that guy's just a faggot.' I get kind of scared sometimes that I might hit a rock and fall on my ass. But as soon as I get warmed up the thought vanishes. I tell myself, 'Just get into what you're doing.' And when I stop watching myself, and stop thinking about how I look—I get into that feeling of power."

"You're making fine progress. You have a fire going inside of you, and the challenge now is to keep it going. After you get a nice fire going, it starts to burn itself out if you don't put another log on it.

"The fire is your developmental momentum and the logs are new challenges. One log will be the challenge of talking to your mother. Still another can be doing those long-distance bike rides. Yet another log will be maintaining those straight male friendships. These are the things that keep the fire going."

A few months later Albert entered my office and spoke excitedly. "The last time I saw you something happened that was absolutely incredible." His voice was much stronger now. Even in his excitement, it had lost that hysterical ring. He no longer avoided meeting my gaze, but addressed me directly.

"Last session I felt weak and lonely. I guess I was feeling sorry for myself. But you gave me hell. You challenged me and I gotta admit it hurt. Then, four nights later, Steve from our group called me up and he also gave me hell."

"Did he?" I was pleasantly surprised that Steve could make such a decisive intervention.

"He lit into me. Like he stabbed me again and again. He said, 'You've got to really get out there and fight.' He told me to stop bitching and grow up. I was insulted, and I said, 'What do you mean? I can't believe you, Steve.' But he just went on, 'You're having the world's greatest pity party for Albert O'Connor. Don't you remember that book by Dr. van den

Aardweg? Stop taking yourself so fuckin' seriously. If you want to get out of that self-pity, first exaggerate it, then laugh at it.' What Steve said hurt.''

He sighed. "Then sure enough, after I hung up I really felt low. I felt betrayed. I'd gotten a double whammy. First you, then him. I thought, 'Shit!' Then I started thinking. Steve was right on the mark. Both of you are. You're both saying the same thing.

"And ever since then when I feel the self-pity coming on, I purposely blow it out of proportion almost ridiculously, and then laugh my ass off.''

He continued, "I've told you I've had very little temptation recently to get into those compulsive masturbation marathons. I feel like I'm really starting to understand now what it's all about.''

"Things are happening.'' I was pleased at his progress. "It's incredible, so freeing! I'm feeling alive for the first time in my life.''

Albert then went on to tell me about his bicycling club. He said, "I felt sort of wimpy at first next to those long-distance racers, but I just went with it. Last week I noticed this girl who came on one of the club rides. She's not a raving beauty by any means—she's got some pimples on her face. But there was something about her personality that turned me on. It wasn't sexual, but for the first time I didn't feel I was just one of the girls. I felt like myself, in my own way.''

Recalling his feelings about the girl led to associations about his body and he went on. "Even right now, just sitting here, I feel no timidity about my body.''

"Why?'' I asked.

"This very moment I feel at ease doing anything with my hands.'' He waved his right hand in the air, then asked, "Is my hand motion a faggot motion . . . you know, effeminate? Either way, it doesn't bother me, whatever you might call it.''

"It's just something moving—a hand,'' I said. Then added, "A lot of good stuff is happening to you.''

For the first time in the session he looked worried. He said, "But of course, you've seen me up like this before, and then you've seen me crash.''

"Yes," I said. "So if you crash, so what? There may be a lot of downs but that's not important. What is important is learning from your setbacks, and reducing your recovery time."

"What do you mean, 'recovery time'?"

I explained, "It's the time between the setback and your return to momentum. Refusing to wallow in self-defeat is essential."

"When I'm in that momentum, I feel like I've been set free." He looked happier. "Just being here, I feel like I'm the real me."

"This *is* the real you," I said. "The you who is spontaneous, equal, talking frankly and directly and intimately with another man. The you who does not need to romanticize or envy other men."

I thought, little by little Albert *is* growing freer.

At the following session Albert brought up an important topic. Right after he sat down, he told me, "I remember that my mom was always really uptight, tense, nervous, anxious—especially about my health. She was really obsessed. Partly because when she was a child her own health was pretty frail.

"My mother had headaches really bad when she was a kid. I think that the panic she felt from those headaches she conveyed to me. As a child I had very bad stomachaches. She panicked about them. It was like the end of the world when those stomachaches hit. She would always be pouring gingerale down me, or tea, and she'd keep me home from school for a week.

"Any sniffle was exaggerated out of proportion into this big horror. My mother never saw illness or aches as natural. It was as if our family had committed some ghastly crime and was being punished for it by illness. I think this is why bike riding is so important to me. I want to push against this fragile body image.

"Whenever I experienced success it was like walking on a tightrope. I knew I could fall any minute, so I never enjoyed it. My mother always reminded me I might end up on my ass, so I never felt good, or happy, or excited."

Albert's no-win predicament reminded me of the significance of Dr. Althea Horner's concept of intrinsic power, which she defines with the motto: "I am," "I can," and "I will." One's worthiness of this power is conveyed by the parents. The boy's sense of power is essentially linked to his maleness. It is through his masculinity that he discovers this intrinsic power. So if he does not feel fully masculine, he will always feel in some way unempowered.

Albert said, "Not only have I been getting up early to bike ride, but today I had the desire to go out and play basketball. I never did this as a child. After all these years I still wanted to get the feel of that ball in my hand and how it feels to sink it in a basket. I didn't care if I looked like an amateur."

I pointed out, "We know that genuine transformation is happening when we discover many little manifestations of change. Together they all point to one thing—that something is truly changing. Something within you is really happening."

"I hear people saying that homosexuals shouldn't try to change," Albert said, irritation in his voice. "That a homosexual man has to follow his feelings, whether or not he likes them." His tone because adamant, "But who are they to say I shouldn't try to change? I never felt right living in the old way. Little by little, I'm becoming a different person. I'm finally becoming me."

The day Albert left therapy was almost three years from the day he had first entered my office. His speech was far more assured. Gone was the occasional hysterical outburst. He smiled more often and talked of one day owning his own nursery.

Some mothers, like Albert's, become too invested in their sons being available to them, at the cost of the boy's masculine individuation. They are so caught up in their own narcissistic needs that they never see their sons' own needs. Robert Bly has said: "Women make boys, but only men can make men." There had been no man to make Albert, for his father had never been strong enough to disrupt the unhealthy mother–son closeness. Albert had had to survive emotionally with a father who did not know how to relate to him. To do so, he had developed a self-protective detachment from men. Originated by the British psychoanalyst John Bowlby, the term *detached defensiveness* was adapted to homosexuality by psychologist Elizabeth Moberly. It describes a child's infantile, self-protective maneuver against emotional hurt.

Albert's hurtful relationship with his father resulted in just such a defensive detachment. Trauma (through neglect, abuse, or hostility) creates fear, which is the basis of alienation. When we are imprisoned by fear, we remain alienated from those who have caused it. Albert's defensive detachment was carried over to his relationship with other males. Emotionally distanced from males and maleness, he romanticized them. They represented the part of himself he had not claimed.

Although he falls in love with other men and is intimate with them sexually, the homosexual never allows himself to identify with maleness. He admires it, he romanticizes it, and he may even wear the male role superficially, but there remains an inner resistance to claiming his full masculine identity. This resistance of defensive detachment emerges in male relationships in the form of criticalness, fault-finding, and promiscuity. The homosexual may love other men, but there is also hostility and fear of them. Thus his relationships with males are invariably ambivalent.

Only in long-term male relationships that are intimate, accepting, honest, and nonsexual can the homosexual man begin to resolve the defensive detachment that causes this same-sex ambivalence. Albert had begun to resolve this detachment through relationships with many men: myself, men at work, and men in group.

Every one of us, man and woman, is driven by the power of romantic love. It is one of nature's ways of making sure the human race endures. Infatuations gain their power from our unconscious drive to become a complete human being. In heterosexuals this strong drive brings together the male and female through the longing for one another. But in homosexuals the drive is an attempt to fulfill a deficit in wholeness of the original gender. Thus, two men can never take in each other in a full and open manner. There is not only a natural anatomical unsuitability, but an inherent psychological insufficiency. Both partners come to the relationship with the same deficit, as each symbolically seeks fulfillment of his original gender.

About one year later, Albert telephoned me for a tune-up, as we called it. Since his termination, he had joined an ex-gay support group, which he told me had been very helpful. With this group, he had continued to explore his past relationship with his parents in order to understand their continuing impact on his life.

Albert told me about a girlfriend, Helene, whom he had met at the nursery. "She loves African violets," he told me enthusiastically. They had been dating steadily for six months.

Before I could ask, Albert said, "Yeah, she knows all about everything." He described Helene as "the best friend I've ever had in my life. I can tell her anything on my mind, and she's there supporting me." He said their relationship was "physical but not yet sexual."

Albert's description of his feelings for Helene was not unusual for a man with a homosexual background. It is common for such men to proceed slowly toward sexual intimacy with a woman. Their relationships often develop in three phases—friendship, then affection, then expression of that affection through sexuality. This is in contrast to the heterosexual man, who is first sexually attracted to the woman, then gets to know her as a friend.

Many men with a homosexual background expect to find themselves attracted to women in the manner of straight men. However their approach to women may always be different. Ex-gay men need to be assured that because of their history, they may take a different path—friendship first, sex second—to the same goal.

About his homosexual attractions, Albert said, "It's very different from what it's been in the past. Now, because of Helene, I've made it my goal to fully claim the heterosexuality that I never developed. And I feel accountable in our relationship. . . . It's not just me any more, it's Helene and me. And so, whenever those old attractions rise up, I say, 'What's going on here?' Then I can track those feelings for other men back to feelings about myself, such as 'I'm afraid,' 'I'm stressed,' or whatever."

Continuing, Albert told me, "I understand these attractions as representing something that I did not receive as a kid—something I deserved. And I'm getting what I need more and more through my support group and opening up to other guys, which has been a wonderful thing for me."

Then I asked, "So, does this mean that your attractions are not completely gone?"

In an unusually decisive tone Albert answered, "I believe they may always come back, now and then—just because of the depth of the deprivation. I see my growth as a continual process. Getting love and support from Helene and the guys in my support group makes all the difference."

As he spoke on, Albert at last seemed to grasp the concept of the false self—the identity structure that lies behind the gay self-label. "I continue to understand my upbringing and its effects on me in the present. The messages I bought into as a little kid were, 'You're weak, you're not macho, you're this little nothing.' In adolescence that got translated into 'You must be gay.' Now I'm rejecting that false identity others tried to impose—an identity that others made me believe was me. No, I'm not gay. Now, I'm determined to *be* the man I want to be—not to fall in love with him."

2

Tom—A Married Man

Thomas James walked into my Encino office—a strikingly handsome man, about six feet tall. His face was smooth, tan, well-scrubbed and moisturized; his eyes were an intense blue that matched the pastel color of his polo shirt. He was wearing crisp chino pants and polished brown loafers.

I offered my hand and gave him a smile. Tom returned my greeting with a quick, forceful handshake, then dropped his lanky frame into the tapestry-print chair toward which I had motioned him.

As he settled into his seat, his eyes swept over the room as if to size it up. Then, evidently having satisfied his curiosity, he drew a pack of Camels from his jacket pocket, leaned forward, and began.

"First, Dr. Nicolosi, let me give you the facts. I'm 40 years old. I've been married fifteen years and have two children, a boy and a girl, 10 and 7.

"I own West Valley Sporting Goods and, to put it bluntly, I've done very well for myself in the ten years I've been in business."

He lit a cigarette, puffed impatiently on it, and set it down in the ashtray.

"My wife Cynthia and I separated a few months ago. I was in a relationship with a young kid, Andy, who worked for me at the store. He's 24." He laughed. "I could be his father.

"When Cynthia found out, she was furious. She said, 'I want you packed and out of this house today.' "

"How long ago was that?" I asked.

"Six months ago. I walked out on my wife and children to live this awful life alone."

There was silence, then he said, "Doc, I really don't like my wife. She's a fine mother to our children, but she's very negative about me, and everything that pertains to me. We're so different. . . . I'm ambitious and outgoing, she's caught up in the house and the children. And she controls everything in the household. I feel like the low man on the totem pole at home."

I nodded. "So tell me, how did she find out about your relationship with Andy?"

"One Saturday night, I felt I had to get out of the house. I was restless—like I so often am—so I called Andy and arranged to meet him at a gay bar we often went to.

"On my way out the door, Cynthia stopped me and wanted to know where I was headed. For the first time, I don't know why, I just impulsively blurted out the whole story. I told her that I was gay, that I was going to see my lover.

"She was stunned. She said, 'In all the years we've been together, why didn't you ever tell me?' At first I didn't know what to say. Then I confessed, 'I guess because I thought I could have my life both ways.'

"Then I told her that it was Andy who had been my lover. The kid had been sort of a family friend. Because his folks live out of town, we had had him to the house last Thanksgiving and Christmas.

"When she heard that my lover was Andy, Cynthia was really furious. She said, 'You mean, you were having sex behind my back with that *boy* while I was entertaining him?' "

Tom paused a moment, reached for his cigarette, and stretched back on the couch. Looking around the room, puffing on his cigarette and exhaling deeply, he seemed to welcome a moment of quiet.

Then he got to the heart of what was bothering him. "I really thought I would be happier away from home. No demands from anyone . . . only myself to answer to. But since I left my family I've felt worthless, empty."

He shook his head sadly. "Sex with a man is a lonely lay. Male-on-male relationships don't last, and part of the reason is the dishonesty in these relationships. Too much deception and cheating going on. That's my biggest fear about being gay. Ending up alone, not having someone to come home to."

His next words were sudden and sharp, as if reprimanding himself. "I don't know why I'm here, Dr. Nicolosi. All I know is that I don't like what I've done with my life. I've lied to my wife, lied to my mother. The last three men came and went. Even Andy left me, and now I'm by myself, completely. I've lost my kids. . . . Now, I'm not even comfortable visiting them. I haven't got any real home. When I go back to the house to see my kids, I wonder, 'Has my wife told our friends about me, about my homosexuality?' I'm terribly depressed, and I don't know where this new life is leading me."

More silence. Then with a shrug of his broad shoulders, he said, "I've lived a lie so long, I don't know if I can be cured. Maybe I don't even want to be cured. I go back and forth, back and forth. Sometimes I think there just isn't an answer."

"Then you must have heard that I help homosexual men change their sexuality."

He nodded. "I've heard that your work is pretty much out of the mainstream. That there are a lot of gay therapists who don't like what you're doing. But I like what I've heard about you, so that's why I'm here."

"Good." I was pleased that he understood my approach from the outset. "Because if you want help divorcing your wife and making a life with your gay lover, I don't do that. On the other hand, if you want to understand *why* you are homosexual and what you can do to change that, we can begin right now."

Tom looked at me appreciatively and laughed. "I like your approach. You don't waste any time, do you?" He drew deeply on the cigarette and set it down in the ashtray. "Where do I begin?"

"Tell me what I need to know to help you."

The following week Tom walked into the room looking serious and preoccupied. Hardly pausing to greet me, he continued with last week's recitation of his history. As he told me about himself, it became apparent that Tom was somewhat different from most of the homosexual men who come to my office. Like most clients, Tom described a deep grievance against his father. Like them, he felt an internal sense of inadequacy as a man. However, Tom showed no external evidence of gender identity deficit. He did not have assertion problems with other men, and he dealt forcefully with others in conducting business. He was generally energetic in pursuing what he wanted. He appeared extroverted and confident. Yet underneath, he still had the emotional fragility of so many other homosexual clients.

Tom did not, however, conduct his personal relationships the way he conducted his business relationships. With loved ones, he tended to become passive, as he did in his relation-ships with Cynthia, Andy, and his children. This compliance was part of a relational pattern begun in early boyhood.

Tom told me about his problems in male relationships. "I've had some wonderful men reach out to me and try to be my friend, but once they get too close I say, 'Back off!' I like it better when I can hold them at arms' length, when they're younger, or less powerful, and I can control them." With an ironic laugh, "I guess that's why I feel so free at work—I'm the boss there.

"But then, I just don't know," he continued. "As much as I need that feeling of being in control, something seems to get *out* of control as soon as sex becomes a part of things. You know," he added, "once you sexualize your feelings for a man you can never really be friends. It's a love 'em and leave 'em life." His voice became serious. "I figure therapy is the only intimacy I will ever have with another man without sexualizing the relationship."

"That's an excellent insight," I said. "In fact that's the

essence of reparative therapy—learning how to build intimate, nonsexual male relationships. Because like most homosexuals, you have much more than just a sexual problem. You *need something* from other men. What are those basic needs you seek to gratify in a male relationship?''

He thought a minute, then answered abruptly, ''I need to be liked.'' His voice was earnest, wanting me to understand the intensity of his need. ''I get a special feeling of excitement from that male attention. There's something that comes alive inside me when I'm having sex with a man.'' Searching for words, he continued, ''There's a moment of electricity, of power from that charge of maleness that comes across to me.''

I thought it was time to explain to Tom how homosexual behavior is evidence of the reparative drive to satisfy three unfulfilled emotional needs, needs never met in the relationship with father—affection, attention, and approval. As with most extroverted types, Tom most craved attention. ''As a boy I never seemed to have male friends, for reasons that may well have been circumstantial. Boys my age always seemed to move away, and I always seemed to end up alone with my sisters. Somehow I've always felt cheated out of boy-friends.''

I urged him to tell me more about his childhood.

''So much of my childhood is a blur. I don't even recall my parents' relationship to me very well, or much of what happened in my early years. It's mostly a blank.''

''Can you remember anything?'' I asked.

He paused, then said off-handedly, ''My father promised to give me a rabbit one time but never did. My sister promised to take me to a carnival one time but then forgot. I never felt much joy as I grew up.''

''What else?''

He thought a moment, then recalled, ''When I was 10 years old, I was really flattered when the older boy next door started asking me along to his baseball games. Later, he got me involved in sexual games and things.''

''That's interesting,'' I remarked.

''What's interesting?''

''That the only memories you can come up with are about betrayal.''

Tom laughed bitterly. "It must be my frame of mind, because of my breakup with Andy." I heard him trying to minimize the importance of my interpretation, and told him I disagreed that this was behind the particular collection of memories. In fact, disappointment and betrayal in childhood is a repeated theme in the lives of my clients. In adulthood, there remains a fear of feeling vulnerable.

I asked, "Did you feel as you grew up that you somehow had to compromise your identity? Did your mother or father somehow convey to you that in order to receive their love or attention you had to be different for their sake?"

A questioning expression crossed those penetrating blue eyes. "I can't really say. I don't recall their relationship to me or what happened in my childhood. It's mostly a blank."

I wasn't surprised. Used children typically have hazy childhood memories, since their true selves were long ago buried in favor of the false selves they've learned to adopt. I knew that as Tom came to trust me more, the memories would flow. But it was clear that for now he needed simply to continue talking, so I decided not to pursue this particular issue. Changing the subject, I asked, "Have you had a lot of exposure to the gay lifestyle?"

"Quite a bit," he said. "I've experienced as many facets of it as I possibly could—the trendy bars, the weekend trips to Castro Street in San Francisco. I even spent a week on a gay cruise ship once—I told Cynthia I had to go away on business. I was curious, I wanted to try everything."

"What have you seen? What have you come away with?"

"Well, from my experience, I found there's a lot of unhappiness. In the heterosexual world, there's more that seems to keep people faithful. The gay world has too many social and sexual opportunities. And gays don't have the social support of marriage."

I asked, "Do you see any inherent problem in male relationships? Or is it social stigma that makes monogamous gay relationships so hard to sustain?"

I pressed Tom to make this distinction. A man who thinks the unhappiness in gay relationships is solely due to society's stigma will not be a candidate for reparative therapy. He must be driven by a deep, personal dissatisfaction with gay life.

"There is something inherently difficult about gay relationships," Tom said, conceding, "It's probably more than society's judgment." Then he admitted, "It's about two men together."

Tom proceeded to share some insights that only a man who had lived a double life could offer. "Men have a tendency to be less giving, not to give as willingly and spontaneously as women do. Women seem secure enough to place themselves in a secondary role. Often they think of their man ahead of themselves. They seem less burdened by their egos."

He continued, "Men have a tendency to be frightened of intimacy."

"Do you think the depth of intimacy between two men can ever go as deeply as that between a man and a woman?" I asked.

His answer got to the real difference. "I don't think so. Because women bring something complementary to the relationship. They balance out the qualities the man brings to it."

I pointed out to him that he was in a good position to know since he had experienced both. Then I asked, "Can you describe how sex between men is different from sex between men and women?"

"The sexual experience with men is more . . ." he searched for the word, " . . . more *sexual*. This sounds strange to say, but sex with women is more tame, more inhibited. There is more raw animal turn-on with a man, while with a woman it's more emotional, more of a total experience."

He went on, "There's another big difference. In many, if not most, gay experiences, the sex starts right at the beginning. Two men together tend to want sex immediately."

"And then what happens?" I asked.

"From my experience, the sexual aspect of the relationship doesn't generally maintain itself. In most cases the relationship fizzles out quickly."

"That seems to support a lot of the research on gay relationships," I said. Then I asked, "How sexually involved have you been with men?"

"Sex with men really dominated my thoughts when I was much younger. It started when my older brother had sex with me when I was 8. Then there was the kid next door on and off for about a year. After that, there were two guys in high school, then a couple in college. Then I fell in love with Cynthia, and I was faithful to her for five years, until our daughter was born. It was shortly after that that Andy came into my life."

It is significant that Tom remained faithful to his wife until the first child was born. It is a common pattern for a husband's homosexual behavior to surface as a problem when the wife becomes pregnant with the first child. This has to do with the need to flee from responsibilities, in this instance, the impending responsibility of parenthood. The man struggling with homosexual impulses feels overwhelmed by the demands of his role as husband and father. These feelings seem to be part of a more general tendency to avoid relational responsibility, which is a frequently seen problem among men struggling with homosexuality.

The prevalence of this pattern suggests very convincingly that the homosexual condition is not so much a problem of sexual orientation as one of relational immaturity. It is often necessary to foster such a client's ability to grow into mature relational self-giving.

What Tom said next confirmed my opinion. "Throughout my relationship with Andy, I also had affairs with other men. At times, especially when Andy and I weren't getting along, sex became an obsession."

"How were you able to have sex with strange guys while you were in a relationship with Andy?"

He shrugged his shoulders. "I don't know," he said unhappily. "Any more than I know why I was having sex with Andy while I was married to Cynthia."

He thought for a moment, then continued, "At home I don't feel like I'm important. With my lovers, I can feel like I'm in charge of things. I just somehow feel uncomfortable with Cynthia.

"But you know," he reconsidered, "in spite of everything, I still rely on Cynthia. After she threw me out of the house, Andy and I shared an apartment. Then Andy moved out—he couldn't handle my emotionality, my mood swings. I was so depressed that I called Cynthia to cry on her shoulder."

"Just a minute," I broke in. "Let me be sure I understand. You expected Cynthia to *comfort* you when Andy left you?"

He nodded like a little boy.

"Wasn't that a little . . . unrealistic?" I asked. "You were having an affair with a young guy from work—a family friend— behind your wife's back. He leaves you, and you expect her to comfort you?"

"I didn't know what to do, who to turn to," he said. "I guess at that moment I was just too tormented, in a crisis." He thought for a moment. "Now that you mention it . . . I can't believe I hurt her so badly. Because I *do* love her. There is a reason I've stayed with her in the marriage. We've been good friends for eighteen years."

Tom's narcissism was obvious to me, but there was a further possibility. "Do you think your insensitivity bordered on hostility?"

Tom looked at me, puzzled. He remained silent for what seemed a long while, and then said, "When I think back, I guess it's pretty obvious."

"Why do you think you hurt her—besides your self-absorption in your own anguish?"

"Well, as you know, I just can't be myself with Cynthia. When I set foot in her home, I become a nothing. It's *her* house, *her* home. So, yes—maybe I was giving her a taste of the treatment I got from Andy."

In Tom's answer I heard repeated a common complaint of many of my married homosexual men—feelings of a loss of control to their wives, with an inevitable resentment toward them.

He fell quiet again and I remained silent. Then he said, in a proud tone, "I did pretty well until I met Andy. That is, until he turned the tables on me, got the better of me—made the old man look like a fool."

I could see that Tom had been propelled into therapy by this acute pain. His double life no longer worked. It had been this trauma that had led him to reflect on the life he had been living.

I wanted to get back to what Tom had been saying earlier. "Tell me about how you feel at home with Cynthia."

"I just have never felt appreciated by her," he said. "And I always feel a restlessness there. Like I have to get out. Do something crazy. Find some excitement.

"Why," he continued, "all of my life, have I felt so driven? So restless and anxious? I'm never satisfied with anything for very long."

This is something I hear repeatedly in the lives of homosexuals. They feel out of control, their needs unrecognized by others, and find themselves trapped behind a compliant, cooperative facade. Their way of getting release from this false self of compliance is to act out sexually. Boredom, anxiety, and depression are the moods most often identified as prompting homosexual behavior. When the affair ends, they return to what psychiatrist Harry Gershman called their "petrified patterns of existence."

Gay apologists argue that the dissatisfactions of these men arise from the unnatural married lifestyle they are forced to adopt. But I am convinced that the problem is much more than that of forced social conformity. Homosexuals who are married are not the only ones troubled by this roller-coaster ride of feelings. I have observed this same pattern of fluctuation—helpless dissatisfaction alternating with homoerotic euphoria—in the lives of homosexuals who are in gay relationships.

Tom's mood suddenly changed and his voice became sharp. "I've lived a lie so long, I don't know if I *can* change. It all seems like a hopeless pattern. I've thought of killing myself sometimes, when I hit bottom in the cycle."

He was quiet after this, and then, with a shrug of his broad shoulders, he said, "Maybe God made me what I am. If I'm gay, God made me gay. But for heaven's sake, why did He have to give me a good wife and children?"

Here I heard the ebb and flow of true desperation mixed with overdramatization. I decided not to comment on the latter, lest I be misunderstood as nonempathic to the former. I knew that the phrase "I was born gay" is shorthand for "I don't want to look at the early childhood experiences that caused me to become homosexual." "There is no gay gene," I told him. "This is a matter of identity."

One day a few months later, Tom came bounding into the office and plopped himself down in the chair. He was in a chatty mood and seemed happy to be with me.

"A few years ago I was in therapy with a gay psychologist. I was struggling with my gayness, my self-image, and my marriage. Cynthia and I weren't getting along very well. I had moved out a couple of times. I wanted to leave her. I was bored. The only thing that kept me in there was that I loved my kids. I was having outrageous flings with guys and Andy was driving me crazy.

"Although the psychologist didn't actively push me toward the lifestyle, he never really discouraged me either. He was quiet and commented very little—" Tom flashed a quick smile, "not like you.

"Honestly I would have liked a little more direction from him. Like, 'Hey, let's get your life in order, let's start doing what's right, let's stop some of this crazy philandering.' I guess he thought I'd work my way through. I didn't."

"How did your therapy end?" I asked.

"It ended abruptly on my daughter's sixth birthday during one of my separations from Cynthia. I was upset and frustrated at losing my family and being told by the therapist, 'You're not losing your family. If you go with your lover, you can still see your children.' I kept thinking, 'But gee, I'm not there at three o'clock in the morning when the kids wake up and cry for their daddy.' "

"You *were* losing your family," I agreed.

"They talk about 'quality time,' " he went on, "yet I say, 'Hey, there's quantity time, too.' On my daughter's birthday I finally just turned to this shrink and said, 'Hey, you can't possibly relate to what I'm going through. I'm a married man, I have an involvement with another man, and my daughter is 6 years old today. Do you know what that really means? Can you possibly understand the feelings that are going on inside of me?' I told him I was through with being gay, if this was the price I'd have to pay."

"You felt he couldn't relate to you?"

"Yeah, I think I frustrated him. He couldn't understand me."

At that moment Tom sat up, looked at me directly, and said, "I'm going to have to find the best way to work within this situation. I will probably always have homosexual attractions; you've warned me about that. But I've also come to realize there's a choice, an act of will involved. I still would like to have sex with men, but the price is just too high. My marriage and my kids are just too important.''

At last, Tom was committing himself completely to overcoming his male attractions. I knew it was a solution the Gay Rights Movement would disdain. They would say it was dishonesty with one's true self, hypocrisy—that sort of rhetoric. I had great respect for Tom James; he had chosen the tough road, yet I believe it was the right one.

Tom came twice a week, regularly. Fighting the late afternoon Los Angeles freeway traffic, he somehow managed to appear punctually for his sessions. Usually he arrived eager to talk, but one day he shuffled in disconsolately and collapsed into his usual chair.

"I've got to do something about my life. I still haven't any real home and I'm staying in a dumpy hotel. I'm lonely and I'm really depressed.''

Tom obviously had to have some clear direction. I asked, "Have you ever had a close male friendship?''

"I think I have," he said. But as Tom recounted his friendships, it became clear that although he had many acquaintances, he had no real friends. Although he was outgoing, friendly, extroverted, even entertaining, no one really knew him. He tended to hide behind a gregarious facade.

I said, "You've never had a comfortable, trusting friendship with a man with whom you could truly be yourself. Rather, the sexual element has always short-circuited friendships by making contact fast and impersonal.''

"I truly believed Andy was my best friend," he continued. "But, looking back, it's clear that that was an illusion. We had an unbalanced relationship—I was his boss, and so much older. . . . I could have been his father. The more I think about it, the more I realize that he used those things to his advantage." Tom fell silent for a moment, then added with a sigh, "I guess we both used each other.

"And you know what, Joe? I've been thinking. I've been using homosexuality as an excuse, a cop-out.''

"What do you mean?" I asked.

"When I get rid of the gay label, I have to face life, face myself. I've been using my problem as a way of not growing up."

I waited for him to continue. "Oh, I don't have to meet my responsibilities! I don't have to think about my family, about others! I'm gay!" His tone was one of angry self-mockery.

It is not uncommon for men to discover in the course of treatment that they find a sense of safety, of justifiable retreat from the challenges of responsible adulthood when they claim the label "gay" for themselves. For some men, this identity serves as a defense against the anxieties of man–woman intimacy and other adult challenges. Tom too used the label of "gay" to free himself from a burdensome sense of responsibility.

Tom said, "I've always put on this devil-may-care display of bravado. But I realize now I've never felt really brave or faced the truth of what I've been escaping."

I said nothing, waiting for him to continue.

"I get depressed and full of anxiety. I can see that I've only been playing at being a real man. I don't believe I can be, not the way I've been living. I don't know if I'll ever be able to settle down and stick with my family responsibilities."

There followed a long silence. At last, pensively, he said, "I wonder if I *want* to be a man, in terms of all that would require of me."

There was a tone of wistfulness in his voice as he then said, "There's nothing sadder than an old queen. That's an ancient quote."

It seemed to me that I was hearing some measure of self-dramatization in this, so I pushed for some accountability. "Many times you've said that you feel like a stranger in your own home, that it seems like 'Cynthia's house.' You complain you feel like an outsider . . . that you have to go to work to feel respected. What's wrong in your home that you can't be strong . . . that you can't assume any authority?"

"I don't know," Tom shrugged, conceding, "but it's something I'd better start talking about. Cynthia called me last week and wanted to know if I'd like to try moving back in with her."

"What did you say?"

"Well, I admit I was happy to hear her voice. I'd really like to make it work with her. I told her that I'd give it a try."

"Good."

"She's been wanting to call you, to see what she can do to help the marriage."

I spoke with Cynthia that night, and she did indeed ask to see me "for Tom's sake," although I did not doubt that she had equally pressing needs of her own. I was about to leave on summer vacation, so we set an appointment for September, when Cynthia would come alone to see me in my office.

After hearing Tom describe their home life as so boring and tedious, I was surprised when I finally met Cynthia to find her to be a charming, outgoing, well-dressed blond. Then again, knowing the importance Tom placed on appearances, I should have expected his wife to be strikingly attractive.

Even though Cynthia and I had never before met, we greeted each other when we met for her appointment like we were old friends. That sense of immediate familiarity came no doubt from the fact that we both knew the same man intimately. Further, she saw in me an ally. I was not just a neutral therapist. I was *for* the marriage and the diminishment of Tom's homosexuality. Some psychotherapists suggest to clients that a wife should be able to accept the husband's homosexual affairs. They rationalize such absurd advice with talk about "respecting the husband's true, bisexual nature." I have never believed that there is such a thing as bisexuality. For me, a so-called bisexual is someone who has not resolved his homosexuality.

Cynthia began by assuring me she had come to help Tom. I urged her to talk about herself and her own background. She had her own story. Her father was alcoholic; her mother, inadequate and emotionally fragile. I could understand why she would have been drawn to the energy and self-possession Tom radiated.

Cynthia told me about the night she learned the truth about Tom's sexuality. "In one hysterical outburst he told me all about his double life. It was the most horrible thing that's ever happened in my life," she admitted. Her voice trailed off as she added, "For awhile, I just couldn't believe it."

I asked, "How did you handle what he had to tell you?"

"I got angry. . . . It was easier than dealing with my horror. I mean, I just couldn't absorb the truth. I asked him to leave immediately. I was so disgusted that I couldn't look at his face. Then afterwards I felt sadness for him, the kids, and myself."

"Had you had any inkling that he might have had this problem?"

"I only vaguely suspected it," she said. "Before we were married, Tom had told me he had had some homosexual experiences. I guess I didn't know what to make of that. Over the years he'd go out at night and come home very late. The thought crossed my mind, but I never really wanted to think about it."

"Do you resent Tom for what he's done to you, to the family?"

"Tom is a good man and I love him very much. But what Tom wants, Tom gets. He really is very self-centered." She added with a slight laugh, "I often felt I had three kids instead of two. Like a child, Tom always expects special attention. He can be very generous to people, but he has to be in the spotlight. For example, I know he loves our children but sometimes it seems he loves them for the love they can give him. He'll say to them, 'What's the matter, why don't you come and kiss daddy?' If they're busy doing something else and won't give him attention, he's quick to get offended."

Cynthia's description was familiar to me; I had heard similar accounts from wives of men like Tom. Such a man is often married and functioning well bisexually. He tends to be exhibitionistic and narcissistic, and to have—at least on the surface—an overinflated sense of his own importance. He is determined to have it all—that is, marriage and family as well as gay relationships. He is quite different from the more typical client who tends to feel inferior, self-doubting, and powerless.

I asked Cynthia, "What sort of a future do you see here?"

"Well, I love Tom very much," she said. "He likes you, Joe, and I'm hoping he can work out his problem."

"Do you think you can forgive him for what's happened?"

"All my life I've had to make compromises," she said. "I believe if we keep on going in the direction we have been, we can be happy. He really has been a lot more connected with the family since we moved back together. But I will always have my doubts, if he goes out at night . . ."

Revealing the strength of the feminine psyche, she added, "I know when Tom and I are connecting. I can *feel* the difference. When Tom pulls away from me, that's when I worry."

"You know the difference?"

"Oh, sure. During the years Tom was involved with Andy, I felt that his energy was somehow going elsewhere—out of the family."

Cynthia's intuition was right on the mark; many homosexual husbands have said that when they are having affairs with other men, they find themselves avoiding their wives and families. As one married man said, "The big obstacle is guilt. After I've acted out, I come home and find myself withdrawing from the family. For days, I don't feel worthy to participate in anything with my wife or the children."

Cynthia's attitude was typical of that of most wives I've worked with. A wife will feel deeply betrayed, hurt, and angry for many months, but most often she will ultimately commit herself to remaining in the marriage. What seems most important is the husband's honesty and sincerity in dealing with the problem. A wife will often be willing to deal with anything as long as her husband is honest. The husband who can patiently and honestly explain to his wife the unmet emotional needs behind his homosexual behavior will usually find he has a powerful ally. His wife will demonstrate remarkable compassion if given the opportunity to understand the *whys* behind his behavior.

Considering the previous level of dishonesty on the part of many such husbands, I have always been amazed at the flexibility and resilience of those wives who determine to keep their marital commitment. A loving wife will walk through hell and back with her man if treated as a loved and respected equal partner.

Particular therapeutic issues exist for married men who, like Tom, have a homosexual background. These men are challenged not only to resolve their same-sex attractions, but to stay in tune with their wives. Such men typically offer many reasons for avoiding their spouses: She's overweight. She's critical. She's mean. Negative. A bitch. Not attentive. Not understanding. Certainly a wife who feels neglected will have her own defensive reactions, and may indeed be guilty of everything with which she is criticized. There may be many reasons for the husband's avoidance of intimacy, not the least of which is guilt. But these obstacles to intimacy must be addressed in therapy.

At our next session, Tom brought up his concern about the long-term problem of feeling detached and restless while home with his family. He often assumed a passive and detached attitude, while in reality he was feeling bored, disconnected, and resentful. Boredom is, in fact, an often-reported feeling of homosexual clients; I consider this mood to be a part of the homosexual condition.

I asked, "Do you know why you are bored in your own home?"

"I don't know," he said. "In the middle of all the family activity I just lose interest and feel like I want to run away."

I explained, "Boredom occurs when you are in a situation that does not permit you to express yourself."

Tom looked confused. I continued, "Most people believe boredom is the result of 'nothing doing, nothing happening.' In fact, on the inside there's always *something* doing, if we'll only respect it.

"Next time you feel bored, ask yourself, 'How would I like to express myself right now? What is it that I am not permitting myself to say or do?' I think you're feeling inhibited and stuck, and there's an element of anger beneath that. Try to feel the real feelings beneath the boredom. If you really allow yourself to do this, I think you won't be bored any more."

In the following weeks, Tom and Cynthia progressed in their work toward achieving mutual honesty and equality in their relationship. Whereas earlier both had felt like victims, they were now far more secure in the marriage. An important part of the treatment had involved getting Tom to connect with his wife and to feel her presence. For many years, he had been so preoccupied with himself that he had virtually shut her out of his consciousness. Now, rather than detach himself, he made the effort to identify his feelings and express them. This process would invariably reconnect him with Cynthia.

"How much I want to make it work with her!" he said. "To cut myself off completely from the gay lifestyle and be only with men who are straight. I'd love to have a real male friend now, not a lover. Maybe some married guy with a family. I need that kind of friendship if I'm going to have a life as a family man."

By this time, Tom had come to understand far more about himself and his deepest priorities, and he had begun to believe he could have a monogamous marriage.

He told me, "The most important thing of all is to keep my family together. My children need a father. My wife needs a husband. And I need a family." He was beginning to see the string of affairs he had had as meaningless and irrelevant.

"I used to resent Cynthia's regimenting my life, but looking back I see I gave her no choice," he said. "I simply abdicated my family responsibilities."

"You did," I told him. "You got into a passive-avoidant role at home. You were showing your resentment at being trapped into family responsibilities by a passive refusal to be involved. You created a vacuum that someone had to fill. Of course Cynthia stepped in to fill the gap. Then you accused her—unfairly—of being controlling."

"Good things have been happening with Cynthia," Tom told me. "She complains sometimes about the house and kids, talking on and on, but then I speak up and let her know how it affects me, and then she catches herself and quietly backs off. She's become very attuned to how I'm feeling.

"The little fights we have now are nothing compared to what they used to be." He added, "Because there's something, somewhere, that feels anchored."

"Where?" I challenged.

Tom looked confused for a moment, then answered, "In me. I feel more centered, more grounded in my place at home. I always had this sense of wanting to float away, get out of there, to escape to someplace else. I don't feel that so much now. And when I do, I know what it's about."

"What *is* it about?"

"It's about not letting myself belong." Tom spoke slowly and thoughtfully, choosing each word carefully. "It's about not being honest with my feelings. And not connecting with the people who are most important to me. For so long, I was feeling isolated and distant from Cynthia."

"Just avoiding," I told him.

"Yes. I'd pull myself into my shell and tune everyone out." There was a long pause. "But then," he said, "there would be those little moments when grace would break through and something beautiful would hit me—something about my children, or some quality of Cynthia's—and suddenly I'd see how thin my shell is.

"One of those moments occurred when Cynthia and I made love and afterwards she began to cry. My first reaction was, what did I do wrong? The tears were a little unsettling. But she said, 'Just hold me.' So I knew everything was all right. Then she said, 'When I feel this way with you, you open up my heart and I'm just lying here completely bare to you. I really want to be totally with you, totally open to you. But when you're distant, not there for us, then I'm left to hold the family together and I have to be the strong person. I have to make the family work, I have to steel myself, harden myself to take care of business and get things done for us. I don't really want to take on the masculine role or these masculine qualities.'

"At these times of closeness," Tom continued, "when the truth of our lives comes through, I open myself up to her, and she becomes soft and feminine."

He sighed. "She opened herself up to me and it felt good, but it was also frightening, because it leaves her vulnerable to being wounded even more deeply. So it's up to me to work toward a place where I'll never hurt her again." He looked at me gravely. "It's a heavy responsibility.

"The other day," he continued, "we were standing in the

kitchen and she asked me, 'If you ever fall again, would you tell me?' I thought about it for a minute and then told her yes. I wanted to say, 'It won't happen,' but a man can never say 'never.' But I am working toward never falling again, and so I could honestly promise that I would tell her. Everything I've been doing has been leading me forward. I don't feel that despair, that hopelessness any longer. I know exactly what's behind the momentary lapses. When I'm not doing well, I know *why* I'm not doing well, and I know what I need to do to get back on track again.

"Understanding the underlying dynamics, the real needs, I see that it's not the male attractions themselves, but something missing within me that gives the male attractions that power. It's not about who's that great-looking guy over there; it's about who I am in here.

"I'll say to myself" (he raised his voice to a dramatic, effeminate pitch), " 'Oh, I can't possibly resist this temptation . . . I was born this way!' But this is really willfulness on my part . . . a *refusal* to go through the necessary thought processes, and a *refusal* to recall the truth about myself. I *permit* the fantasy to overwhelm me." Once Tom had seen the truth about himself, he could only pretend to forget.

Tom's therapeutic formula depended on three things: confronting the unfulfilled emotional needs behind his homosexual behavior; developing nonerotic male friendships; and breaking through the emotional detachment from Cynthia. At Cynthia's request, Tom asked his old lover, Andy, to leave the store and helped him find work elsewhere. Tom was determined to see him as a person of the past, and to move with Cynthia and their children into the future.

As Tom approached the last days of his third year in therapy, we talked about termination.

"So, what do you say, Doc?" he asked. "Am I ready to graduate?"

"I think you are," I assured him.

"I wish I could feel totally confident that I won't fall back into the old traps that brought me here originally."

I told him, "You have already committed yourself to

honesty. You are more honest with yourself today than you have ever been before in your life. You may have a fall, you may experience some setbacks, but I'm not worried about that because the insights are there. You have the understanding. Just stay honest with yourself, and with Cynthia."

Tom nodded gravely.

"Genuine insights can never be lost or forgotten," I told him. "You can never go back to the place you were, psychologically, when you first came here."

Speaking in a low, slow voice, Tom said, "I enjoyed what I've learned with you, Joe. You have given me a lot that is very important. I'm really going to miss the giving, the sharing, that has come from you."

I realized that Tom clearly felt intensely ambivalent about ending our relationship. When the final moments of his last session had arrived, I told him, "Any time you need to, you can, of course, come back—even if it's only for a single session."

"Thank you," he said, standing up and shaking my hand briskly. "I'll miss you and the guys in the group. I've learned a lot from you." There was bravado in his voice, but as we walked to the door, he looked back one more time, wistfully.

Two years after his termination of therapy with me, Tom learned he was HIV-positive. I remained in touch with both Tom and Cynthia, receiving calls from them off and on over the next three years. From time to time we discussed a variety of problems—communication between them, parenting issues, especially about their son, Sean, who was now in adolescence.

Tom began to show more of the symptoms of AIDS, and when it became increasingly evident he would soon die, Cynthia asked me to provide family counseling. It was time to prepare the children for the end. Tom and Cynthia asked me to assist them in telling the children. I saw their incredible strength as all four sat on the living room couch. For two hours there were questions and tears and a sharing of love.

I visited Tom at home in the final weeks as he grew more and more feeble. It had been five years since he had ended therapy. One day as I was about to leave him, he called me aside. His voice surprisingly strong, he told me, "If it hadn't been for you, I wouldn't be here now with my family. I will have the blessing of dying with my wife and children beside me."

"I'm very thankful for that," I said.

"And Doc—" he winked, "you'll be happy to know I've kept my promises to Cynthia."

One month later, Cynthia called early one evening. Her voice was low and sad. She told me Tom had passed away that morning.

After Tom's death I continued to stay in touch with Cynthia and the children, and I did my best to help them through their grieving period. She told me how her relationship with Tom had deepened, and that their family life was the best it had ever been. Tom had developed a deep relationship with both his children, who helped nurse him at home as he became weaker. Cynthia too had cared for him faithfully. He died in his own bedroom in the care of his family and a nun from his parish who had come to bring him communion.

Reparative therapy helped Tom to put aside his double life. It afforded him the insights with which to follow through and live according to his convictions. I feel satisfied that I was able to help him find what he was looking for.

3

Father John—
The Double Life

Father John was a Roman Catholic priest, 52 years old, who had an extremely rich, deep, elegant voice. He was an articulate man, perhaps the most articulate man I have ever treated. I could imagine him delivering a thunderous sermon in his charming brogue from the pulpit of a cathedral.

He came from a staunchly Irish family and possessed a bittersweet sense of humor, which he often called upon to laugh at himself. But in spite of all the laughter over the wild absurdities of his life, he was a deeply spiritual man who was embroiled in a terrible battle with what he called his "dark side."

At his first session he reported that he was compulsively drawn to gay baths and bookstores. In an anxious rush to confess it all, he could hardly get the words out fast enough.

"My addiction to pornography works like a magnet to draw me out of the rectory every weekend. Every Friday night I drive to West Hollywood and go to my favorite source." He laughed cynically. "The Circus of Books."

"The what?" I asked.

"Yep. . . . It's a gay cultural landmark on Santa Monica Boulevard, and it is a *circus*," he informed me. "It's this supermarket—if you will—of pornographic material for every taste and inclination."

He went on, "Anyway, I usually take out two or three all-male videos and bring them back to a room I rent at this little dumpy motel, the exclusive—" he pronounced the name in a feigned haughty tone—"Tropicana Peaks Motel. I carry my own VCR and hook it up to the T.V. in the room." He looked at me, then continued in a somewhat abashed manner, "I have what I call a marathon masturbation party all by myself there."

He rushed on, "Sometimes I'll call this escort service to send a young guy to my room. You know, for sex." He looked at me, took a deep breath and confessed, "But I always feel terribly guilty afterwards."

Father John followed with an incisive description of the psychology of pornography: "Pornography anesthetizes—it numbs the pain, gives me a 'fix' of excitement."

This priest, I would learn, was a man of many facets. He did not follow in the path of the typical man of the cloth. He was critical of the Catholic Church because he felt unsupported in his personal struggle against homosexual behavior. He was also critical of God, and expressed this feeling often in our sessions.

Father John's case was not merely one of the scandal of a priest who has broken his vows. It was not merely a case of a priest who was "just a man, like other men." What is significant about Father John's struggle with homosexuality is how it challenged him to push beyond the frustrating cycle of sin, guilt, repentance, and more sin to achieve an intimate relationship with God. Paradoxically, it was through his struggle with homosexuality that Father John really came to know God.

For the first three months of his therapy, Father John seemed to be making great strides forward. He had in fact been fulfilling the role of the good patient. Then one day he came in and told me the truth. "I haven't been honest with you. I've been getting worse, actually." Then he admitted, his charming voice laced with irony, "I was pretending to be making a new life through you."

After a short, tense silence, he continued. "I've tried to do with you what I've been doing with my superiors—live up to *their* expectations. I haven't been facing the feelings inside. The truth is, I've all but decided that I'll never have success in this battle." His shoulders heaved in a sigh of despair. "At some deep level I think that I don't want to get better. I want to push all thoughts of my life away. Push you away. I think, 'I can't handle this. I'm too weak. I deserve pity and gentle handling.' I even want God to back off.

"I don't know." There was sadness in that elegant voice. "For so many years, I've played at being a real man, but it's all been a cover-up. At some deep level, I don't believe I ever can be. Maybe I don't even *want* to be a man. Somehow I can't imagine myself really living a normal life."

"In all great literature and mythology," I said, "the hero first refuses the opportunity for higher consciousness. Even Jesus prayed to be released from his cross—'Let this cup pass from me.'"

Father John went on in a sad voice, "So much of my life is still caught up in these perverted, juvenile fetishes. I don't know why I have this big preoccupation with looking at penises. I know it's ridiculous, but it's so compelling."

He was silent for so long that I finally spoke. "Try to go beyond the fixation, to focus on the intent of the penis . . . its anatomical compatibility with the vagina, its natural purpose of procreation."

"It is an infantile preoccupation, that's what I must remind myself," he said sheepishly.

"Absolutely. Most homosexuals overfocus on the penis. So much of homosexual behavior is like two little boys playing *show me yours, I'll show you mine*. It's fetishistic behavior. The penis has an important symbolic power. It's a symbol of the masculinity that you feel you need but don't have. Some trauma, some gap in your development seeks fulfillment in phallic fixation. That's part of the homosexuality."

Father John said thoughtfully, "Most gay men I know are fixated on their own penises. They are fascinated by their own anatomy. 'My penis is my best friend!' one gay guy said to me. It's sad."

"Exactly. The homosexual has not integrated his masculinity into his own identity. He is alienated from his own male anatomy. He sees his penis as something other than himself."

"But why does he do this? Why all these 'size queens' in the gay world? Why such preoccupation with the penis?"

"Maybe in his childhood, the boy's role in the family necessitated the denial of his budding masculinity. His special place with Mom probably required the abandonment of his masculine strivings. So now he wants to protect his fragile maleness. He is always afraid it is going to be taken away from him."

I continued, "The boy's gender orientation is dependent upon his place in the family. The way the mother treats him. The way the father treats him. The way both parents show esteem for his masculinity."

Father John nodded. I could see that he had been listening attentively. "I think of my poor mother, God love her. She tried the best she could do. Because if my Dad was not satisfying my emotional needs, he probably wasn't satisfying hers, either. He was just a nonentity in our home. I needed someone, and Mother seemed like a feminine father whom I could relate to."

Silence again, then, "I suppose she was frustrated in her marriage. I know she felt alone and tried to fill that gap with me."

A smile and a faraway look came over his face. "Every so often she'd take out a few dollars she'd saved. We'd get dressed up and she'd announce to my father, 'Johnnie and I are going on a splurge.' She'd use that word 'splurge' to mean that we were going downtown to see a movie. I'd wear my church clothes, and she'd put on her little hat and white gloves. They did that in those days. Afterward we'd head to a little restaurant and have a nice supper together, talking about anything that came into our heads. When we got home, Dad would be in front of the television and he'd hardly notice we'd walked in the door. Mother and I would be as happy as two people who'd been out on a date."

He once more fell into thought, then shortly divulged it: "I wonder if my father or my grandfather was homosexual." I often hear this question from my clients. Although these relatives probably were not homosexual, the question arises out of some perceived masculine weakness of their fathers. "I know my father never had much love to give because his own dad was always out of the house when he was little. He was a journeyman carpenter. And my dad hardly said a word about his dad's father."

I thought, so rarely do the fathers of homosexual men speak about their own fathers. Often the inadequate father–son relationship goes back to the grandfather or great-grandfather. Not only did Father John have an inadequate father, he had an overintimate mother as well. As a result, this particularly sensitive and vulnerable boy grew up homosexual.

Father John shook his head sadly. "I always felt like my father was a missing person. There was no sense of a masculine presence in the house. My mother was the one who always stepped in to fill the void. She had to move in and fill his place, as well as hold her own." He added, "I grew up feeling that Mother was both mother and father." There was anger in his voice, as though he felt this had not been fair to her.

I pointed out, "The mother can never be the father. A completely different emotional process exists between mother and son, and father and son. It takes a man to raise a man."

"I knew that, I guess." He sighed, but still the sound of anger tinged his voice. Changing the subject, he said, "My strongest perception of childhood was always the fear."

I have heard these same words from nearly every client who has come to me with a homosexual problem. Nearly every man's overriding childhood feeling was vulnerability and uncertainty, long before sexuality ever became a conscious issue.

Father John's hour was nearly up. I asked him, "Now that you've been coming for three months, are you satisfied that we're doing everything that can be done for you?"

He admitted honestly, "Well, I must admit that *I'm* not doing everything I can for myself. I've been sort of waiting."

"Waiting for what?"

"Just waiting. Every good thing that ever happened to me simply came to me."

Father John was describing one of the fundamental resistances of the homosexual condition, namely, avoidance of the painful challenges of life. It was time to confront an essential dimension of his therapy—the claiming of his intrinsic power.

"I hope you don't judge me by my passivity," Father John said gravely.

I shook my head. "I'm not concerned about judging you. But I'm concerned about what this attitude means in terms of your ability and willingness to take charge of your life. This passivity is a part of your identity that will have to change."

He looked puzzled. "I need to get a clearer picture of what you mean."

"Reparative therapy is not about sex, sex, sex," I said. "We're here to understand the total picture of your identity formation. Essential to healing homosexuality is changing this perception you have of yourself as the passive, helpless victim. Real change requires more than just putting the lid on a sexual behavior. We're looking for a larger transformation."

"Well, I'm ready," he said earnestly. "This homosexual obsession is consuming my life. I want to heal this once and for all. For once in my life, I want to feel like a whole person."

"But this is something you will have to fight for. Forever— I'm not talking about a week. Some days will be big battles; some, small battles. But every day has to be a battle of some sort," I warned him. "Otherwise, as they say, it ain't gonna happen."

Critics of reparative therapy believe that the technique uses guilt as a tool to manipulate suppression of homosexual behavior. Paradoxically, many men, like Father John, pass through a sometimes necessary and healthy phase early in therapy in which, instead of suppression, there is an increase in homosexual behavior. Although this may appear contradictory to the goal of therapy, it offers the client the opportunity to evaluate for himself the subjective effects of his behavior. Whereas some men never need to experience such behavior to know it is not for them, these others need to see the personal consequences. For them, homosexual acting-out serves as an expression of the self-understanding and personal empowerment that they have discovered in the early stages of therapy. Sex and assertion are interrelated for the male, and when therapy first begins to empower the client, he may misdirect that power in a sexual way. Further, within the transference relationship with the therapist, increased homosexual activity can be a way the client tests the therapist's acceptance of him.

During his first three months in therapy, Father John lived in mixed moods. Sometimes he faced the truth of his life, and other times he slipped into passive denial.

One morning he told me, "Last Saturday night I had nothing to do, so I thought I'd take a ride. I did something I hadn't done in several months—I went to a gay bar. I felt a little uncomfortable at first, but then I thought, 'What the hell!' and began to relax. Had a beer. After a while this guy about my age came up to me. That felt good, and we started to talk—"

I interrupted, "What felt good?"

"Oh, that somebody . . . some guy . . . should make the first move on me in a place where middle-aged guys like me usually don't get attention." He went on, "Anyway, we just stood there talking for about an hour. He said he was married. We really hit it off and we went back to my room at the Tropicana Peaks. We sat there on the couch and talked for another three hours. Talked about all kinds of things. We had a lot in common, lots of the same experience. We really understood each other. I felt for the fellow . . . a real gentle, sweet guy."

"Sounds like you made a real connection," I said. "Then what?"

"Then nothing," Father John said. "Well, then we went into the bedroom and just had sex. Safe sex," he added. "Mutual masturbation."

"Are you going to see him again?"

"No. I don't think so."

"But it sounds like there was a compatibility. The foundation for a potential friendship. You guys had so much in common."

"I don't think so. It was pleasant for that moment, but I don't think I'd want to follow up on it." He sighed. "Honest to God, Joe—I really don't care any more if I end up having sex with men. Sometimes the whole thing seems to take too much effort.''

"Why did you have sex with this guy?"

"I don't know."

His indifference was becoming irritating. I waited.

Finally, "It just seemed like the thing to do. You know, it was implied by our just being there."

"Being there?"

"Yeah. You know, on the couch, at the Peaks."

"Did you feel the desire to get sexual with him?"

"Not really. I guess I just let it happen."

"Because of pressure from him?"

"Not really. He was probably as indifferent as I was."

As we explored Father John's motivations, we were both pleased to note a diminishing of his compulsivity; yet evidently, he was still unable to muster the conviction to draw the line between male friendship and sexuality. Beneath this difficulty in maintaining boundaries was the deeper issue of self-identity. I remembered what he had told me in an earlier session—"I don't feel like a real man, and I don't believe I ever *can* be. Maybe I don't *want* to be a man." Could Father John ever see himself as a man who receives male attention and approval, yet tolerates the absence of sex?

Like so many of my homosexual clients, Father John lived a life of emotional isolation. He desired relationships of male closeness and affection, but found only short-term sex.

"Your same-sex deficits will be satisfied through male bonding, not male sexuality. Healing won't happen through sexual behavior. Look at what you did last Saturday. You go and sit on the couch with a stranger and talk for three or four hours, you like him a great deal, then you have sex. But what's this . . . you never want to see the guy again? There's a contradiction there. What is your attitude about such behavior? It is O.K. or is it not O.K?"

Father John replied, "I'm not sure if it bothers me that much one way or the other. I'm not sure I'll go to hell over being intimate with a man for one evening."

"Look," I said abruptly. "Let's stop with the illusionary euphemisms. Let's not call it *intimacy* when it was just plain sex. How could it be intimate when you never want to see the guy again?"

He spoke more loudly, and now he sounded angry. "I'm not going to give you an answer about myself at this point because I don't know what the answer is."

"Do you feel that I'm pushing you too hard now?"

He seemed relieved by my question. "No," he answered. "It's O.K., Joe."

"It's O.K. not to have an answer right now," I said. I appreciate that you answered my question honestly."

There was a long silence between us. I asked, "How do you feel about being out there cruising?"

"To some extent, I like it. Certainly I get satisfaction those couple of hours. And there's a validity to following my feelings. 'This is where I am in my life right now.' I've acknowledged these feelings. I've accepted them and I'm starting to understand them. Maybe understanding them is all I can ask of myself."

He shrugged his shoulders. "You know, I sometimes feel, 'Well, this is my life. Whatever made me this way, I'm stuck with it. I should quit knocking myself over the head, trying to change.' But on the other hand, therapy has helped me a lot. Much of my recent happiness and self-acceptance is a tribute to the understanding I've gained from it. You could say, the truth has set me free.

"But you know, Joe . . . what concerns me is that while the concepts may be fine and true—I think you're right, I'm trying to fulfill same-sex deficits—there may be a failure in the therapeutic process. It may be useless to try to change myself." He looked up at me earnestly. "What about the process, Joe?"

Before I could answer, he continued. "I look back at this little boy that I was, who lived in nothing but shame and fear and isolation. Nobody to talk to, no real friends, giving sexual favors behind the barn to a cousin eight years older. I had no identity. I was scared to death. I was drifting, empty, lonely. All I had for friendship and closeness was jerking off this older kid."

"Always that deep, deep sense of disconnectedness," I said.

"Yes," he said. "Sex got me out of that disconnectedness. And Joe . . . this part of me may not change. I may be stuck forever looking for that quick fix. I don't want to place a guilt trip on myself about what I do—in case I do it again.

"I want to be realistic," he continued. "If this is going to be as far as I'm going to grow and change in life, I want to accept this. I want to have sex if I feel like having sex. And I don't care to have to carry any guilt."

Then he added, "I guess what I'm saying is that I want you to contradict me. I want to hear you say, 'But you can't!' "

"Why?" I asked.

"I want you to tell me that this is not really where I'm at in my development. This is the kid in me, the boy, talking right now—the boy challenging his father."

"That's what it is," I agreed.

Father John paused, then suddenly slipped into angry profanity. "I know I'm not fuckin' feminine, that I'm not a woman—but I also know that I'm not a damn man. What the shit am I? A male–female hybrid? Or just a little boy in the body of a balding middle-aged man?"

"There *is* a hurting little boy there," I assured him. "There is a hurting little boy."

"Certainly there is." Father John showed a faint sign of pleasure on his face. "It's something you've talked about many times in theory, but now I can see it. You're right—this little boy has got to be dealt with." He looked up at me quizzically. "But I want to know how I went from being a hurt 5-year-old kid, to acting out sexually like I do today. Why?"

"To fill an inner emptiness."

"Maybe you're right," he admitted. "But if acting out sexually, as I do, comes out of pain, it's not current pain. I don't have any cause for pain today. My parents passed on long ago, God love them. I have a religious vocation. I must say I've never had a better life situation."

"A man who finds himself acting out unacceptable feelings is living with an emptiness carried over from early relationships," I explained.

Father John turned to me with a voice full of frustration. "Why did I get involved in this? The porno shops, the allure of things I hate, the double life that betrays the vow I made when I became a priest. . . . Why am I so conflicted?''

Before I could answer, he ran on. ''You know, sometimes I've felt these sessions are full of shit. I could sit at home and ponder this stuff myself, by God. But now I see that I really *do* need you to get to the bottom of this.'' His voice grew tense. ''Because I'm really feeling that little boy. I'm feeling the isolation and the suffering that little boy endured.''

He sighed heavily. ''I can see that unless we get back to that little boy—heal that little boy—I'm never going to be a man.''

He leaned out of his chair, gesturing imploringly at me as he asked, ''So what is it that I should do now?''

I told him, ''You need close, honest male relationships—*intimacy*, with all that word implies. We're not talking sex. You need two or three men in your life so you can really have the experience of knowing them—not sexually, but as peers. To know them in the way you never knew or understood your father. Our relationship satisfies these needs to some extent, but it is artificial because of the necessary therapeutic boundaries.''

''It's not artificial to me,'' Father John protested. ''I have built up a tremendous trust in you. I have told you many things about myself about which I have never spoken before.''

He looked at me, his eyes betraying a mixture of affection and anger. ''I don't want to sit at some fucking bar and talk to a stranger, telling him the same things I've been telling you.''

''Of course not,'' I agreed. ''You need genuine friendship—a man from group, for example, who will understand your struggles. But at some point you'll hit up against the homosexual guy's defensive detachment—so you'll also need to be close to a guy who's straight and can give you a different perspective.''

Father John said, ''But first I need to understand more about that hurt little boy.'' And with that we concluded our session.

Over time, Father John's sexual behaviors began to diminish. He spoke less about his sexual attractions and more about his relationship to God. As he grew stronger in keeping his vow of celibacy, he seemed more free to grow in spiritual understanding.

"My attitude toward God has been so screwed up for so long now," Father John said one day. "I never would have dreamed that I'd be saying this, but—I hated God, I really *hated* him."

He was silent, then said, "Unfortunately, I've projected a lot of my own shit onto this being I've been calling God."

"Of course," I said.

He went on—this man who was always so very verbal— "When I feel severed from God, I go into this dark, twisted thought pattern. My whole life has been a perverted sort of self-atonement in order to buy God off. For ten years of my priesthood there has been this compulsive, empty cycle of jerking off and sucking cock. Then I'd run to the magic wand of the confessional to make it right with God, and be clean again. . . . Then the whole sexual thing would blow up all over again. It's sick. My whole sick approach to religion has been to buy God off. I've been trying to bribe him, saying, 'Don't condemn me for living this double life and I'll give all the rest of my life to you.' Throughout this whole, empty, cyclical relationship to God, I've felt nothing but anger and hatred.

"I've even been scared to go to Jesus because Jesus is a man, and I've been completely alienated from men and masculinity."

He took a deep breath and continued. "Even though this sex addiction is still strong in me, I'm not feeling the great helplessness I used to feel. I'm coming to feel that maybe God *can* deal with this mess. That he understands my struggle."

Silence again. Then, "Freud was right. God *is* a projection of the father figure. The relationships we have with our loved ones on earth can expand or constrict our experience of God. I've been stunted in my relationship with my earthly father, so I have a hard time knowing my heavenly father."

"This new relationship you have with God is very heterosexual," I pointed out.

"What do you mean?" Father John seemed surprised.

"A homosexual boy fears and distrusts his father, and he

associates those feelings with God. Not only does he hide from his earthly and heavenly fathers, but also from the other boys, his bosses and his landlords.''

I continued, ''The homosexual boy turns away and hides from his father—as you have been turning away from a relationship with God, the Father. When the straight kid feels hostility toward his father, he allows the hostility to emerge— he puts it right out there. When you turned away from God and excluded him from your struggle, it was the homosexual boy's way of hiding—a turning away from the father's challenge.

''The first challenge the prehomosexual boy rejected was the challenge of the father. As he grew up he continued to turn away from masculine challenge. Soon there was a painful tension between himself and other males. Alienating himself from a man's world, he romanticized males and he tried to short-circuit this tension with erotic contact.''

Father John nodded. For a long time, there was silence between us. At last he said, ''So much good is coming out of this. The saints be praised . . . I can feel the response within me. I am finally reaching something real. Everything in my heart has been opening up to this new God I've been seeing.''

He went on, ''The Christian challenge, I believe, is to reestablish harmony with our Creator. In some very important ways I've disrupted the link between God and myself. I'm overworked, I've lost the joy of life, I've been depressed and bitter. The result, if I stay alienated, is death.

''Even in the midst of the alienation of my homosexuality, I've been challenged to fight to hold onto Christ's righteousness. I'm starting to see that in some unexpected ways, this curse of the homosexual struggle has brought me blessing.''

''In some surprising ways,'' I told him, ''we are blessed by our struggles. They can end up as nothing more than a neurotic and futile cycle. Or, they can redeem us.''

Father John replied, ''I believe my own fellow priests don't understand how to deal with this. The traditional Catholic advice for homosexual behavior is repent, repent, repent, then take cold showers and get a hobby. But if you haven't resolved anything, you're only thrown back into the neverending sin–confession–sin cycle. Then, there's the advice of liberal and gay priests—'God loves you no matter what you do. You want to sleep with some guy, God digs it.' Both extremes miss the essential truth.''

As I listened to his words, I felt privileged to hear the flow of revelations that come only through a man's personal struggle. Father John was at last finding what he had so long been seeking.

Several weeks later, he and I sat down to a discussion of the sadomasochism in same-sex relationships. Father John had asked me why he felt so drawn to this type of pornography.

"There's a certain amount of masochism in the homosexual's relationship with other men. It's a pattern that began in relationship with the father. When the little boy wants closeness with his father and doesn't get it, there's a willingness to degrade himself in order to receive that attention. It's a hostile, self-defeating way of winning points with the father. This is why the homosexual's fantasy life and pornography often contain sadomasochistic themes. He wants the love and attention of someone he feels hostility toward. It's not always chains and whips you see, but the more subtle themes of control and dominance that are so characteristic of gay pornography.''

Father John responded, "I'll never forget that my dad was a big, strapping man. He had large arms and he used to taunt me because I was this little, anemic, gangly kid. He would say, 'Do you think you'll ever have big muscles like these? Do you think you'll ever be a big, strapping man like me?' ''

"A good father would have said, 'Wow! Look at that little muscle. It's really getting bigger.' ''

Father John went on, "My dad always seemed to hide his maleness from me, as though we weren't the same. If ever I caught him changing out of his work clothes, he'd quickly close the door as if to say, 'You're different; you're not part of the company of males.' I can never remember even seeing my father bare his lower limbs. It makes me mad to think my father would not share his masculinity with me.''

I said, "That's how the homosexual feels when he looks at men. He feels cheated and angry; the world of men is a mystery. Straight men seem to possess this quality of masculinity that is so easy, so un-self-conscious, so natural—and the gay man just doesn't have it. Where there's an intense dependency and hunger for something, there's simply got to be anger.''

I continued, ''Most of the guys are very angry at their fathers because they feel they didn't get enough masculine affirmation. Left with this feeling of hostile dependency and anger, they feel a masochistic excitement in being degraded. Even though they're being treated roughly, there's an excitement because they've made a connection—they've broken down the barriers. 'The only way I can be close to the masculine is to lower myself,' the guy says. This explains the pleasure so often taken in sadomasochistic relationships.''

I thought of the first client who taught me this insight into masculine deprivation and sadomasochism. In graduate school, it was not politically correct to discuss the cause or treatment of homosexuality, so my training as a psychologist did not prepare me for my work. But as an intern at a hospital, I was faced with the case of 8-year-old Ryan, whose mother was concerned about his childish and socially inappropriate behavior as well as his sexual experimentation with other boys.

My only clue to Ryan's problem was his ongoing, bitter complaint that his father ignored him. Hungry for male attention, Ryan loved seeing me each week and as our relationship grew, he hated to leave when our session was over. His behavior became more and more physically aggressive toward me, and physical boundaries soon became a problem. His way of liking me felt like an assault. He would climb all over me aggressively, demandingly, almost angrily, as if he could not get enough satisfaction. I knew this intense love–hate relationship had a great deal to do with the boy's ambivalent feelings toward his father.

''You know, Joe,'' Father John said, ''I had an insight last week. I have been using pornography to show me what men are. When I'm into porn or checking out men, I'm into this need to know what it's like to *be him*.''

His words echoed in my ears. The foundation of homoerotic attraction—*the need to find out what it's like to be him*.

''Somehow, in my little boy mind, those guys on the

screen were *real men,* like I wanted to be. Somehow porn actors represented to me what men really are.

"Then it struck me, 'Who are these guys, anyway? Why would they be doing this—on camera, no less—if they were so normal?'

"I began considering, 'Do they have nine-to-five jobs? or do these poor bastards need the money that badly? What's their self-esteem level? Do they have girlfriends?' The gay fantasy is that these porn actors are regular guys in every way except they do this stuff on camera. Give me a break!

"As I grow in my own manhood, I see these poor guys not as male images to look up to, but as men who are just as broken as I have been.''

"Nothing is ever finished, Joe." Father John used those words to open our next session. He was talking about his search for an expanded awareness of the past, saying if we were to spend all day every day delving into our memories, we still would never know ourselves fully. Nor would we be totally freed from our early conflicts.

"The desires I've felt are still a part of me. Sometimes I still drive by The Circus of Books, you know. Yet there's a strange reaction when I get there." Father John looked pleased with himself. "After a few moments, I get a feeling of aversion. I'm filled with hatred toward that garbage, and an anger that I've wasted so much precious time and energy on it. Porn is a psychic violation of my goodness and my person-hood. It's emotionally and spiritually hurtful. It drains me, and then it takes me a couple of days to get back my sense of dignity.

"When I feel those old familiar urges to go to Circus of Books or out cruising, I say, 'Lord Jesus, there is a deep pain inside me that masquerades as this desire to act out sexually. Help me heal it.'

"And you know, Joe, as messed up as my parents were— God love them—I believe they've been forgiven and they're in heaven, so I pray to them, too. I say, 'Father and Mother, you are now in a different place where, God willing, you are totally at one with your sexuality. Let some of the goodness that you're experiencing flow down to me now so that I can be the wholesome person I want to be.'

"I'm no longer cowering in a corner and feeling shame about myself. Even when I get this compulsive urge, I talk to God, saying, 'I give you permission to use this experience with all its negativity. Use it to teach me, as that writer Colin Cook says, to *fail successfully*. Lord, if I fail you sometimes, bring me back to victory.'

"This helps me, Joe, praying and praising God. Then when I see a good-looking guy now, I look down toward his dick and then I praise God for just being able to look at him and then get on with my life. It's an exercise I do in my mind. I imagine the guy as a loving husband and father. I picture his sexuality within a natural context.

"And you know what else? A beautiful thing has been happening to me recently. I notice women! It's not forced, not a mind trip I'm putting on myself. I'm discovering this openness in myself to just taking in a woman's beauty. I'm open to her strengths and mental abilities, even her physical attributes. When I see a beautiful woman I praise God. It's just a normal, natural thing that's started to happen.

"I don't try to figure it out, I just praise God that a woman is there and that she is beautiful. There are no strings attached, there's no sexual compulsion, she's just there and praise God.

"There was a time fifteen years ago when I would buy a *Playboy* magazine and look at the centerfold and try to masturbate, try to be normal. But now I'm getting to feel more comfortable with whatever level of attraction I feel or don't feel.

"I used to go into a men's room and stand next to another guy and struggle to pee. It was always like such a defensive feeling, such pressure I put on myself—like 'this is a test of the emergency broadcast system'—and if I couldn't pee I wasn't a man.

"All through high school and even into the seminary I went through hell holding my bladder—I think I had the biggest bladder in Los Angeles from all this tension. But now I can do it. I think because I'm more at peace with who I am as a man."

For many years, Father John had been in a predicament common to many priests. He had used his role of priest as a way of hiding. The priesthood can be a lonely place, with the priest alienated not only from fellow clergy, but parishioners. "Today I called one of our deacons and shared something with him that happened during the week," Father John continued. "His closing words to me were 'I love you.' I said to myself when I hung up, 'How beautiful. I really needed that.' "

He went on, "You may listen to the same sonata a million times, then suddenly one day at a concert, one movement begins and you think, 'I never really knew *that* piece was there!' Then you get into this unfamiliar part, and all of a sudden it is beautiful to you. You could say the lovely melody I've discovered recently is good relationships with married fellows like this deacon."

Father John had also struck up a friendship with Tom James, the one married member of our psychotherapy group. He said, "I was with Tom the other night, getting into some of the pain I've been dealing with. Tom said, 'I just want to hold you,' and he held me. I was rigid, like an ice cube—scared to death. Tom said, 'You're trembling, you're shaking!' I was so determined to take in the warmth of his friendship but to keep out any unwholesome feelings. Then I relaxed. What Tom gave me was a shot-in-the-arm, and I needed it. Caring relationships such as this one are freeing me to focus on my real needs, such as strengthening the male identity that I've sought for myself in other people.

"This whole process is not just psychological, but actually spiritual. I've flown light years in just the last twelve months of working with you, Joe. I am reaching out to others and allowing them to help me. And I'm also finding the confidence to allow myself to offer guidance. Last week, this young kid came into confession and talked about his struggle with homosexual feelings—'The Big H,' Lord help him. He was upset with the guilt the Catholic Church lays on you. I was able to offer him understanding and specific direction because of what I'm learning about myself.

"I explained to this kid that if his natural, genuine needs for maleness remain unfulfilled, then he will continue to experience homosexual feelings. That if he can meet these needs authentically through platonic same-sex relationships, he can diffuse that sexual drive which seeks to break the barriers down erotically. He can break that tension down in healthy ways . . . constructively.''

He added softly, ''I'm not sure homosexual behavior is *the* mortal sin. God understands the deficit that leads us to it.'' He added thoughtfully, ''I wish the Church could be as understanding.''

He sighed, settled deep in his chair, and smiled. ''Joe, it's been wonderful. Even though I know it's not finished yet.''

''It's hard work,'' I agreed. ''And you're right—nothing of this sort is ever finished. Alcoholics rarely completely lose the urge to drink. People who grew up with low self-esteem aren't transformed into people bursting with self-confidence. We never become fully whole in this life.''

''But I'm doing so much better—the saints be praised. Now my sexual temptations are a background temptation; they've stopped preoccupying me,'' he said.

''That's the essence of it. You're aware of the attractions, but you've grown in consciousness.''

''That's just what it is,'' he agreed. ''It's an expanded consciousness. A fuller awareness. I understand these feelings and they're no longer enslaving me.''

One sunny spring morning four months later, Father John came in, took his seat on the couch, and gave me a peaceful, self-satisfied smile. We both knew he was nearing the end of his therapy.

''Today is June third, the feast day of St. Charles Lwanga— the patron saint of homosexuals,'' he told me. ''I believe the spirit of St. Charles has been guiding me. I was cleaning out my closet last week, and I came across an old porno film that I used to take with me to the Tropicana. To my surprise, I could only watch a little segment of it before something shut down and said, 'This is sick! This is definitely not healthy.' Watching the film felt like it diminished my integrity. As I looked at it I said to God, 'This is not a thing from you. This is a man-made thing, and it's not good for me.'

''Now, when I get that familiar urge to go to Circus of Books, I'm aware that this is a deeper need I'm feeling, masquerading as eroticism. I start talking immediately to Christ. I say, 'Jesus, help me with this emptiness that masquerades as erotic desire.' After all, Joe, how does a man fill an empty spot in his heart with porno movies?"

I warned, "Those addictions can really creep back into your life if you don't take care of yourself."

"Yes, I know. But one of the most hopeful changes I see," Father John told me, "is that now when I do slip, I don't go overboard and wallow in the misery of a long guilt trip. That was the story of my life—going to confession and admitting my failure, then getting right back into the same endless cycle. I'd put a lid on the thing, I'd screw it down—but then the whole thing would blow up again."

In a confessional tone, he told me, "For the first time in my life I've been really facing my homosexual feelings. Not just bottling them up. I'm really facing what I'm doing. I can say the truth now: 'I am an addict, and I am dealing with it.'

"I've been thinking about this whole problem of masturbation. I want to be free of it, too—to keep my vow of chastity. I think I just have to be honest with Christ. I say something like, 'I feel like masturbating at this moment, and I'm not happy I'm giving in to it. But Jesus, stay in the battle with me in spite of my feelings.' "

He thought for a few seconds, then said, "My way of dealing with God in the past was to shut him out, to avoid him. To go into the dark and jerk off in the corner. I know now that God would rather that I face him.

"I had no relationship with God the father because I had no concept of father. I can see how some feminists who had horrible relationships with their fathers want a God who is feminine. They can't trust God, the father."

During his final session Father John complained, "This therapy has taken the fun out of a homosexual encounter. Even though I know I may fall once in awhile, I know it isn't going to satisfy me. The act has become a burden. It no longer holds the excitement—the hope, the fantasy—that once made it so appealing.

"I know now where it leads me," he said emphatically. "It leads me nowhere."

4

Charlie—The Search for the Masculine Self

One of the most intelligent and insightful men I have ever had the privilege to know was Charles Keenan, or Charlie, as he asked me to call him. Charlie had a slight build and somewhat effeminate mannerisms, but this certainly indicated no softness of character. Charlie was a man of unusual strength and clarity of purpose.

Thirty-two years old, Charlie was head of a large university biomedical library where he had worked for several years. He was well read, well spoken and highly educated.

At Charlie's first session he walked across the room and sat down quickly like someone who knew exactly what he wanted. "In the past ten years I've done quite a bit of flirting with the gay lifestyle," he said. "For a year now I've been in a gay relationship. A guy named Derek. It's not a bad relationship—we treat each other well—but I want much more in life. I can see this isn't all of it."

"What do you mean by 'all of it'?" I asked.

"I'm not getting a wife, I'm not getting children, and I'm not getting the kind of relationship I want to grow old with."

"And what kind of a relationship is it that you're looking for?"

"Well . . . I just feel there's something missing from what one man can give another."

He paused and sighed, trying to find the right words to continue. "You know, most of the gay guys I've met insist that homosexuals are born that way. But I can't help seeing it as an insult to my dignity to be told I'm this way because of something genetic. I have been a part of the gay lifestyle long enough to tell you that when a man craves masculinity so badly that he has to try to suck it out of another guy, then there is—undeniably—a big problem.

"I don't want to be gay," he continued angrily. "I'll never believe that that's been decided for me by some kind of genetics."

I lit my pipe and leaned forward, eager to hear more of what this man had to tell me.

"I've read a lot about homosexuality," Charlie said. "Working at a university library has given me the opportunity to read dozens of volumes on the subject." He chuckled. "I spend my lunch hour around the WM 16 section. In fact, one of the books I've read is your *Reparative Therapy of Male Homosexuality*. It made a lot of sense to me, and I decided to call you when I found out you were here in the Los Angeles area."

"I'm glad you got something from it," I told him. "What about the syndrome of male gender identity deficit, which I describe in it? Does this reflect your own experience accurately?"

Charlie laughed. "It is my life story!"

"Well, tell me about yourself, then. Let's begin with your childhood."

We both sat back in our chairs and made ourselves comfortable. Charlie sighed and looked out the window. "You know, looking back at myself as a boy," he said, "I can see I was born artistic, maybe a little unassertive."

I could see that he was eager to speak, but finding the right words was an obvious struggle. "I guess I didn't have the . . . the usual male buddies because I was . . . kind of different, more on the sensitive side. I had an operation on my knee when

I was young, which has left me with a bit of a limp, and that kept me out of a lot of masculine things—all that usual sandlot baseball stuff. But I don't think that any of that in itself means I had to be homosexual.''

"I agree," I said. "Many prehomosexual boys fit the picture you have given me—sensitive, nonaggressive, not being on the inside of male activities. But some other boys who grow up heterosexual also fit this picture. It takes something more than that to make a boy homosexual.''

"Well," Charlie continued, laughing, "I'm afraid I had that something more—I had the classic homosexual background. I was raised by a household of women, with a smothering mother, a domineering grandmother, and two older sisters. My father basically decided very early on, 'I can't handle this family stuff. I'll be around, I'll pay the bills, but I'm not actually getting involved with anything that goes on in this household.' So he didn't have much of a relationship with any one of us. He was basically a wimp, a nice guy but an outsider.''

After a brief pause Charlie proceeded. "I'm sure my dad had his own private inferiorities. There was really something wrong with him. Whether he was gay or not, there was some kind of a problem with his maleness, because he certainly didn't know how to conduct himself as a man in his own household. I really doubt he knew what to do with a son. He gets this little boy and he thinks, 'What the hell do I *do* with this?'

"My mother and grandmother made me into a sissy. I read, I drew, I stayed at home—you know, all that classic stuff. You could say that for many years Mom *absorbed* me. She took my life for her own purposes. Her relationship with her own father was horrendous, also with her brother, and later her husband. So I was the new little male, the moldable one, that she could work out all her shit on. She wanted the kind of relationship with a male she had never had before, so she took me for herself and drained me.''

"I imagine you never wanted to be close again to women," I commented.

"Well, actually, I have had a couple of girlfriends. But every woman I dated was like my mom. I had no self, no dignity, no boundaries with my mom. And I refuse to marry

Mom!'' Laughing, he said, "I pick 'em perfectly. I always get trapped into what you've so aptly referred to as that good little boy role.''

He continued, "I hate it. I was drained of my life being that good little boy.'' He pounded his fist on the armrest of the chair, his face betraying anger and embarrassment.

"So when did you figure out you were homosexual?''

Charlie sighed and relaxed back in the deep cushions, closing his eyes for a moment. "I was about 13,'' he said. "I was invited to this camp-out party with a bunch of teenage guys. They invited me because I hung around with the girls and I think they thought I could be an 'in' for them. But then the stud of the group, Andy, got really friendly with me, it got sexual, and bingo! Here I'm accepted by the stud! I have this special relationship with the leader of the pack. I take care of his sexual needs and he protects me.''

I interpreted, "Sex became your instant entry into the world of males.''

"That's right,'' he said. "So here I am feeling like I'm a man, I'm one of them. I'd discovered a way to relate to this guy I'd always admired from a distance. I didn't know what was going on but I thought, whatever it takes . . . and . . . I had to admit, it was pretty exciting.''

"So you were into sex with guys pretty much from that point on?''

"Not really. It was a few more years before I got into the lifestyle. I had a couple of relationships with women in college, but this particular guy Andy was still in my fantasies. In fact I always liked to imagine him joining us.''

I was confused. "Do you mean while you were making love to a girlfriend, you fantasized having sex with Andy?''

"No. Andy was there supporting what I was doing. Encouraging me.''

"That's interesting. I think this fantasy of Andy was actually symbolically bolstering your injured masculine self,'' I said.

"Well . . . maybe so. Because I'd imagine he would stand alongside of the bed and encourage me and . . .'' he searched for the word, "*support* me in having sex with my girlfriend. He'd tell me I was a stud, that I was doing the right thing, and he'd cheer me on while we were doing it.''

I clarified, "This fantasy man serves as the support that symbolically repaired your deficit male identity."

"I guess you'd say that," Charlie conceded. "Because I *was* there for her, and to some degree I was enjoying it . . . but somehow I needed Andy."

Charlie was able to function heterosexually, but he needed the image of another man's maleness. His use of the fantasy of Andy revealed one way the reparative drive is used to heal a man's injured masculinity. He also gave me a way of expressing what we would be doing in his therapy.

"Charlie, this whole therapy will be the actualization of that fantasy man from within the depths of your own psyche. So that you'll find him within, and you won't need to take another man's maleness sexually."

"To find him within. I like that idea. To draw on what I already *am*, but haven't actualized." Charlie said he wanted to give that idea some thought, and with that in mind, we closed our session.

The following week we decided to delve into some child-hood issues. "You know, Joe, as a kid I got shortchanged," he said. He sat on the edge of the chair. "You could say, being Mom's little man is how I got cheated."

He opened a silver cigarette lighter. "Excuse me . . . I hope you don't mind if I smoke? When I'm tense and excited I just feel like I have to occupy my hands."

"That's all right." I passed him an ashtray from the bookcase and settled back to listen.

"I've done a lot of thinking about what you said in the last session. In a way," he gestured forcefully in the air with his cigarette, "in a way, I've continued to cheat myself by getting stuck in gay relationships and not challenging myself to *become* those men I fall in love with.

"I was born a man. It is my identity, and it's something I want to be, completely." He leaned forward, his voice rising in frustration. "It's not that I never liked the idea . . . I've just felt insecure about my maleness. Do you know what I mean? I've always felt somehow that I was left out of the club of men.

"I really want to change that feeling. I want to claim the sense of manliness I envy in others, and I want to stop admiring other men. But you know what makes me angriest?" He set down the cigarette and spoke emphatically. "Society, psychology, the gay world—they want to tell me I was *born* desiring other guys. I wasn't born that way; it was a wound inflicted on me!"

As I listened, I couldn't help but feel admiration for this bright young man's hard-earned acquisition of self-understanding. He had struggled and questioned and fought with himself, and what he believed was clearly not an opinion that would have won him friends in the gay world.

"As I explained to you, my job offers me the opportunity to read lots of books on homosexuality," Charlie said. "A lot of the older psychoanalytic books really fit my experience. The classic family of inadequate Dad and overinvolved Mom. The kid who didn't like rough and tumble play. But if you read the recent books by gay psychologists you'd think the whole world agreed that homosexuality was inborn, impossible to change, and in every way as normal as heterosexuality. How could it be normal?" His voice rose, and he shifted into angry profanity. "You know, Joe, Mother Nature didn't make a dick to go in an asshole! It's sick! It's perverted! Even in the animal world . . . when one dog mounts another, it's a dominance thing and not something he'd do if there was a bitch in heat he could get to."

Charlie laughed and settled back comfortably onto the chair cushions. Then he sighed, looked around, and said mischievously in a low voice, "Want to hear a dirty joke? You know why scientists haven't found a cure for AIDS yet? You can't guess? Because they can't get those little white mice to butt-fuck!" Charlie seemed pleased with himself for the uncharacteristic expression of profanity.

I told him, "You know, it's true, you sometimes see mounting behavior in animals. But no species of animal *prefers* homosexuality. As for homosexuality in other societies, all cultures strongly favor heterosexuality."

Now I felt just as intense a need to express my convictions as Charlie had a moment before. "Gay spokesmen say we're presumptuous to use our values when we decide if something is normal. But then where *does* society draw the line on normality? Don't you think pedophilia feels normal to the child molester?''

''I don't know,'' Charlie said. ''That's an interesting question. Does it?''

''There was an article in a 1990 issue of the *Journal of Homosexuality*,'' I said. ''One-third of the pedophiles in it claimed that their sexual desire for children was a natural part of their constitution. They felt it was 'innate,' 'a fact of nature,' 'inherent in them,' and so forth, and they explained it by saying, 'This is just the way I am.' '' Because they believed they were born that way, they felt they could not change. Therefore they said they had the same right as other people to pursue the expression of their sexuality.''

''That's incredible,'' Charlie said.

''Now I'm not putting homosexuality in the same category as pedophilia,'' I said. ''Gay men are consenting adult partners. But *both* conditions are erroneously justified by the claim that they *feel* normal.''

Charlie pounded his fist to his knee and looked up at me intently. ''Don't our bodies proclaim the wisdom of nature by their design? Aren't we supposed to live out the natural male–female complementarity? Shouldn't this all make perfectly good, obvious sense to everyone?''

''Any man with that vision,'' I summed up, ''will never be satisfied being gay.''

The next week, Charlie decided he wanted to tell me about his previous therapists. He was eager to express his frustrations.

''I've been with three therapists in the last five years,'' he said. ''The first I'm sure was gay, although he never said so. He told me that I was gay, and that I should accept it. He kept telling me to go to the Gay and Lesbian Community Services Center to make a circle of friends in the gay community. I went a few times and the people I met there were nice, but I felt sorry for a lot of them. I really couldn't relate to them and where they were going.

''That psychologist had no concept of why I might be attracted to guys, and he did not want to help me explore the subject. He'd say, 'We don't need to know why a guy is *heterosexual*, do we? So why should we be concerned about why you're homosexual?' He totally avoided discussing how my relationship with my parents might have contributed. Before I left, I said to him, 'Look, I need you to support me in where *I* want to go in my life, not where *you* think I should be headed.' Of course, he felt I was denying some integral part of my nature.

"My second therapist was a young straight guy. He said I was lucky to be bisexual because I would have more sex partners to choose from!" A loud laugh. "Such idiocy! Forget him! Then I found a woman therapist, a really well-meaning Christian woman. She tried to support me in overcoming my gayness but she just didn't know what to do. I spent my money teaching her what I knew from what I'd read! Finally I discovered your book and I came to you."

I said, "Charlie, I've been amazed at your understanding of the condition. About what it means, and where it comes from."

He countered, "I'm amazed how others in my position *don't* seem to know, or don't *want* to know. I've asked a lot of gay guys, 'Hey, why do you think you're gay?' They don't want to talk about it—they're scared to death!"

He thought for a moment, then said, "Choosing to live the gay lifestyle feels like a last resort— a convenient way of having some contact with someone. I had to waste too many years to find out that what I'm living is a shortcut. I could have gone on like that, kept on doing it, but then I realized that I'm not the kind of person who will just settle for something forever."

Then Charlie verbalized a core issue of the homosexual condition. "I've always known I have an intimacy problem with both men and women, and I know it has to do with my homosexuality, but I'm not quite sure of the connection."

He continued, "My biggest problem is feeling lonely all the time. Disconnected. Even though I'm surrounded by people all day at work, I live in emotional isolation. Last week I felt empty, anxious, like jello. I didn't have the ambition to do a single thing, and every task simply felt like too much effort."

A hopeless expression took over his attractive, gentle face. I waited for him to say more. He sighed and continued, "I've been successful recently in avoiding homosexual contacts . . . but maybe my success is just due to old age and waning libido?'' He smiled ruefully.

In his little joke I heard a clear tendency to discredit himself, not to give himself credit for his achievements. Many homosexual men in treatment are slow to give themselves credit for what they have accomplished. They have not been taught to recognize their personal power.

Charlie sighed impatiently and looked me directly in the eye. "I'm doing without the sex but I'm lonely and . . . I want to know how I can give up having sex with men forever. It's just too difficult to do by sheer willpower.''

"I'm glad you realize that," I said.

"I feel too blah, too tired, too weary. Like I'm in a rut with no way out.''

"This blahness," I said, "is a cover-up for an untapped energy that's just under the surface. If you don't get in touch with that energy and draw on it, you'll fall into a full-scale depression, and then guess what will happen?" I warned him. "Depression is the lull before the storm of sexual acting-out again.''

"That I know all too well," Charlie agreed. "I can imagine myself hitting the bars in a big way if I don't do something about getting myself reconnected. I hope you can help me light the right fires and get back on track again. Funny thing—even though I know a lot about my problem intellectually, I still don't feel healed emotionally.''

"Well, Charlie, time's up for this week. So let's think on that paradox until the next session. Because yes, you're right; there's a world of difference between making change intellec- tually, and making change emotionally.''

When we met again the following Tuesday, Charlie con- tinued with the previous week's discussion. "You know, you were right when you told me that I'm very hard on myself. It's part of my problem. I never give myself credit for anything. I have a hard time patting myself on the back. I'll get enthused about a new idea and then I drop the ball, second-guess myself, and create all kinds of doubts and fears which I know are needless and unrealistic. I feel a constant dull, deep hurt somewhere inside.''

Then he confessed, ''One of the things that keeps coming back to paralyze and depress me is that I don't seem to know how to leave my parents, emotionally speaking. How to cut the umbilical cord and still . . . '' he searched for the right words, ''remain friends with them.''

''To remain in a relationship with them but not as a child,'' I clarified.

''Yes. To have some kind of equal relationship with them.'' He thought for a moment, then added, ''I don't know how to be real, to be myself around them. How to relate in a genuine way. I'm not sure what my feelings are toward them.''

As he began to confront how he had not been treated honestly by his parents, Charlie entered one of the more painful stages of reparative therapy. Out of their own narcissistic needs, his parents, especially his mother, had required him to be the good little boy and thus compromise his own masculine, autonomous development.

''The hurt you feel inside comes from realizing you were not recognized for who you are as an individual,'' I said. ''In some ways you were neglected, and in others, overindulged. Your parents did not give you a strong sense of who you were.'' It is this kind of childhood that has led authors Leanne Payne and Colin Cook to describe the homosexual as an orphan.

''Perhaps that's it,'' he said. ''Intellectually I feel sure of myself, but emotionally . . . I've felt like in some ways I'm nothing, I'm nobody, and it makes me angry. . . .''

I said, ''Going back and claiming your true identity will mean beginning to work your way back through the hurt.''

''What about my anger?'' he asked. ''I also have a lot of anger.''

''Of course. The anger is a defense against the hurt, the injustice. That's why so many of the guys are angry. Their anger is not just about the intolerance of society toward homosexuality. It comes from their awareness, on some deep level, that part of their essential identity was ripped off from them in their early years.''

"But how do I acknowledge these feelings of anger toward my parents? Do I have to emotionally disown them?"

"I don't think you *can* disown them," I said. "The task is to be an adult *with* them, not a little boy manipulated *by* them."

He sighed and said, "I feel paralyzed when I think of what lies ahead of me."

I said, "This is a critical, transitional phase in your therapy. You're not the manipulated little boy any more but you don't know yet how to be the autonomous adult."

"That's exactly where I'm at," he agreed. "How do I become an adult in relationship to my parents? I know I can't change my dad. As a kid I could never get him to acknowledge me in any way. Maybe if I had gone out for the sports Dad liked—he loved river rafting and fishing. I didn't go along with him more than a couple of times because I don't like swatting mosquitoes all night and listening to coyotes howl in the bushes. . . . When I started refusing to go along with him on his trips I really think he felt I was rejecting him. In some ways, I guess it was my fault that he abandoned me to Mom and my sisters."

"If you focus your therapy on changing your dad you'll sabotage your treatment. You probably can't change your dad, but you can change how you relate to him. You don't want to set yourself up to be frustrated, because that will lead you—"

"Back to some other guy, and that's not what I want any more," he said abruptly.

"And you'll come back next week with the same issues anyway," I added.

"Yeah, you're right." Then he added thoughtfully, "As soon as I turn my back on dealing with my dad, I face the struggles again. I can forget for awhile, put the struggle out of my mind, but it's clear that I'm just buying time, that eventually I'm going to have to deal with this problem. If not by changing him, then by changing how I relate to him."

I sensed the pressure Charlie was putting on himself and felt I needed to reassure him. "It's not something you have to resolve instantaneously. The great benefit of this therapy is that there are so many ways of moving forward—physical activity, developing healthy male friendships, starting a dialogue based on respect and mutuality with both your parents. There are lots of challenges that will get you moving forward.''

"Because I've just felt so stuck. . . .''

"The active, initiatory nature of reparative therapy emphasizes daily challenges in the world,'' I explained. "But when you're stuck on a conscious level, look to the unconscious. Pay attention to what comes up in your dreams.'' Even though Charlie felt stalemated, there was much to be learned from the everflowing undercurrent of his unconscious.

Pondering my words, Charlie said suddenly, "Last night I had a weird dream, which I can only recall vaguely. I had a hard time bringing it back into focus when I awoke, it was so brief. . . .'' He hesitated, then said, "Ah! It's coming back. I'm standing naked in front of my father.''

He looked at me and said, "That was all.''

"Any feelings?'' I asked.

"No. Not particularly.'' He shrugged his shoulders.

"Were there any sexual feelings?''

"Nothing. Just a very matter-of-fact attitude of 'Here I am.' ''

"How do you understand this dream?''

"I have no idea. I've never dreamed anything like that before.''

"What might you be trying to say by standing naked in front of your father?''

He answered, "This is me. I want you to look at me!''

"This dream has a reparative theme,'' I said. "It is an attempt at self-healing. Your father represents the masculinity never reflected back to you. The masculine affirmation you wish you'd had. You're saying to him, '*Look* at me! *See* me for what I am! I'm a man, acknowledge me!' This is what you want. I think it's an important dream that represents exactly what you want to achieve here in therapy.''

Charlie smiled. "Precisely! The image is really so simple but so perfectly symbolic. That's exactly what I want.'' A look of wonder crossed his face. "It's amazing. On some deep level of my psyche I know what I need, and I'm already striving toward it.''

He laughed. "I guess I'm not as stuck as I think I am." And on that note, we concluded our session.

A few sessions later Charlie recalled how, as a youngster, he had submitted to sexually serving an older boy. Then with considerable shame and embarrassment, he admitted that this had not just been a one-time incident, but in fact a regular pattern. He tried now to reenter the world of that little boy—what had he been seeking?

He asked, "What makes a kid do that kind of stuff, Joe?" The pain and shame still showed on his face.

"Something had to be acted out, some need had to be fulfilled," I answered.

"But why like *that*?" He sat stiffly in the chair, his face flushed and angry.

Then Charlie answered his own question: "It was a search for me. Something I wasn't finding in myself."

Charlie had touched upon an essential truth about the homosexual condition—that it represents a striving toward a lost part of the self. When I began clinical work with homosexual men, at first I thought it was simply a sexual problem. Later, I saw it as a male gender-identity problem. Today I see it as a core identity problem. Homosexuality represents a loss of the true self and of aspects of one's masculine power.

"Most of those boys I had sex with are married today," Charlie said. "They didn't get hung up on homosexuality like I did."

Charlie's perception was accurate. For many boys, homoeroticism satisfies a normal curiosity. But for other boys, like himself, such behavior expresses a deeper emotional hunger. In Charlie there was a need to fulfill his essential masculine identity—a need that he sought to meet in sexual intimacy with other males.

I asked Charlie, "Did you find any satisfaction during the later years when you were a part of gay life?"

"In some ways, yes," he said. "It could give me a very freeing feeling. I'd spend a couple of hours in a gay bar after a day of working so hard at the library. At last I'd be in a world

of guys who were in the same mess I was, and there was no
pretense, nothing to hide. . . . I might meet a guy and go home
with him for a couple of hours—it would be like the pleasure of
enjoying a good meal after a hard day of work.''

His use of the word *meal* struck me. Was the homosexual
act comparable to eating, devouring? Could fellatio signify the
same unconscious drive to take in something needed? *Dinner*
can be both primitive and pleasurable, sparking fantasies of the
other man inside the self, making the self stronger. I thought of
the male initiation rites of primitive tribes such as the Sambia of
New Guinea, where young boys are initiated into manhood and
strengthened through the ritual of taking in the semen of older
males.

I was also reminded of Carl Jung's insight into the homosexual condition. As paraphased by his biographer, homosexuality was, according to Jung, ''a repressed, undifferentiated
element of masculinity in the man . . . which instead of being
developed . . . from the depths of his own psyche, is sought on
a biological plane through 'fusion' with another man'' (Jacobi
1969, p. 51).

Charlie and I went on to talk about the patterns so often
seen in families of homosexuals. While insisting that homosexuality is strictly genetic, gay apologists have discouraged research into the family origins of homosexuality. They offhand-
edly dismiss classic psychoanalytic findings on homosexuality
as ''disproven'' and ''outdated.'' They fear that if we can prove
a connection with unhealthy family patterns, then society will
be more intolerant of homosexuality. Yet, I've often asked
myself, as important as tolerance is, should it come at the
expense of truth? Why can't we have both truth and tolerance?

I explained to Charlie how the prehomosexual boy is in a
general way what Alice Miller (1987) calls the ''used child,'' but
that he is used in a particular manner. The mother may use the
prehomosexual son to gratify those emotional needs that have
been unmet by her husband. The good little boy she raises is the
creation of a distorted feminine perception of what a male is
supposed to be. The father, on the other hand, uses the
prehomosexual boy in a more subtle way. He may be loving but
inadequate, or well-intentioned but neglectful. Sometimes the

father has sacrificed the boy to the mother's needs for a pet; he gives the boy up to keep Mother happy. In any case, the use of the boy in this triadic relationship sacrifices his maleness.

Charlie said slowly, "In other words, the boy may have been unacceptable to his mother until he extinguished his masculinity."

"He never extinguished it," I pointed out, "he simply never had any encouragement to claim it. To remain in the good graces of Mother, he may have even had to deny his *desire* for maleness. For Mother's love he had to submerge what we call his masculine strivings."

"Was it because she wanted him to be her little boy forever?" Charlie asked.

"Often. Many mothers want their sons to be good, pure, there for them as Mommy's little pet. The role of the good little boy excludes maleness, since maleness carries with it independence, autonomy, and exercise of personal power," I explained. "What makes the boy different from the mother is precisely his masculinity. If he expresses it, his mother thinks, 'He's going to be *not* like me.' Some mothers feel threatened by this gender difference."

"Kind of like she'd like him to be her partner," Charlie said, screwing up his face with a disgusted expression.

"Yes," I said, adding, "these mothers do not consciously wish their sons to be homosexual. When they discover twenty years later that their son has a homosexual problem, they're very often shocked and saddened. They don't realize that they themselves helped to lay the foundation for this condition."

"And when the mother is creating this nice, neutered little boy, the father doesn't intervene!" Charlie's voice carried a hint of anger.

I answered, "Exactly. One important role of the strong and nurturant father is to disrupt the comfortable symbiotic bond of the mother–son relationship. Many fathers mean well, like yours, but simply don't see what is happening."

"So there may be many boys out there who had the same mother I had, but their fathers stepped in and stopped what was happening. If I'd had a stronger father who was more involved, the equation might have balanced out differently."

"Absolutely. And perhaps if you, yourself, had been a little tougher and more resilient, maybe you could have pushed your mother away, and broken through your father's reserve and uninvolvement. But you were a sensitive child, and not the type who is apt to take on emotional challenges. This is why homosexuality is usually not a mother–son problem or a father–son problem, but a mother–father–son problem," I explained. "It's a balance among the three. The eminent psychiatrist Irving Bieber referred to it as the triadic relationship."

Charlie recalled, "It's funny, I was recently looking at some family pictures and my sister told me that every time we took a family photo I didn't want to be part of it. I kept slipping off out of range of the camera."

"A withdrawal. A feeling of differentness. I hear this all the time. The prehomosexual boy doesn't feel like part of the family."

"I sure didn't," Charlie said.

"I can understand that, because you weren't taken seriously by your parents."

"I was treated like a possession," he said. Then added, "When I was in grammar school, I had a weight problem and the kids at school used to tease me and called me klutz and fatso. Yet my mother watched me proudly one day while I ate a whole chocolate cream pie by myself. To this day she'll talk fondly about how cute Charlie looked when he finished that whole pie in one sitting."

"You were an adorable possession," I said.

"Like the two little poodles she got as pets when we three kids had grown up and left her." He laughed. "Those dogs took our places!"

"You were made to live a false self that sacrificed both your autonomy and your masculine identity," I said. "People often don't realize they've been living a false self until they start to experience some freedom from it. As you start to live through your true self you'll feel a sense of liberation, spontaneity, and inner power. The false self usually leaves a person feeling self-conscious, rigid, and somehow empty or dead inside."

"And the feeling of the true self will stay with me, in

time?'' Charlie asked. Then he said, a note of pleasure in his voice, ''I've been starting to feel stronger. I've been making progress in my straight friendships, and I've been thinking of joining a gym.''

''Good. You're moving in the right direction.''

''I want to feel better about my body,'' he said. ''I'm getting older and I'm getting flabby,'' he said, patting his stomach, ''which makes me depressed. I used to look really good—about the time I was in college. I had thrown off that fat boy image by losing a lot of weight and exercising so I'd feel sexy. It felt good to get noticed by the guys in the bars. You know, that sort of vanity thing.''

This ''vanity thing'' led to a discussion of the male homosexual's condition that I call *alienation from the body*. There is a tendency for gay men to perceive their own male body with a detached fascination, as though it were object rather than subject. The homosexual's body, particularly the penis, is something he carries but does not own. This feeling of not owning one's own body may take the form of a sense of inferiority or superiority, but there is never a relaxed connectedness with it. Many clients express a sense of disconnectedness with their bodies starting in early boyhood. There is also an excessive modesty, which usually continues into adulthood. They may describe an unwillingness to take their shirts off, even at the beach or in hot weather. They describe a reticence to undress in front of other boys, even their brothers. The shyness may alternate with exhibitionism, which is an attempt to overcompensate for shyness. Both shyness and exhibitionism are forms of alienation from the body.

This same sense of inferiority and discomfort resurfaces in later years when the young man typically develops an overconcern about penis size. Associated with this is the phenomenon of being pee shy, or having difficulty urinating in the presence of other men in public restrooms. What we are seeing in this dynamic of alienation is a failure of the family (and father in particular) to integrate the boy with his masculinity by way of his own body.

Even when describing his participation in sports, the homosexual often experiences an objective detachment. His tendency is to observe himself and his bodily movements, rather than sense himself as *being* his moving body. Because he lacks this trust and confidence in his natural movements, he is likely to envy this quality in straight guys. For this reason and others, I see homosexuality as not simply a sexual problem, but a larger problem in one's way of *being in the world*.

Returning to the vanity problem, I said to Charlie, "Your wanting to become involved in physical improvement is great, but it shouldn't be pursued for vanity's sake. You don't want your body to be an object to show off. That's a need that comes out of the false self. The goal is to develop an internal sense of ownership. You *are* your body, you are centered in your maleness. You don't carry it, it carries you. The pride you feel about your body should arise from your identification with other men. Do you understand the distinction?"

"Absolutely," he said. "I've known both sides. The look-at-my-body trip, which comes from narcissism, and on the other hand the sense of centeredness in my masculinity. I know the difference, but sometimes it's hard to hang onto that other way of perceiving myself."

"That's O.K.," I assured him. "What's important is that you know the difference."

"For a long time after I got my weight down, I felt proud because I had a good body that got me the attention of other guys. In the bars, guys would look at me and that really made me feel good about myself. Yet in a way I hated it—it stood in the way of what I really wanted."

"Which was what?"

"A man."

Startled by this contradiction, I asked, "Your body stood in the way of your getting a man?"

"Right."

"Explain that to me."

"All I've ever wanted is to be close to a man. Not a gay man, someone straight—a 100 percent natural and masculine man. But those men don't fall in love with me—they want what they can't be, and that's a woman. That's the paradox of the homosexual condition."

Thinking on that, we ended our session.

Charlie was soon making excellent progress in his male friendships. He joined a gym, where he was discovering he could develop male friendships without being overwhelmed by sexual temptation. He now spoke of a new friend, Rich, whom he described as "a great guy, very affirming. Straight, and he has no idea what I'm dealing with."

"I have one question," I said. "Any attraction to him?"

"A slight one," Charlie admitted after a reflective pause. "Yeah, sort of. Sometimes I compare him to myself and find myself thinking, 'He's got something I don't have.' From that, it sort of slips into a little bit of sexual attraction."

He continued, "One day last week Rich walked into the locker room. He had a tee shirt on and his muscles were really bulging. I wasn't feeling good about my skinny arms and chest and I felt that attraction welling up in me. I said to myself, 'Hey, if you want what he has, you'll have to work for it like he did. If you think he got that way overnight, you're crazy. He paid in sweat for that body.'"

Of all the men I've worked with, Charlie was best at utilizing a valuable technique of reparative therapy called *self-mentor talk*, the practice of talking to himself in the voice of an internalized strong, benevolent father.

He continued to talk about his new friend. "Rich always makes me laugh. He helps me be a little less serious. I like that sense of spontaneity in him, that enthusiasm and crazy humor. He doesn't blow every little thing out of proportion, like I do."

He was quiet a moment, then he reported the following. "The other day I was hit with a truth that I really think came to me by the grace of God. I realized there is no one on the face of this earth who can give me my masculine identity. No other guy. It lies within me, only dormant. No one can give it to me. Nor can I get it by changing my external image. The real key to change is actualizing what I already have in me."

Charlie seemed eager to talk on. "Rich and I went hiking a couple of weeks ago, and it looked like it was going to rain before we got back to the car. Rich didn't seem to care so I kept quiet, but it was making me nervous. My mother always used to say, 'It's going to rain!' as though getting wet would be the death of me, like I would die of pneumonia. Most guys don't care if they get wet, of course, but Mother's voice has always played on like an old tape inside me. So I thought, 'If I get wet, I get wet. So what?' Well, we were soaked. I thought, 'Now what do we do?' Rich kept walking so I said nothing, as though it wasn't important.''

Charlie tossed me a faint smile. As if he felt happy to have burst out of one more bond by which his mother had constricted him.

"I really think I'm making progress," Charlie said. "I've felt it in some dreams I've been having lately. Last night I dreamed I was standing at the base of a mountain trail with my friend Eric. We were wearing backpacks and hiking boots and we had our shirts off in the afternoon sun. We were both looking muscular and I was feeling pretty good about myself. Suddenly two blond girls walked past and I said, 'Hey, Eric, don't they look good?' He said yes, and I was feeling this really lighthearted friendship.''

"Very interesting. And how would you interpret that dream? Remember the two basic rules of dream interpretation—everything in the dream is significant, and every part of the dream represents a part of you.''

He began, "There was a feeling in the dream of being happy about just being me and I loved it. The sensation of being carefree and strong. I wanted to grab onto that feeling and just hold onto it. I don't feel that way often, and it was a real high for me.''

I asked, "My question now is, why is Eric in the dream?''

"Let me think about that," Charlie said. Sitting back, he squinted upwards and pondered. "Well . . . maybe I see qualities in him of which I wish I was in possession.''

"Sure," I said. "Do you feel you are gaining those qualities?''

"Slowly, yes.''

"What qualities?''

"The spontaneity, the freedom. That's what Eric represents—those are the qualities that I most admire in him.''

"What part of you is represented by the mountain?''

Charlie thought for a moment, then answered, "I suppose it's my struggle. This therapy feels like climbing a mountain.

And you could say that in some ways Eric is my companion and guide.''

Charlie seemed reassured by this dream. I saw in him the satisfaction that comes from understanding how his dreams, in perfect symbolism, reflected his conscious strivings. Charlie had come a long way, and for that we were both happy.

Many men have come to me chronically depressed and unhappy, going through the motions of life while missing some sort of essential vitality. Gay spokesmen would say that these men were full of self-hatred because they had internalized society's homophobia. Or they would say that these men felt chronically empty because they didn't allow themselves to find fulfillment in a male lover. But that vitality had been missing for as long as Charlie could remember, and he knew it had to do with his lost masculinity.

During the course of psychotherapy, each client goes through despairing times during which I try to make him aware of the new life that will emerge on the other side of his struggle. I stand by him while he endures the pain that is always a part of healing, as he asks, time and time again, why it is he who must suffer. There were many months during which Charlie wondered whether he would ever make it over that mountain.

In the final year of treatment Charlie entered group therapy, where he contributed a strikingly thoughtful and insightful presence. Before long the respect he was accorded by the members of the group was readily apparent: whenever Charlie spoke, everyone listened. His clarity of expression and penetrating vision earned him the position of much-admired leader. Charlie often set the direction of our group discussion. He made many close friends among the men, supporting them when they lost their direction. When he walked out of my office for the final time, I knew I wasn't the only man who would miss him.

Charlie Keenan changed in many ways. What he wanted most from reparative therapy was to find a centeredness in his own masculine identity. Through that achievement, he hoped to find a diminishing of his homosexual distractions. After just over two years, he left my office feeling that he had achieved what he had come to therapy for.

I still keep in my desk a piece of paper on which Charlie once wrote some reflections:

Today, my therapy unravels the lies that inflicted this male insecurity upon me. My therapy has been a sophisticated process of discovering the truth, trying it on, and living it out confidently for the first time in my life. My therapy shows me I'm a full member of the club of men because I was born a man. My therapy puts me in the company of men with the same struggle. We believe in one another and help each other to live out our masculine energy and identity, rather than perpetuate the mythic message that we are unworthy of the healthy male identity that all men are meant to enjoy.

These two and one half years have been a blessing of freedom and empowerment. My sense of satisfaction with my masculinity is now alive and growing:

1. I don't crave masculinity any more. Instead, I have claimed it.
2. I no longer overvalue (sexually desire) or undervalue (defensively detach from) the men in my life. Instead, I stand with them as an equal.
3. I have lost my antagonism toward my father and find myself identifying more and more with him.
4. I speak up more often and am far more assertive.
5. In spirit, I am less repressed.
6. In action, I'm more in control. I'm more willing to take risks.
7. Through exercise I've made better friends with, and I have less hatred toward my body. I may never be completely free of this limp I've had since I was a boy, but I've been making the most I can of my body.
8. I am able better to appreciate the feminine in my women friends because their contrast to myself is now more apparent.
9. I look for the masculine energy in all things and find ways to experience or express it genuinely from within because to do so is to live, and to heal.

I know there are homosexual men who accept the idea that they were "born that way." I challenge them; they are selling themselves short. They refuse to admit that they might be broken (as every human being is). They refuse to look for roots to their problem because it is repugnant to see where one has, perhaps unwittingly, said "no" to the responsibility that is placed upon us to live as we were created. It is a sin of pride that blinds these individuals, that tricks them into believing that brokenness is shameful. It is not. The real shame is in not *accepting* forgiveness and in not *giving* forgiveness. I have forgiven the men who have failed me, as I have forgiven myself for years of running away.

It is my hope that every man who hurts from homosexuality may open himself to receiving the same grace that I have known. It was this grace that enabled me to see that my homosexual tendencies were not a cry to have another man— but a cry to have a manly me.

Charlie still drops me a note now and then, and I am always happy to hear from him. The men in the group still miss him.

5

Dan—The Angriest Man

My secretary Jennie knocked on the door. "Your six o'clock appointment's here to see you." The door opened a crack and Jennie looked through it. "This fellow looks a little . . . intense," she whispered.

A minute later, Jennie showed Dan Prescott into my office. A tall, muscular man about 40 years old, Dan swaggered into the room, flashing brown eyes at me that were unnervingly penetrating. He looked like a teenager from the fifties, with his tight blue jeans and a white tee shirt, the sleeves rolled up above the biceps. We shook hands, and I motioned him to a chair as I took the seat opposite him.

Almost before he sat down, Dan began. "Let me give you some background information. I don't want to waste time. After all, at a shrink's office, time is money." His laughter was cynical.

He leaned forward and spoke intently. "I've been fooling around in the gay scene since the sixties. Seen it all. Got heavy into drugs, all sorts of shit, alcohol. Must have had sex with a few hundred guys. Really fucked up my life."

He sighed deeply and looked down, his brashness suddenly softening. "I've come to the conclusion that it's just not worth it." He shook his head sadly. "The pain is just too much. The brief hope of meeting that special friend, finding that lifetime relationship. . . ." He hesitated, seemingly groping. "Well—I can see it's just not possible."

He stopped, looking for a response from me. Receiving none, he continued.

"For the past three years, I've worked hard at staying sober, and I've been pretty successful." In spite of himself, Dan's eyes showed a glimmer of pride. It was obviously difficult for him to feel good about any personal accomplishment.

"And why are you coming to me now?"

"I heard about what you do here," he gestured around the room, "and I thought you could help me. I want to give up sex with guys just like I gave up drugs and alcohol. For me, sex with men is just another addiction."

He hesitated, then added, "I thought you could give me some advice beyond 'Just Say No.' " Momentarily, he surrendered a chuckle.

Quickly turning serious again, he continued, "I want to know more about myself, to get more for myself. And I want to get out of this continual . . . this . . . well, unhappiness."

As I spoke to him, I would often find Dan regarding me with a look of smoldering anger. Indeed, this was one of the most hostile men who had ever entered my office. Dan was always irritable, always ready to sense an affront. His anger was just below the surface, and seemed ready to explode at any moment. Yet beneath the rage I would discover an equally intense, paralyzing fear which he bore from childhood.

In a self-mocking tone, Dan told me that he worked as an "assistant to an assistant producer" of a children's television show. Little by little I heard the story of his struggle with an addiction to one-night stands he picked up in adult bookstores or on the streets of West Hollywood.

In time, I learned that Dan's anger served as a defense against the vulnerability necessary for authentic interpersonal contact. Observing his body in the chair, I discovered that whenever Dan made an emotional connection with me, however brief, his physical restlessness immediately ceased. He sat still and calm. His verbal expression became focused, strikingly insightful and lucid. For Dan, anger was a form of defensive detachment. It kept people away from him and protected him from the hurt he always anticipated.

He announced, "I'm angry at my friends, my bosses, every one of those sons of bitches. But no one pisses me off more than my mother. A two-minute visit with her can make me positively crazy." He twisted tensely in his seat.

"Like the other day. She's always saying that I don't come by enough. I have the key to her house so I walk in, making plenty of noise. She comes around the turn in the hall and jumps [he imitated a high-pitched, hysterical female voice], 'Oh, my God! It's you!' She grabs her breast and shrieks, 'Why didn't you say something?' Then for the whole time I'm there, all she can talk about is what I've done to screw up her nervous system!

"I feel like walking the hell out of there. The woman is, and always has been, nothing but a hysterical basket case!"

Regaining his composure, he continued, "I realize she's an old lady, but this is just so typical of my mother's way of acting. I keep hoping someday she'll quit being so wrapped up in herself and her hysteria, and try and get the message."

"What *is* the message?" I asked.

Caught by the question, Dan paused for a long moment, then said bitterly, "To see me . . . to think about me . . . to . . ."

"To *acknowledge* you," I nodded. Speaking for him, I continued, " 'Mom, it's me, your son! Can you forget your nerves for a minute and remember that this is your son standing in front of you?' Maybe that's what you'd like to say to her."

Dan nodded. His expression told me that I had understood him.

As Dan described his early childhood, it was clear that his mother had, in effect, emotionally abandoned him. This fear of abandonment had left him with an inner emptiness and anger, which nothing in his life seemed to assuage.

Dan said, "There's a musical instrument called the Indian

sitar, and there's one note that's played over and over, the sruti note.'' He shook his head. ''My sruti note is, 'I'm not getting what other people get in life. Relationships don't work out for me.' ''

''That same frustration, anger, bitterness, and disappointment are always just beneath the surface,'' I nodded. ''And you can be distracted for awhile—get some relief—but when the distraction stops, that background note is still there playing.''

For a moment the anger and restless motion ceased, and it seemed that Dan smiled at me, if only slightly.

The following week Dan hurled himself into the chair and got right into hashing out his grievances. Although he wasn't yet making an emotional connection with me—in fact, he often seemed to ignore what I had to say—he had no trouble describing the things that bothered him.

''As far back as I can remember there was always a power struggle between me and my dad,'' he said, punctuating the statement with a jab of his fist in the air. ''The only time we had any relationship was when we were fighting.

''It often happened around the dinner table, and this goes back to when I was walking around in diapers. I just plain wouldn't eat. It was this big power struggle between us. He was going to make me eat and I wasn't going to eat. I would sit there at the table for what felt like hours. It became a battle of wills— we would carry on for the longest time, with him yelling and me crying. And of course my mother was hysterical, totally helpless.''

''What do you think the battle was about?'' I asked.

''It was more than food, I know that.'' He shook his head, unable to speculate further.

I pushed, ''Whatever it was it must have been very important. Imagine the great emotional cost to this little kid who certainly must have been hungry.''

Dan shrugged his shoulders helplessly.

''Fighting your dad was somehow of great importance.''

''I guess so.''

''Because you were not just fighting for the sake of being stubborn. You were struggling for a vital aspect of your own identity—your power and autonomy. Negative attention was better than no attention—it was better to have your father fight you than just ignore you."

Dan stayed silent.

I continued, "The killer is that the battle became self-defeating. You thought you were gaining autonomy, but you just ended up locked into a destructive pattern."

I could see clearly how Dan's battles with his dad had established a lifelong pattern of hostile male relationships. His self-defeating way of relating to men was a twisted attempt to gain male attention and recognition. Women were scorned as untrustworthy, weak, and manipulative; men were seen by him as exciting and powerful, but frustratingly unapproachable.

"My father. My father! The thought of the man makes me cry. Just a big, fat, sloppy, loud-mouthed dummy. Reminds me of Jackie Gleason. Good heart, but a jerk. Had no friends, and half the time he didn't even want us kids around—he'd scream, 'Brats, shut your goddamned mouths, get 'em out of here!' Right in front of us. What a fucker! He was a shithead. I hated him. Can you believe, when he died, they gave me a picture of him? I don't want no fuckin' picture of that man hanging in my house!"

In a soft voice, he added, "And yet I miss him."

"There's anger, but . . ." I said.

"Yeah."

"But love *and* anger."

"Yeah. Which makes a conflict. Love–hate."

"Turned into self-hate," I added.

There was a long silence.

Suddenly Dan said, "There's this flaming queen named Tyrone at work, and the very sight of him makes me nauseous. I laugh and joke with the other guys about him. We scapegoat the poor bastard all the time, and I say things like, 'As long as he doesn't touch me, ha ha ha.' I don't like being identified with Tyrone, and I don't like feeling attracted to other guys, the way he is.

"But I am," he added. "And I don't like masturbating to thoughts of men. I'm stuck in that shit and I want out. I'm frustrated and I'm angry.

"I've got a lot of 'Call me a faggot and I'll knock your teeth in!' I've got a lot of that kind of anger."

"Remember what these feelings for men represent," I said. "They're perfectly natural and understandable strivings for male love and understanding. Of *course* you need men— you never had enough of the love of men when you were young and vulnerable. There's a deep hurt that these feelings are trying to answer."

Dan wasn't yet willing to acknowledge these needs. He laughed, that familiar cynical snort, as if to dismiss any sympathy or sentimentality sent in his direction.

One month later, Dan recounted an old memory that he felt had great significance. "It was the cellar," he told me wistfully. "I still have dreams about that cellar. We had an old farmhouse outside Sioux City, and you opened up this rickety trapdoor and went down these creaky steps into a dark and damp-smelling basement. My father would escape from the rest of us and spend hours there in his machine shop. But I was forbidden to go there—I might break his tools or get hurt, is what he told me. So I would lie on my belly up above, looking down and watching Dad work.

"What I'll never forget," Dan said, "is that feeling of mystery about what was going on down below. Eventually my Dad let my two older brothers help him, and they'd be talking and working and laughing. It wasn't just the mystery of what was being *done* in the cellar . . . it was the whole mystery of who Dad was, because to this day, I really don't understand him." He hesitated. "I'm not even sure if I love him or hate him."

"He didn't permit you to enter the world of men," I said. "He never taught you how to develop your masculine identity."

He repeated wistfully, "That cellar is about Dad. When I think about Dad, I think about the cellar."

Dan continued, "If I had to draw just one picture that would represent my entire childhood, it would be of me peering down into the darkness at my father and my brothers. If I felt shut out of the cellar, I know I felt shut out even more in other ways. I remember one Sunday morning my brother Dick called up to me, 'Guess what Daddy is doing down here?' I called down, 'What?' But he was just teasing me. He never answered.''

He thought for a moment, then added, "I think this is how I still feel about men.''

How many other times had I heard homosexual clients describe men as mysteries? Like Dan's father and brothers working in the cellar, men are exciting and unknowable. A boy's natural curiosity and healthy need to know other men, when frustrated in childhood, is later eroticized.

As the months passed, I began to see a vulnerable side of Dan which had been hidden deep within the bristling, swaggering man who had originally entered my office. Soon it wasn't unusual for Dan to cry during his sessions.

Our work brought up many painfully repressed memories of his father. During one session Dan got out of his chair and, imitating his father, glared directly into my face. "Don't think you can stand up to me. You are a nothing!"

He bellowed again, "You are a nobody!" Gesturing at me with his little finger, "You are this big. Don't you ever think you can fight me!"

Collapsing back into the chair, he continued, "I remember, I must have been no older than 4 or 5, I made a fuss about something and he yelled, 'You don't like the way we do things? Things don't suit you? Get out! Get out of my house, kid!' "

He stared at me, eyes wide, with a stunned, blank expression. For a moment the anger was gone, and there was a little boy's face, filled with paralyzing terror. I could see that Dan—tense, cold, angry Dan—had been frightened out of his heart.

Dan's father belonged to that small minority of fathers who are explicitly punitive, even cruel. Fathers like Dan's seem to need a little boy to be the weaker masculine figure whom they can intimidate to enhance their own sense of power. The majority of my clients' fathers were not so much hostile as they were inadequate, passive, or emotionally distant. Many of these characteristics of fathers were demonstrated in the classic case study by the psychiatrist Irving Bieber.

"Sometimes my father would try to help me with my homework. He'd tell me to sit down at the kitchen table and keep working until I figured out how to do it. I'd be crying, but he'd keep needling me. 'Just shut up and *think*, you'll solve the problem.' That was his way of helping!''

There was a long pause. "I truly hated the man." Dan's voice was surprisingly husky. For a long time he sat silent. "Oh, why can't I talk about my father?''

Besides occasional traumatic assaults from his father, Dan described an ongoing, day-to-day emotional neglect from both mother and father. Like many of my clients, Dan felt he had never been taken seriously. He said at one session, "I never felt that the real me mattered. I don't think either my mother or my father ever really *knew* me. Even my feelings were twisted around and misinterpreted.'' In these words I glimpsed the ultimate cause of the lack of personal identity so often found in the homosexual condition. This sense of not being taken seriously is the foundation for the false self so often seen in the homosexual.

"Do you remember, Joe, back in the sixties, when they had those haircuts with the straight, square backs—not tapered?''

I nodded.

"When I was about 13, I told the barber to give me a square back. I guess I was trying to look cool or something. When I got home my mother started screaming, 'That's disgusting! Who do you think you are, some hood?' She marched me right back to the barber and in front of everyone, demanded to have it tapered.'' He snorted. "It was one of the most humiliating experiences of my life. In fact, Joe, I was never again able to face that barber.''

Dan continued, "I never felt like I was heard or understood, and I guess that feeling is still with me. At the weekly studio meetings, I can often feel myself getting very hyper, very melodramatic just to get a simple point across. I end up exaggerating just to get acknowledgment. I feel like I'm struggling to get people to hear me.''

I nodded. "You always felt your opinions, judgments, and decisions were dismissed or ignored.''

Dr. Gerard van den Aardweg has observed that the homosexual often has a tendency for overdramatization. The fear that he is not having any impact may also explain the exaggerated, larger-than-life characteristics of behavior so often seen in gay culture. Gay rights parades, protests, and demonstrations—mounted as if in defense against not being heard—are often presented in a theatrical, outrageous, carnival-like manner. Someone once dryly observed, "Gay people are like any other people—only more so."

Like most prehomosexual boys, Dan had developed the stereotypical false self of the polite and accommodating good little boy during his childhood. His compliant demeanor, however, was easily shattered by his angry outbursts. This "problem child" side of his personality was as false as the good little boy facade, as it too was a role created out of a dysfunctional family structure. These hostile outbursts alternated with long periods of quiet withdrawal whenever he felt the same sense of abandonment and not being understood that so many other prehomosexual children experience.

These boyhood swings between rage and quiet despair obliterated his true spontaneous, receptive, joyful nature. As I pondered this death of his true nature, I could feel the rage of baby Dan in his highchair, and I could understand his refusal to eat his dinner.

As the months progressed and Dan grew in peace and self-understanding, he came to understand some factors that were motivating his behavior. He saw his anger as a cover-up for deep abandonment fears from his earliest relationship with his mother. Preoccupied with her own anxieties and obsessions, she had neglected Dan pathetically.

While the groundwork for Dan's deeper characterological problems had been been laid by his mother, Dan's father was responsible for setting the stage for his erotic longing for males. The homosexual attractions Dan developed in adulthood were an attempt to bridge the gap between himself and other males, which had been symbolized by the cellar.

Dan said, "I look back and see that my homosexuality came from a desire to belong to the company of men, to be connected. In the beginning, it wasn't sex at all that I was seeking.''

He hesitated, struggling to put words to an important memory. "When I was still in high school, I remember I wanted to be friends with this guy, Jerry. But he didn't want to be friends with me. Simple as that. [His voice rose in frustration.] But it was sheer hell! Like it was this incredible isolation. I blurted it out one day—I told him, 'Man, I am sexually attracted to you!' I was crying. I look back on all that now and see him as being a nice guy with whom I just wanted to be friends—but I didn't know how to be just friends, without the sexual thing.'' Dan was wide-eyed as he spoke, with a helpless expression.

I nodded, saying nothing.

"Looking back,'' he said, "I realize that having sex with guys was a way of filling an emptiness. Sex would be an emotional catharsis. I needed to have the sex to get through to a feeling with a guy, even if it only lasted for a moment.

"That need to be held!'' Dan continued, despair in his voice. "There's such a deep hunger for that contact. The need continues to this day. For a long, long time it wasn't sexual. I just wanted to . . . you know, squeeze the guy.''

He continued, "A few months after I got out of high school, I met a guy at a bar. I was loaded, and after we had sex I started sobbing and telling him about Jerry. [He laughed.] I scared the guy, like he must have thought, 'Wow, I picked up a freak!' I never saw the guy again—he was probably glad to get rid of me—but I walked out very relieved, like at last I had reached a core feeling.

"The wound, the pain inside . . .'' Dan continued, "I'm always wanting to show it to someone, to have them draw it out of me. But when I find someone who might be able to draw out the pain''—his frustration punctuated his every word—''I-can't-let-it-out-of-me!

"I'm always bored with people,'' he continued, twisting tensely in his chair. "Always. I've felt bored and restless all my life, since I was little. Even when I'm with a guy I'm attracted to, I end up feeling this boredom, as if I'm just killing time until the really exciting guy comes along to replace him.'' He paused.

"But I know now there is no such guy. It's all been a pipe dream."

"You feel empty, anxious," I said.

"And then I run away from it."

"How do you run away from it?"

"The usual addictive things—drugs, alcohol, picking up on guys." He thought for a moment, then added, "And on the few occasions I've spent a few weeks with one guy, I've gotten into a destructive, dependent relationship. The more I'd get, the more I wanted—it would never be enough."

"Because it was the wrong thing."

Dan seemed confused.

I clarified, "If it was the right thing—true affirmation of you—it would feel satisfying. But the wrong thing—that romantic high, that overidealization—it never satisfies. It just feels good for awhile. Takes away the pain of aloneness."

Dan nodded in agreement.

"And along with that, there's the need to possess—not just to be with—but to *possess* him. You begin to see him as a missing piece of yourself."

Dan laughed ruefully. "Pretty soon I'd actually find myself taking on the guy's personality! I'd start imitating things about him. Do I need an identity so desperately that I look to other guys to tell me who I am?" He snorted. "It got so humiliating, I just quit trying to have relationships."

Dan's account evoked once again the three needs unfulfilled in boyhood that underlie homosexual attractions, the three A's—affectional needs, attentional needs, and approval needs. For each client, these needs may vary in relative importance. However they each represent a way in which men strive toward masculine identification.

For men like Dan—severely neglected in early childhood—not only masculine identification, but personal identification needs lay behind his homoerotic attractions. Dan's need for identification was so desperate that he often found himself trapped in dependent relationships that made him feel vulnerable and violated.

A large proportion of homosexual clients find themselves

in dependent relationships and suffer interpersonal boundary problems. I've often thought that this is because gender identification is so closely related to ego formation. The man who is weak in gender identity is also likely to have a weaker sense of self and of personal boundaries.

The existential predicament of the homosexual is that until he identifies fully with males, he will want them erotically. Yet he cannot identify with maleness as long as he continues to eroticize it. To identify with men, he must *surrender the eroticization* of men. The only way a man *can* absorb masculinity into his identity is through the challenge of nonsexual male friendships characterized by mutuality, intimacy, affirmation, and fellowship.

In consulting a male psychotherapist, the homosexual man hopes for perhaps the first time in his life to find another man who understands and accepts him. Through his relationship with a same-sex therapist and the understanding of similarly committed group therapy members, he can work to restore what his relationship with earlier significant males failed to provide.

In every case of homosexuality, successful treatment depends heavily on the building of close, nonsexual male relationships. The client must grow beyond his defensive detachment to reconcile his ambivalent love/fear of men if he is to resolve his homosexual conflict. Dan described this very ambivalence during one session:

"I don't want to depend on anyone. I've got a lot of 'Get away from me!' inside. I *need* friends but I don't *want* friends. Like the other day, this guy Brent said, 'Let's go to my house after work.' I said O.K., then a few minutes later I thought, 'Screw you, I don't want to see you! Why would I want to go to this fucker's house?' So I told him something had come up, that I was busy.

"So you went home, back to your little isolated world," I reminded him.

"Yeah. Why can't I be normal? I need friends," Dan said. "I need *you*." There was a long and painful silence. "It was tough for me to say that."

One day Dan confessed to a strange behavioral pattern. "The 'Jerry' thing I told you about—when I cried in front of a guy—that was almost twenty years ago. Since then, I guess I've gotten a lot more cynical about love. During the past few years I've been attracted to guys who you'd consider controlling— typically an older, domineering man. But when the doors are closed and we're alone, I like to turn the tables on them." He chuckled.

"How's that?"

"I like to know I can beat a person who is trying to control me. So, here is a man who is a domineering figure, but I become the top man in the sexual arrangement."

"How do you control?"

"I like to—um, I will decide if we will kiss, I'll decide what we do in bed. I like to persuade my partner to do things he'd rather not do, things that he thinks will humiliate him." He hesitated, seeming to evaluate my reaction. "And if the guy doesn't like to get fucked, I'll persuade him to let me fuck him." He half smiled. "There's a lot of emotional gratification in domination, in getting a guy to subordinate himself to me. For me, that's a particularly satisfying arrangement. And I'll never let him see any emotion from me."

"How's that?"

"Like, even when I come, I won't show any pleasure."

"Why?"

"Well, the control thing. I like to show that I can hide my feelings."

Dan began to recognize the anger that he felt toward the very persons from whom he sought sexual gratification. This sadomasochistic characteristic often found in homosexuality traces back to the unattainable father whom the boy desires, yet despises.

Dan spent many months in therapy working through his feelings for his father and mother. It was those core feelings of love and painful dependency that he sought to feel again in order to heal. Uncovering these feelings in a safe and under-standing relationship offered the only hope of relief from the sense of hollowness he lived with. As with all persons whose character structure has been damaged by neglect in earliest infancy, Dan would have a painful struggle to fill that emptiness. He was well aware now that the hole in his heart could not be filled by drugs, alcohol, or homosexual relations. He had begun to surrender the perennial gay dream—that of finding that one special person, that one solution, that one fix. Rather, he realized that the real healing would come from a slow accumulation of positive introjects—that is, the taking in of good feelings from healthy relationships.

As he told the group in one therapy session, "The gay scene was like taking speed. A real high in the moment, but totally destructive to my spirit."

Dan eventually made peace with the memory of his father. Even though it was painful, he had needed to do this in order to be at peace with himself.

There is a particular quality of anger that characterizes the homosexual's relationship with his father. While straight men may also report problems with fathers, I have noticed a qualitative difference in their anger. The straight man's anger is usually framed within a realistic acceptance of the father's shortcomings. But the homosexual man holds a profound grievance, a grudge and a deep hurt that block any kind of understanding of his father as a man.

A frequent misunderstanding of many a client is that in order to grow and change, he must gain his father's acceptance in the present. This error is based on the unconscious assumption that the father possesses the key to the son's healing—again, the projection of the omnipotent father. A significant step in the client's development is the realization that it is *he*—not father—who now holds the power that can give him his masculine identity. The client also needs to be reminded that the damage was done not just by his father, but by *his own participation* as a small boy, through his own defensive detachment. In fact, many of my clients' fathers see their sons as having rejected *them* from earliest childhood.

Dan was being called upon to give up his defensive attitude toward all men, starting with his father. To forgive the father is not an easy task. It often means accepting the father with all his limitations, including a limited ability to show love, affection, and acceptance.

Many clients must accept the fact that their fathers cannot change, as they had hoped they would. As one client expressed it, "I know my father will never be different. I'll get as close to him as I can. But what he can't give, I'll have to find in emotional intimacy with other men."

It may feel like death for a young man to realize he must give up once and for all the fantasy of ever receiving his father's love. To understand, forgive, and love his father is, ironically, to be father to his father—to give his father what he, the son, once himself desired so desperately. Often compassion for the father grows out of an understanding of his father's father and how he treated his own son.

Almost all my clients report that their fathers had very little to say about their own fathers. The shadow father—the man who is uninvolved and ineffectual—can often be traced back to father, grandfather, and great-grandfather. Thus the foundation of one man's homosexuality may lie in earlier generations.

I find it interesting that gay ideology continues to deny this important common denominator in homosexuality—problems in the father–son relationship. There is, in fact, a stubborn refusal within gay psychology to concede any significance whatsoever to fathers.

Dan's self-esteem continued to improve over the course of the three years he was in therapy. "I have got to keep working on self-acceptance. It is essential to my well-being. Without it I have no hope of survival," he told me. He became better able to develop trusting relationships, to avoid anticipating betrayal. Little by little he came to let go of his angry defensiveness with me, the group members, and all the other men in his world.

His second most important goal was the continued pursuit of nonsexual, close relationships with men. As these needs were being satisfied, he told me, "For the first time in my life I can see the possibility of having a relationship with a woman."

Dan had been free of drugs and alcohol for three years before entering therapy. As he told me in our first session, his

next goal was to be celibate—what he called "sexually sober."
After the first year of treatment, he had achieved his goal of
sexual sobriety, except for very occasional masturbation to
homosexual fantasies. Critics of reparative therapy might say
Dan merely suppressed his desires, and did not truly resolve
them. Yet for Dan, sexual involvement threw all relational
structure out the window. He could not handle this dimension
of relationships. In his case, the choice to remain celibate while
he was working through his issues was very wise. As he often
told me, "It's just an easier way to live."

The goal of celibacy was reached through commitment to
a structured lifestyle—weekly individual sessions as well as
weekly group psychotherapy; maintaining his commitment to
Alcoholics Anonymous; and maintaining nonsexual male
friendships. He also kept up an involvement with his church,
and made a commitment to jogging daily.

Structure was an essential key to Dan's healing, and
through this structure he slowly learned to build up a higher
level of trust and to penetrate the pain of his profound inner
emptiness. He learned that with time, maturity, and life structure, the pain diminishes.

But even though structure brought Dan to his goal of
abstinence, abstinence is only one step toward healing. What
Dan also needed to heal himself was the slow absorption of
positive introjects. Through therapy, he began to allow himself
to be touched by other human beings, and in turn he began to
see beyond his own pain to empathize with another person's
feelings.

Dan's early childhood deprivation and resulting characterological damage ran deeper than his sexual orientation difficulties. Indeed, this characterological wound, more fundamental than his homosexuality, would not heal itself quickly.
There are quite a few homosexually oriented men in therapy
who struggle with characterological deficits. Their pain is
profound and their therapeutic work particularly difficult.

As our sessions came to an end, Dan understood more
clearly the contrast between his true needs and his false pursuits.

As he told me in our last session, "Abstinence keeps me
out of trouble, but I know now that man-to-man intimacy is
where the real healing happens."

6

Steve—The Seeker of Male Symbols

Steve Johnson was a 24-year-old clean-cut, collegiate type. He arrived for his first appointment wearing khaki cords and a pinstriped shirt and tie. Yet although Steve was strikingly handsome, his looks were a bit studied, even effeminate. He worked as a legal researcher for a prominent Los Angeles litigation firm.

Steve had a charming, gregarious social style. Yet behind this outward energy he hid a deeply troubling depressive side of himself as well as an inner softness and passivity, which he particularly hated.

Steve's flirtatious search for male attention, combined with his attractive preppie look, made him particularly appealing in gay social circles. He told me he had been leading a frenzied social life of short-term relationships, which made him feel out of control and very unhappy. "Out of control" is an often heard complaint in the lives of many homosexual men.

In this first session, Steve described the classic family background—a weak, emotionally ineffectual father, and a close relationship with an overindulging mother. There were two older brothers with whom Steve had never gotten along.

Steve was more manipulative and extroverted than most of my clients. His personality could be classified as narcissistic—that is, he tended to evaluate the worth of others in terms of how they made him feel about himself. If someone reflected him in a flattering way, then he liked him. Everyone else he dismissed as unimportant. With his characterological problem of narcissism, Steve's homosexuality posed a particular challenge.

Steve needed to be in control of others, yet he constantly felt out of control of himself and his relationships. In fact, he often found himself in the painful position of being manipulated. The combination of passivity and craving for positive attention caused him a great deal of conflict.

In his first session, Steve complained, "My insides feel so weak. I get swept off my feet by a man who's strong. I've experienced this problem most of my life. I feel like I just lack a forward thrust."

"You lack the forward *male* thrust," I said.

He nodded thoughtfully. "You could say that for me, sex with a man serves. . . ." He halted, as though searching for the words, "ah, it validates that I'm good looking, that guys like me. You see, sex with men is real easy, instantaneous," snapping his fingers, "and it gives me some sort of, well, a feeling of life."

"Life?" I asked.

With an embarrassed laugh, he said, "Yeah. If I'm having sex, it means that I have a social life. I'm not isolated." Then sadly, "In actuality, I still am isolated."

He then said, "I trust you can help me develop some hope of feeling like a man." His voice sounded sad. "I'm shocked at my lack of confidence in myself as a male." He added, "But at least I do feel better now that I've made the decision to come here and face my problems."

Narcissism is a heightened emotional investment in one's own image. The narcissist shields against hurt by armoring himself with materialism and the latest fashions and accoutrements, as well as fostering an extreme concern with every detail of his body. This self-absorption extends beyond his own body to include a preoccupation with his choice of car, his home, his interior decor, and every other personal detail. This overconcern with image is how the narcissist protects himself against an internal sense of vulnerability. Homosexuality is so often connected with narcissism because both conditions can be traced to a hurtful relationship with parents in earliest childhood. There has been an injury to the deepest sense of self—a narcissistic injury.

Just as the body sends a flow of blood to repair a physical wound, so, too, does the psyche center itself on repairing a psychological injury. The person with an injury to the sense of self is forever focused on protecting that injury, and the result, just as with a bodily injury, is an overcompensation, in this case in the form of the grandiose narcissistic style.

The narcissistically wounded person relates to others in terms of whether they will intensify or allay his pain. Those who cannot allay it are devalued. Such relationships are not I–thou, but rather I–it. In homosexually oriented males, this is sometimes seen in a compulsive search for anonymous sex.

As Steve described his relationships with other men, he spoke of becoming swiftly disillusioned as soon as he discovered something unmasculine about each man.

"I'm always searching for that magic—the man who can fulfill my ideal," Steve continued.

"Tell me what your ideal is," I requested.

"Let me see." He thought a moment, then said, "Masculinity. He has to be very secure in himself. Very together. Very confident." He added, "But there are not many such men around, so my selection has necessarily been limited."

I asked, "Why are these certain men so attractive?"

He hesitated, then answered, "Well, I don't feel very strong in those areas. So I'm just drawn to them. I always have been, since I was little."

"Exactly," I said. "You understand that your attraction to them is really a projection of the ideals of masculinity."

He nodded. "I want and expect them to be masculine, to be a stronger person than I am, and when I find out they're just like I am, it's like a huge flaw. I drop them immediately."

Steve then spoke on at great length about his unhappy relationships, and before I had the chance to say much in response, it was time to end our first session. As he stood up to go, Steve admitted, "I know these patterns I'm into are sick." There was sadness and defeat in his voice. "And I know they're a large part of why I'm always lonely." He looked back at me searchingly. "I just hope that you can be the one who will finally help me."

After several months of therapy, Steve had broken the pattern of frenzied short-term relationships. We were both very happy that he had made this progress. Still, all was not going well for him. He came into my office one sunny morning and dropped himself dejectedly into his usual chair.

"I'm controlling myself sexually a lot better now," he said. "I still think a masculine, well-built man is gorgeous . . . I still have the aesthetic appreciation. But now I don't have to lust after a man like that. I don't *have* to have him.

"Yet," he said, "my *real* Achilles heel is still this sense of loneliness. It's the hardest thing for me to deal with."

Steve and I went into a discussion of the importance of establishing nonsexual male friendships. He had been making good progress over the weeks in terms of insight, even behavioral change. Yet his passivity and depression were still preventing him from seeking out male friendships. He felt stuck.

We talked about how these relationships would be different from those with his lovers. "I've been thinking about the relationships I had with some of the men I dated, and I remembered that when I dated a man I considered very masculine and I felt accepted by him, I felt a corresponding increase in the feeling of *my own* masculinity."

"This is an underlying motivation of homosexuality," I said. "You feel that you can absorb the other man's masculinity. That's what fellatio symbolizes. You vicariously take in the other guy's maleness."

"But the feeling never lasts," Steve said. "It's only momentary."

"That's just it," I replied. "When masculinity is eroticized, it can never be internalized."

Steve looked puzzled and asked, "But why is that?"

"Because your lover remains an erotic symbol, not a real

person who can affect you. The lasting transformation occurs when you experience man-to-man, authentic intimacy. *That's* what will heal you. Honest intimacy with men is what the homosexual really desires—but it's also what he's very afraid of. Honest relationships will get you out of that deadly cycle of loneliness. In fact, we should spend some time working on ways you can get these relationships started."

Steve suddenly brushed aside the subject with a sigh of frustration. "Well, anyway . . . I guess I should tell you I had a rotten day."

I decided he had had enough lecturing on male relationships and asked, "Why did you have a rotten day?"

"I don't want to go into all the details. Everything was just very difficult, very much against me."

He sat silent for a minute, then said, "I saw this gorgeous pair of lovers today." His voice was tinged with envy.

"Which only stimulates the longing and the loneliness," I said.

"Right. It was like, 'Oh, they've got this close relationship, they're both so good looking.' I felt sorry for myself, that I didn't somehow fit into the picture. This is something I've lived with for years," he admitted. "I feel sorry for myself and I expect other people to feel sorry for me. Recently I've been getting so bummed out about being deprived, that the temptation gets worse than ever."

"And that self-pity gives you permission to give up on the abstinence you've been working so hard on. 'Oh, poor me! I need a break. I'm going to pick up some guy and act out my fantasies.' " I continued, trying to be gentle, "Do you understand how self-pity can lay the foundation for such regressions?"

"I still have no real significant male friendship," he said, his voice plaintive.

"So, indeed, you've set yourself up for this loneliness," I pointed out. "You need friendships, Steve. You need men. You've got to take steps to start things happening."

"I guess I do." He sighed and shrugged his shoulders sadly. Steve could see how depriving himself of intimate male friendships would lead to loneliness, self-pity, and compulsive sexual contacts. He could go on and on with "poor me" descriptions of his problems, but when I counseled him about doing something, the conversation fell flat. Although he usually *agreed* with what I said, I suspected that my words weren't having much of an impact.

Steve could talk about himself in endless, dramatic detail—his memories, life experiences, clothing, men he found attractive, injustices he had suffered. Yet I wondered if he was allowing himself to be moved on a deeper level by what I said.

A few weeks later Steve walked in and, as though he could hardly wait to talk, sped to his chair. He described an incident in childhood that spoke of his thwarted desire to connect with the masculine.

He said excitedly, "I remember that in sixth grade they were going to have this father and son event sponsored by the school system, to teach the boys about sexuality. I must have been about 12 years old. It was on a Saturday and I was all excited. It was supposed to be a film in a city auditorium, followed by a discussion. My mom pushed my dad to take me—it wasn't easy getting him to budge from the TV set. I remember we went by train together.

"What was special about this event was that one of the presenters was a male teacher who I looked up to and admired. I guess I had a crush on him."

Steve looked almost embarrassed and went on, "I was so excited. I even made a point of dressing seductively for the occasion." A slight laugh.

"What do you mean by 'dressed seductively'?"

"I wore these very tight shorts that I liked myself in." He reflected for a few moments, then said, "Even then, I liked tight clothing."

I was surprised to hear that a 12-year-old boy could think so flirtatiously.

He continued, "But when I got there, who was leading this whole thing but a woman, not my man teacher. She was the principal and a *woman!*"

He added with an outraged laugh, "And a bitch, yet." He went on, "And everybody hated her! She's gonna teach male sexuality? Here is this father–son day and *she's* gonna lead us? Like yeah, right!

"And to think—I dressed up for her!"

We both laughed at this absurd situation. Steve went on, "It was horrible."

Beneath the outrageous humor I could feel the painful disappointment for the boy who had been deprived of the opportunity to have a needed experience with males, about maleness. Suddenly Steve became more serious. He said, "I was really hoping for the opportunity to share some intimacies."

Those words—*share some intimacies*—capture so well what the prehomosexual boy desires so intensely from males.

"Anyway," Steve continued, "they discussed masturbation but I still didn't know what it was. So on the train going home I tried to talk with my father about what we had seen and he gave me very short answers. I asked if masturbation was bad and—" he giggled and waved his arms in the air, "my father gave this *very* bizarre answer. He said, 'Yes, masturbation is wrong, unless you do it when you're married.' Even at the age of 12 I thought, 'Man, this doesn't make sense! What's he talking about?' There wasn't going to be any sharing of intimacies with *this* guy."

Steve now looked tired. Sighing, he said, "I was always looking for these men and these inside experiences with them."

"And you can still find them," I assured him. "Let's put you in group therapy. I believe you're ready."

Putting Steve in group was important because he would not take enough initiative on his own to develop a circle of male friends. Yet I was also concerned that the group would put temptation in his path. Steve was attractive, flirtatious, and particularly vulnerable.

It was Father John that I was particularly concerned about. Father John would surely find Steve his type—the personable, good-looking young man he sought in his porno fantasies. I hoped that Father John, twenty years older than Steve, would resist any temptation that might arise to become more than the platonic good father whom Steve had always longed for. Their symbolic attraction would be a risk, but it was time to take it.

Steve was now into his third month of treatment. He was doing well in group, and we were both encouraged. I decided to broach a problem in our individual sessions that he had hinted at previously.

"A couple of weeks ago," I reminded him, "you said there was a long-term problem we should talk about. Some kind of sexual problem."

"Oh, right. I . . ." Awkward and groping for words, he threw his hands up in exasperation.

Finally, "This 'thing' has been a problem for me for a long time." Silence. Then, "It's embarrassing."

"Just get into it," I encouraged.

"Well, as I've told you, I hate my job. Everyone is so demanding of me. 'Steve, get me this.' 'Steve get me that.' I come home feeling no energy for anything, and the only thing that gives me a lift is thinking about going through this—this crazy, repetitive cycle."

He fell silent again. I said gently, "Tell me about this cycle."

"Well, I have this fetish about certain western clothes and riding around in certain kinds of cars and trucks."

"Like what?"

"Well, I go through these buying sprees where I get all this western-style clothing. I normally dress like this," he said, pointing to his Calvin Klein shirt. "Conservative. You know, semi-preppie. But every once in awhile I just have to have these western clothes—Levi jeans, cowboy shirt and hat, snakeskin boots, things like that." He paused, adding, "Maybe a brown suede jacket.

"It all makes me feel more masculine. I imagine myself going on a date with a girl dressed like that."

"And then what?" I asked.

"Well, I imagine making love to her when I have these clothes on. I'll masturbate all dressed up. . . . Sometimes I'll do it in front of the mirror. It's a ridiculous cycle . . . kind of sick. I don't understand it." Then he added, "I usually don't buy top-quality western stuff—not the grade I'd I wear to work, for example—because I know I won't keep the clothes around afterward."

"Why?"

"Because if I keep the stuff around the house, I know I'll fall into the cycle again. If I know they're there, then when I feel upset or angry, I'll use the clothes as an outlet. Then I'll just feel like shit afterwards."

"So what do you do with the stuff?"

"I try to return as much of the clothing as possible or else I give it away to the poor, like I'm doing a penance."

He continued, "It's time wasted. I have to go drive to the stores, buy the stuff, wait in line, go home. Then, after I've had a couple of thrills, I have to go through the craziness of getting rid of it. Sometimes I'll bring it back to the store and try to get my money back. Then I feel like a jerk going back to the same salesperson." A frustrated laugh. "They must all recognize me by now."

He laughed. "I'm glad I can imagine making love to a girl. But the weird part is, I have to have these clothes on and be in a jeep or something." He said seriously, "I feel so perverted and silly."

Hearing this self-deprecation, I intervened, "Steve, if you understand how and why this came to be, you will be less self-condemning."

He went on, as if he didn't hear me, "At one time I actually drove all the way to Los Angeles to rent a brand-new Land Rover to go with all this western gear, and I acted out in it."

" 'Acted out?' "

"Yeah. I mean I drove out into the hills and masturbated in it. Or sometimes when I'm out hiking, I'll find an abandoned vehicle."

"O.K. So, what are your associations with western clothes and cars?"

Steve looked at me blankly.

"Male symbols?" I suggested.

"Sure."

"Any memories in particular?"

Again, he seemed to draw a blank, as if never having considered the origins of his behavior. "I remember when I was a kid, the boy next door, Robbie, would dress up sort of western. He would say, 'Oh, these cool Levi jeans, they're really in, I really dig them.' I was really turned on by him. Robbie was the trendsetter in our neighborhood.''

"What else did he say?''

"Well, he mentioned how much he liked the metal parts in the jeans.''

"The metal parts?''

"Yeah. You know, the rivets.''

"The rivets?''

"Oh, yeah. I try to get jeans with the rivets but they're harder to find today. Copper has gone up, you know.''

I could see we were only scratching the surface of the detailed world of fashion. I decided to stick with the psychodynamics. I said, "Somehow, I think Bobbie's—''

"Robbie,'' he corrected firmly.

"Thank you,'' I said. "Somehow you found Robbie's comments on the jeans significant. Stay with that.''

"I always admired Robbie. As I said, he was the trendsetter, and I really envied his family. His father was an attorney, and his mother was elegant.'' He added wistfully, "Unlike my family, who were always screaming and fighting.''

"How old were you and Bobbie at this time?''

"Robbie. *Robbie.* I was 13 and he was two years older— 15.''

"Did you look up to Robbie? Did you admire him?''

"Oh, yeah. I did. But Robbie was never—you could say he was never affirmative to me. In fact, I don't think he even liked me. His attitude was, 'Well, not everyone can achieve like me.' You know.''

"Do you think your western fetish started with Robbie?''

"It might have. But my father also loved westerns, and he watched them on the TV all the time. I'd sit with him and be turned on by Lee Majors in 'Big Valley' and Michael Landon in 'Bonanza.' I remember a dream I had over and over, about someone stepping out of a truck dressed in western clothing, a macho-type male.

"I've been thinking, 'My God, if I get married, will I have to wear this western stuff to bed in order to perform sexually? And if I did, would she wonder, 'Is he getting off on *me* or *himself?*' ''

"Hmm. Well, let's not worry about marriage just yet," I assured him.

Steve suddenly said in a desperate tone, "I don't know how to stop!"

The fetish was Steve's way of compensating for his sense of powerlessness. Unable to maintain interpersonal boundaries, he often allowed himself to be used by others. This had been a problem for a long time at the office, where he was manipulated by his boss and co-workers. On the outside he was the cooperative, congenial pleaser, never saying no to extra work. On the inside, Steve built up anger which he could only express indirectly. His pattern was to return home at the end of the day feeling manipulated and emotionally depleted, then to use his western fetish to give himself the feeling of power he could not find internally.

I explained, "The western clothes are armor to bolster your masculine power. You get sexually aroused by your image, so that you become your own sexual object."

"Yeah," he said. "I always felt it was somehow weird, but I never understood what was happening."

"What you need to do is *internalize* symbols of masculinity, *own* them—not objectify them. Your masculinity is a form of imitation. Like the little boy who puts on daddy's shaving cream or tries on daddy's hat."

"I guess that means I'm still a little kid," Steve said, blushing a bit.

"In that way, yes. The imitating you are doing is inappropriate because it's a bit late, developmentally. Erotic energy has been attached to these masculine symbols. At this point, what you're stuck in is called a fetish."

In the following weeks, Steve began to understand how Robbie represented his own unactualized masculine identity. Steve was caught in a false masculine identification consisting of no more than imitation. He had never fully identified with Robbie (or maleness in general) and had never genuinely internalized masculine attributes.

The question of *why* Steve had never identified fully with males has no simple answer; but we may suspect that his father's indifference was one key factor. He evidently found no other affirming males with whom he felt secure enough to share masculine identity. His friend Robbie was attractive but rejecting. Steve saw Robbie as like his father—distant, unapproachable, and therefore unidentifiable.

A fetish occurs when free-floating sexual energy becomes attached to a particular object. The fetish of western clothing symbolically connected Steve to the masculinity he wanted. Fetish objects are chosen and infused with sexual energy because of some powerful personal significance.

Steve could achieve only false identification—that is, *imitation*—using admired male symbols. While imitation offers temporary gratification, it never leads to a deeper identity change. A *real* identity change would require real contact with real men, not just the appropriation of masculine symbols.

When driving a jeep or wearing cowboy clothes, Steve felt himself becoming the cowboy-masculine image. Because it was an image, something external, he aroused himself by it. One cannot sexualize what is subjective—what feels to be within and a part of oneself. We only sexualize what we do not feel ourselves to be.

As he progressed, Steve began to identify the all-important emotions that always preceeded his compulsive fetish behavior. He was able to identify the feelings of loneliness, stress, and being out of control that triggered the fetish impulse. Through understanding the symbolism of this fetish and knowing when he was most vulnerable to it, he would strip it of much of its power.

One day, he bounced in looking particularly cheerful. "Last weekend I was driving along Pacific Coast Highway with a guy who knows what's going on with me. As we drove along I told him, 'For the first time in years, I am starting to control my sexuality and my weight.' " He spoke happily.

"Your—weight?" I asked him.

"Yeah. All my life, I've had a diet problem."

"You look trim enough," I assured him.

"Well, I've got this overeating compulsion that I sometimes get into. I'm addicted to Almond Joys."

"I like Mounds myself," I blurted out reflexively.

"Oh," he said animatedly. "You like the coconut with the *dark* chocolate!"

I could feel that I was getting pulled into another one of Steve's detailed digressions. I quickly steered the conversation back to his progress in therapy.

As Steve discussed his diet problem, it became obvious he had a serious eating disorder, which included a cycle of binging and purging. Food and sex, the two fundamental passions out of control in Steve's life, were both abused to soothe the inner desperation.

As we evaluated what had been accomplished so far, we could see that Steve had done fairly well during our twenty sessions together. He had far less need to act out his western fetish. He and Father John had become friends and saw each other outside of therapy. Fortunately, Father John was able to see beyond Steve's physical attractiveness, and they had a good relationship, which seemed to be mutually healing. Father John became a mentor of sorts, and was able to help Steve stay away from his fetish compulsion.

Then for two or three months, the group saw that Steve was becoming quieter. One day, his silence was challenged by Charlie. Forced to speak up to the group, he told them what was happening.

Nervously clearing his throat, Steve began, "I've really gotten a lot of strength from you guys." He looked around at the others. "But for the last couple of months—I've been feeling I need a break." The group members looked at him expectantly.

"I still have faith in this therapy," Steve stammered.

Then he got to the heart of the matter. "But I don't have much faith in me. Actually . . . . I don't think I can handle it." The men tried to reason with him, but he could not be convinced to stay any longer.

That was Steve's final session.

What had kept Steve in therapy for five months was his great need for undivided male attention. Therapy offered him the opportunity to receive the three A's from men—attention, affection, and approval. I'm not sure how much he really listened to what I had had to say to him. Rather than really taking in what I had to offer, I think he was enjoying his chance to talk and be attended to.

Yet, while Steve enjoyed the attention, he never really trusted me. This lack of trust was evidenced by his secret struggle with bulimia, which he kept hidden until near the end of our sessions.

A couple of months later, Father John met Steve for lunch. Steve said he was back in the gay lifestyle and had changed his mind—he no longer believed in the idea of any sort of change therapy.

Hearing Steve's change of heart, I felt a certain sadness. Steve had gained some insight into his behavior and now better understood his male relationships. But people choose their ideologies to meet their needs. I believe he ultimately went back to a gay ideology because he couldn't meet the demands of reparative therapy. He could never develop the compelling belief that he could change. How I wished I had found a way to communicate the conviction to him that change *was* possible.

7

Edward—Agony of a Youth

Sixteen-year-old Edward Paterson was brought to me by his mother because she had found some gay pornographic magazines in his bedroom. This discovery prompted the painful confession from Edward that he was homosexual. Upset and confused, Mrs. Paterson insisted that Edward consult a psychologist.

Mother and son lived in a large house overlooking the ocean in Pacific Palisades, while Edward's brother and sister lived with Mrs. Paterson's ex-husband in the city of Los Angeles. Their father was a well-known criminal lawyer.

Mrs. Paterson was dressed in a crisp linen suit with matching alligator bag and shoes. Her handshake was strong and her manner direct. She introduced her son with a grim expression, then turned to leave us. Looking over her shoulder she said sadly, "I hope you can help him, Dr. Nicolosi."

It is usually the mother who recognizes the homosexual son's problem, and many mothers have been instrumental in bringing their sons into treatment. The father often seems oblivious to the difficulties, and even if he does see them, he is rarely an active force in initiating his son's treatment. Indeed, Edward's mother had been concerned about his effeminacy and his lack of male friends for years. She had often suspected that this might lead to homosexuality. On the other hand, his father had been completely surprised when he heard of Edward's interest in gay pornography.

I felt a particular ache for this teenage boy trying to do the right thing as he sat facing me, half frightened, half defiant. Was he boy or man? Ed was clearly a little of both. His dark hair tumbled about his pale, sensitive face. He was slim and somewhat slight, but showed a developing chest and arms under a bulky sweatshirt. Left alone with me, he was clearly frightened.

After a few pleasantries, I got right to the point: "Let's talk frankly about why you're here. Your mother is unhappy with your homosexuality."

Edward shifted in his chair and laughed nervously.

"How do you feel about it? Is it something you want to work on changing? Or is it something you want help in accepting?" He looked puzzled, then said in a low, rather slow-speaking voice, "Well, it's kinda like I never talked to many people about it before. . . ." He paused, then added, "It's obvious homosexuality is not socially acceptable. I mean, for that reason alone, I don't like being gay."

"But you yourself aren't motivated to change the feelings?"

"No, I don't think so." He half smiled and seemed embarrassed.

This is the essential quandary of the adolescent—his wish to set his life on a healthy course, in conflict with the compelling desire to satisfy intense erotic attractions. Unlike the adult who comes to me after grappling with the pull of gay life for several years, and has decided unequivocally he does not want it, a teenager cannot be expected to sublimate sexual gratification for long-term vision. Especially when popular culture is telling him he must embrace his gayness.

"The reason I ask you," I said, "is that I can't help you grow into a gay identity. That's not the kind of work I do. If that's what you want, you'll need to see a gay-affirmative psychologist."

Edward looked unsure. "I don't know. We have a gay counseling office at school. This counselor gave me lots of advice, some gay books and pamphlets, and kinda took me under his wing . . . so I guess I should hear how you are different."

I knew Edward was talking about Project 10, a service of the public schools staffed by volunteer gay counselors. These programs, which I strongly oppose, do not make students aware that there is any other alternative. The message is, "You will never change. Your only choice is to accept and embrace a gay identity."

I sensed Ed was becoming confused by conflicting messages. Comparing ideologies was not what he had come for, and he was becoming disinterested. I decided to focus on what he himself saw as his needs.

"Of course, I understand that your attractions toward other guys are very strong and very important to you now. We will not focus on getting rid of the feelings unless you decide you want to. If you like, for now we could spend a couple of sessions understanding you, what's going on in your life."

He nodded, seemingly relieved. He said, "My biggest problem right now is school. I have this school phobia."

"What exactly is your fear of school?" I asked.

"The whole thing," he answered. "I don't know . . . just everything." He seemed stuck.

"But your mother told me you had a leading part in the school play, and you're on the dean's list. How can you have a school phobia and be an honor student?"

"Oh, it's not the work," he corrected. "It's just that I get nervous as soon as I approach the building."

"Well, let's try to focus on just what about school makes you nervous."

My concerned tone seemed to comfort him. For the first time that session, he was beginning to focus.

"I don't know. There's just the fear of being under the control of something, maybe the teachers and the principals. I can handle other social things like drama class, stuff like that.

"For most kids, high school is O.K.," he continued. "They fit perfectly into it. But for some reason I'm different."

"Why do you think you're different?"

"I don't know," he said, puzzled. "I don't know the reason. I just know that I am." He looked at me helplessly.

"All right, let's not worry about the reasons," I said. "Let's start with the experience. What do you feel?"

"It's kinda like I'm in prison, and everyone is telling me what to do."

I suspected the true problem was that Ed lacked social support. Without understanding friends in whom he could confide his conflicts, he felt alone and alienated, turning for satisfaction to academic work, and seeking self-expression in drama.

"Anything would be better than school," he continued, his tone self-pitying.

I challenged, "Anything would be better than having to deal with people your own age?"

"Well, except for acting class," Ed corrected. "I feel really comfortable dealing with drama students."

"Maybe you don't want to fit in with the other students, especially the guys?"

Ed looked at me. "That's true," he said solemnly. "I don't *want* to fit in with the other guys. I'm different."

Ed was using his theatrical interest to justify the feeling of differentness that came from his homosexuality. ("I'm too *artistic* and too *different* and too *special* to be with the other kids at school.") This artistic-gay package justified his detachment from "boring" straight guys. This was to become a repeated theme in our early months together.

"And that's the big problem," I said. "The biggest fork in the road of your life. You'll keep confronting that fork for the rest of your life—'Do I fit into the straight world? Or do I stay in the gay world?' "

Gay spokespersons themselves are in disagreement about how to handle this issue. Some argue the gay man is just like the straight in every way except for his sexual "preference." Others maintain that a "gay sensibility" invariably sets gay people apart from conventional society.

I sensed that Ed could not handle this question right now—it was too abstract and futuristic. At any rate, the clock told us our session was over.

"Well, Ed," I asked, "have you had enough of me forever? Or do you want to try one more session?"

"I don't know." He shrugged indifferently.

I waited.

He thought a minute. "I'll come back one more time, I guess. I'd like to talk a little more about my school phobia."

The following week, Ed plodded in with the same hangdog look he'd worn in our earlier session. I wondered how much of this was acting. Since he had nothing to say on his own, I prodded him to tackle his relationship with his mother. "You and your mom live together, and your brother and sister live with Dad. How did this happen?"

"Well, my brother and sister are older, so they went with my dad. Living with him is like living by yourself."

"More freedom?"

"Yeah. That's why I want to move in with him." He laughed bitterly. "My dad never knows what's going on—he's too busy with his law practice. He's never been too much involved in our lives. I guess that makes him easier to live with." He sounded disgusted.

"There's another reason I'd like to get out of the house now," he added. "I'd like to get away from my mom."

"Why?"

"I'm sick of the fights with her all the time." Ed's voice was still low but more determined.

"How does she make you angry?"

"Well—we used to be really close. Maybe because I was the youngest, Mom kind of took me around with her. I always did things with her. I guess I never had a lot of friends. But now, she's just very annoying to me at times." He retreated into silence.

"How does she annoy you?"

He shrugged his shoulders, saying nothing.

"Come on," I urged. "It's important to identify how she annoys you." Ed's passivity was beginning to get to me.

There was a long pause. "It's just—just like she's too nosy. We used to do everything together. I mean, we never used to fight until last year."

"Perhaps when your sexual feelings emerged, it created a conflict and you pushed Mom away?"

He went on, as if I had not asked the question. "I just feel so—I don't know, it's like I have all this anger toward her but really don't want to have it."

This was the typical adolescent conflict—but experienced all the more intensely by a homosexual teenager. Ed loved his mother very much, but there was also a long overdue drive to separate from her. Perhaps unconsciously, he sensed their closeness had contributed to his homosexuality. Heterosexual boys typically achieve autonomy from their mothers many years earlier.

"All right," I said. "We need to understand why you're angry with your mother. Because we already know why you're angry with your father. Your father is ineffectual."

"What's 'ineffectual'?" Ed asked.

"As in 'effect.' To have an *effect*. Your father had little effect on you. He was absent in his influence on you."

"Yeah, a wimp." There was unveiled contempt in his voice.

He went on, "Mom has trouble making up her mind. One week she says having my own car would be good for me, the next week it's 'dangerous.' "

"A car?" I asked.

"I thought a car would make me feel better about school. That's the whole kind of freedom thing."

"So she gives you encouragement, then disappoints."

"Yes." Relief in his voice. "She makes me feel guilty about everything."

Here I heard the foundation for his sense of powerlessness. "You feel she confuses and frustrates?"

"Yeah, like, I never know if I can believe her. Last night I heard her call my dad and say, 'Come over and take Ed out to dinner or something.' Then she comes into my room and it's like, 'Dad called and he said he wants to go out to dinner with you.' And I thought, well that's strange. Why would he just call? It's not like him."

"Sure," I said.

"So I get on the extension and I hear my dad say to her,

'But Beatrice, I don't want to take him out. I already ate!' I hung up and I'm like, 'Forget it, Mom, I just don't feel like going out tonight.' "

"But you never told her why."

"No. I didn't bother. What's the use?"

"Instead of expressing your anger or telling her that you feel manipulated, you sulk. Then your parents wonder, 'Why is Ed so quiet? Why is he so moody?' "

"Now that I think about it, I realize those kinds of things happened when I was little. My mom would say, 'Dad's going to take you kids to Disneyland' or someplace, and he would take us, but he would be in a bad mood the whole day, like he didn't want to be there."

"Right," I said, encouraging him to go on.

"And it was probably because she had told him to."

I heard the familiar pattern from the lives of so many of my homosexual clients—a manipulative family communication pattern that gives the child no choice but to retreat into self-protective isolationism.

"She always has to be in control," Ed said helplessly.

He paused, a sad expression on his face. "But still, I know she cares a lot. She does all the things a mother is supposed to do, like make nice dinners and take me to church and stuff like that. But—it's like she cares too much and she's too involved and just too—" words failed him.

He thought for a minute, then continued, "It's like I never want to talk to her about anything personal. Like she'll try to start a conversation and say, real nicely, 'What kind of car would you like to buy, Eddie?' and I'll just get all huffy. But then other times I think, 'Oh God, I'm just being a jerk and she's trying to be a nice mother!' "

Father doesn't care enough and Mother cares too much, I thought. "These same feelings of intrusion and loss of personal power will be carried on to the girls you meet," I said. "If a girl gets too close, you'll push her away."

"Yeah," he admitted. "It's funny you bring that up. Like last year I was very popular and had lots of girlfriends and stuff. I remember that whenever a girl would start to like me too much I would be completely rude, like I am with my mom."

"Exactly. First, you are afraid she will expect a romantic response. But more than that, you don't want to get entrapped in the same situation you have with your mom—feeling manipulated by her and responsible for her feelings."

Edward had been gazing down and fidgeting, but now he looked back up at me, startled.

I knew I had identified a conflict familiar to most homosexual men. I continued, "When you were a little boy and Mom was unhappy, it was your job to make her happy. This sense of responsibility for your mother's feelings gets carried over to relationships with the girls who get too close to you. Unconsciously, you are affected by the girl's feelings and her expectations. Taking care of her feels uncomfortably familiar—it's an old entrapment, and it means the denial of your own needs."

Edward nodded slowly.

"Besides, you're rude to girls because there's too much feminine in you already. What feels attractive is the masculine that's missing in you."

Changing the subject, he went on, "I just auditioned for *Oklahoma!* at the summer theater. I tried for Curly, the lead role."

"It's no coincidence that you love theater," I pointed out. "Drama is a way of hiding yourself. You want to be an artist, above the regular guys. Drama is a perpetuation of the false self."

I looked at the clock. "Anyway, it's time for us to end this session. Do you want to make another appointment, or have you heard more than you want from me already?"

Ed said, "I've got to see about the drama rehearsal schedule."

"Remember, it's up to you, if and when you want to continue."

"I know." There was a faint smile on his face as though he enjoyed being the one in command. Finally he said, "I'll see you next week, same time. O.K. Doc?"

Ed did not see his problem as homosexuality. For the time being, it was a sort of distant issue, something he didn't tackle because he did not know how to begin to deal with it. Instead, he spoke only of school and "relationship problems."

Ed's case exemplifies challenges typical of any adolescent. However, he was also dealing with a number of issues typical of a homosexually oriented adolescent male: (1) anger at an ineffectual, uninvolved father; (2) anger at an intrusive, confusing mother; (3) avoidance of peers (especially male); (4) interest in drama and theater as a way of avoiding his identity and social challenges; (5) authority problems—fear of school officials; and (6) an attitude of superiority as compensation for a sense of masculine inferiority.

Ed showed up regularly, soon requesting two sessions a week on the grounds that his parents were "driving him crazy." After a month of therapy he walked in one afternoon, sat down in the chair, and gave me a very serious look. He had shed most of his earlier attitude of indifference.

"I've been so mad at my father lately."

"Sure." I wanted to reassure him he had committed no crime by expressing a lifelong grievance.

He said, "I mean really angry—in the past couple of weeks."

"Sure." More reassurance.

"It just seems like he's so—" words failed Ed.

I waited. He went on, "There's this whole ordeal with getting a car. My parents both agreed, but then at the last minute they decided not to. My dad said stuff like, you know, 'Just humor him until we can find an excuse to get out of this.' That's what my mom told me."

"How did you feel about that?"

"He always does stuff like that, and then he denies everything. Like the other day, I got about thirty CD's in the mail that I'd ordered from a club catalogue, but I don't have any money to pay for them. And so my dad's like, 'Oh, just don't pay for them. They really can't come after you 'cause you're a minor.'

"And so my mom's like [in a shrill voice], 'Edward, what are you going to do? This is the third time they've billed you! Are you going to pay for these or what?' And I'm like, 'Well, there's really no point in my paying. Dad told me not to pay.' And so Mom has a whole fit and goes to tell him off, and of course he denies it. So he gets in trouble with her and says to me, 'Why did you tell Mom that I said that?' So I tell him, 'Well, because you did!' And he says, 'No, I didn't. I never said that.'

"I don't feel like he even—" Then he interrupted himself, continuing, "Half the time when I talk to him, I mean, it seems like he's listening, but it's like you'll bring it up the next day and he doesn't even remember." Ed's voice was a whine, his shoulders slumping.

"It's like he just doesn't take you seriously," I said.

I saw clearly why Edward came in regularly. More than anything else, it was because *I* took him seriously.

There was a long pause, then, "I told my mom I don't want to go to his house any more because there's really no point. I mean, I go there and he either has to be in court or take out his girlfriend."

"Then why do you go?" I asked.

"I don't know. It's not so much a matter of hating him, as just not wanting to be around him."

"O.K.," I said, "So why are you avoiding him?"

He sat back, shrugged, and said simply, "He doesn't understand me. I'm just different from him."

I took a deep breath, as one does when beginning a long lecture. I hate to lecture, especially to a 16-year-old who already admits he hates—or fears—being told anything, but I wanted to challenge his passive and complacent attitude.

"You think you're so unique," I pushed. "But most guys with a homosexual problem have fear and anger toward male authority figures, who they believe don't understand them. Remember, you've been disappointed by your parents, your first authority figures. They've hurt and abandoned you. You can't trust their authority—their parenting—over you.

"It's especially true for your dad who is supposed to care for you through his adult strength. How can you trust your father's power over you when he constantly disappoints you? So you see," I knew I was pushing Ed to the edge, "you're not so unusual or so special."

Ed began to understand that the homosexual's feeling of differentness is defensive. I explained to him that he retreats into this fantasy of differentness and specialness as a way to justify his unwillingness to meet other boys on equal terms. That way, he can dismiss other males as he dismissed his father, returning to the protected and privileged place with his mother. At the same time, he resents his mother for permitting him to avoid the challenge of claiming his masculinity and the intrinsic power that would be part of it.

I explained that this sense of specialness probably originated in early childhood, back in the gender identity phase, when he first avoided the challenges of masculine identification. It was then that he decided to avoid the challenges of separation and individuation, and the challenge to be autonomous from his mother. In so doing, he had given up much of the personal power that was essential for developing his masculinity. In short, specialness was a convenient defense that allowed him to avoid the challenges of claiming both masculinity and intrinsic power.

Ed sat up in his chair, listening intently. As if relieved to be free of the burden of specialness, he said, "It seems like all the things I didn't necessarily associate with homosexuality, like acting, the authority thing, and stuff like that—it's all related, it all makes sense."

"You've been keeping all this stuff to yourself, not sharing it with anybody. Now, you can reinforce that sense of differentness and specialness, or you can work on being a regular guy, learning how to connect with guys your age. You see, it's not such a coincidence you're into drama because this is a way to escape these everyday challenges."

Ed looked puzzled, then angry. "So if I'm just like everyone else and I don't have any special problems, is there any point at all in me continuing to come to these sessions?"

I heard his inference: "If I'm not someone special, then *Just who am I?*" I decided not to address this, but to keep the discussion practical.

"There are two reasons why you might want to continue therapy," I told him. "First, to diminish the hurt and confusion in your life, and second, to try to develop the heterosexual side of yourself."

He sighed. "It's hard to be sure what I want." A long pause. "I think I do want to develop the heterosexual side of myself, but I hear so many other things—people saying I have to be gay in order to be true to myself . . . stuff like that.''

"You'll be hearing a lot of that. From the gay world, you'll get a whole different set of answers. But remember this basic principle, Ed. If you do nothing, if you decide to float along and follow the crowd—you will become gay.''

"Well, for now,'' Ed said, "I'd just like to begin by understanding how to deal with my father.''

The father, I thought, nodding to Edward. How often I hear this refrain from my clients. How often is the issue at hand one of *problems with father.*

I went away on vacation after that session with Edward. When we saw each other again one rainy Monday three weeks later, Edward arrived looking very sad and discouraged. He shrugged off his coat, tossed a soggy umbrella on the carpet beside him, and plopped down in front of me.

"I've been thinking I'm not so happy with having these homosexual feelings.''

"What happened?''

"Well . . . you know how lonely I've been because I don't have any friends. So, a couple of weeks ago I'm walking alone in the park and I see this old guy—probably about your age—and we started talking. I thought he might be gay because he was, like, a little too friendly. We talked for a bit—his name was Jason—and we exchanged phone numbers, and that night he called me and asked me if I wanted to go out and see a movie.

"Then he invited me to a party that turned out to be all gay guys, mostly his age.'' He laughed bitterly. "It was the best party I've ever been to. I was the center of attention.''

"So you got what you couldn't find with straight guys at school. This is why the gay scene is so appealing—you get instant acceptance.''

Edward laughed, but his face was unhappy. "I know. It's so hard with the other guys. With them, I'm nothing special.''

"So what happened?''

"Well . . .'' He sounded bashful. "Although it really wasn't what I wanted, it got sexual. I wish he had just been affectionate and we could have had a friendship. Maybe if he had just ruffled my hair or something, hugged me a little . . .

stuff like that." He laughed, embarrassed. "But he gave me a massage and then—well, one thing led to another."

"I see."

"So I was pretty interested in him. But then, the next day he called and said his former lover, Harold, had asked him to move back in with him. Jason said not to worry, it wouldn't affect our friendship."

"So are you still friends?"

"Well, on Friday night Jason asked me to help him move his stuff over to Harold's, and it turned out Harold was very nice to me, very friendly. He took me out for pizza and stuff, said he really wanted to be friends, too. I didn't want to lose Jason, so I went along with it. Then we went back to their apartment and they put on a porno movie. Jason and Harold both undressed me and . . ."

"And what?"

"And . . ." He blushed, "they took turns giving me a blow job." Attempting a French accent, "A *ménage à trois,* Jason called it." Edward grinned at me shyly. "Afterwards they both said they loved me and I could move in with them. That the three of us could have lots of fun together."

After a long, silent pause I asked him, "So did you get what you wanted?"

Ed's voice sounded weary. "No. I really only wanted some friendship. Some affection. I told Harold and Jason I couldn't be a part of their relationship."

Edward's story illustrates the false allure of special attention so often offered by the gay world. Young men like Edward—who so badly need male attention, affection, and approval—are so often seduced into sexual affairs and misled or discarded.

"There's lots of wild, outrageous fun, and it's very attractive to a young person like you. You'll find instant attention—and it's going to feel like a dream come true. For a while, that is," I told him.

"But what about straight guys?" I continued. "Have you been developing any straight friendships?"

"I'm afraid to try to strike up a friendship. I can't just go up to a guy and talk. . . . He'll think I'm hitting up on him."

This is the confused thinking of the gay world, I thought to myself. These sexual relationships between gay guys aren't *friendships*. Gays can't separate friendship from sexuality. Edward, too, was unclear about that separation. He needed to make the conscious distinction between friendship and sex. Now he was projecting his own confusion onto the heterosexual males he'd been attempting to become friends with.

"Why would a straight guy think a friendly conversation was a come-on? To him, male friendships don't involve sexuality." Before Ed could answer, I continued, "There's nothing wrong with wanting attention—but you don't know the right way to get it. *Speak* to these straight guys you find attractive. Make them real people. If you don't speak to them they'll remain objects—larger than life. If you remain isolated, your erotic feelings will intensify. Sexual interest increases when you are lonely and isolated."

Ed nodded, considering this.

"If you want to join my group—it's Monday nights—you can listen to the guys who have been in the gay lifestyle and have left it. I want you to hear them describe their experiences."

He agreed. "I'd like to join the group. Meet the guys. I'm ready to work on dealing with my homosexuality."

That spring Ed graduated from high school and began his summer vacation. His concern about school phobia faded into the background, and he continued to work on his father issues and his need for male friendships.

He soon established some close relationships with men in the group, especially Charlie. Although Ed was a few years younger than the other guys, he had a lot to learn from the perspective of men who had already had a taste of gay life. And for the first time in his life he could have honest and intimate, nonsexual relationships with men who understood his temptations.

Over the next few weeks, Ed experienced no more than the typical ups and downs of an adolescent with a homosexual struggle. Overall, he was doing much better.

Then he admitted how difficult things had become during the summer with his mother. He described how he had ridden his bike to his father's house recently, just to get away from her.

His shuttling between Mom and Dad symbolized a predicament common to homosexual youth who feel caught between an overinvolved, intrusive mother and an underinvolved, uninterested father.

"On Saturday night I had nothing to do, so I went to see a horror movie with Mom. I was bored, but I had nothing else going. When I got back, I felt really bummed out. So many Saturday nights I end up spending with my mother."

"So why don't you have a few good friends to go out with?"

With his little lost boy look he answered, "'Cause I can't find any."

"Can't *make* any," I corrected.

Ed seemed stuck.

"Hmm. Well, have you heard the story about the tuna sandwich?" I asked him.

"The *tuna sandwich*?" He shook his head.

"Yeah. Every day, two men would eat lunch together. The first day, the older man unwraps his sandwich. Pastrami on rye, pickle on the side, potato salad. The younger man opens his sandwich—tunafish.

"The second day, the older man takes out a sandwich of imported swiss cheese on a kaiser roll, dijon mustard, coleslaw. The younger man takes out his sandwich—tunafish.

"On the third day, the older man unwraps his lunch—avocado, sprouts, and tomato on whole wheat bread. The younger man opens his sandwich and exclaims, "Tuna again!"

The older man asks, "Why don't you ask your wife to prepare some other kind of sandwich?"

"What wife!" the younger man says. "I make my own sandwiches."

Edward smiled.

"So, you don't want to go to the movies with your mother again next Saturday, do you?"

"No."

"You're using your mother as a substitute for peer friendships. Make some kind of plans, and don't wait until the last minute to call a friend. You've been making your own tuna sandwich!"

A bit irritated, Ed changed the subject. "Yesterday, I ran

into this girl I used to sit next to in homeroom. She asked me if I wanted to go to the mall with her to exchange some dresses she bought.''

"And did you go?''

"I kind of stalled her. I'm not sure I want to get back with people I knew in high school—people who knew me as quiet . . . you know . . . not masculine. And now, if I act different with her, she may see me as just pretending.'' He hesitated, choosing his words carefully. "The fact is, I've been going through a lot of changes recently. I've been feeling different about myself. Now, I can't see myself going along with a girl to exchange her dresses. I'm not sure she'll understand that I feel different about this.''

I nodded. "Our friends and family have a vested interest in our being the same for them. Old friends from high school will resist seeing a different Edward, a maturing Edward.''

"I just don't have as much patience now for girls, their gossip and stuff. It doesn't feel comfortable like it used to.''

I explained, "You're starting to do now what you missed in early boyhood—the necessary rejection of females that latency-age boys go through. It's the 'I hate girls' phase.''

"Yeah. The 'girls are yukky' phase—I know. I never went through that.''

I continued, "This whole therapy centers around overcoming your defensive detachment from males. Remember, as a little boy you made the decision to stick close to Mom and stay away from Dad. You looked at him and said, 'I don't *need* you. I don't *want* you. I don't *trust* you.' Right? And you said that same thing to the boys with whom you should have been bonding. You avoided them, stayed away from them—then you'd try to break down that alienation with a sexual connection.''

The following week, Ed bounded in with a smile of triumph.

"Well, I got the part!''

"What part?''

"The summer theater. I'll be Curly in *Oklahoma!*''

"Congratulations.''

"Rehearsals may interfere with our appointments," he told me. "They'll probably work us every day."

"I'm really glad to see you so excited, so happy. Of course, you'll have to make your own decisions about priorities. But just remember that when the show is over and the curtain goes down—"

Ed nodded. "I know." His voice was grave. "I'll still be alone with the same problems."

In spite of the rigors of his rehearsal schedule, Ed managed to find time for our weekly sessions. He also continued to come faithfully to our group meetings.

One morning he surprised me by asking if he could bring his father to his next appointment. I welcomed this suggestion. However, I explained to Ed that there would be no value in exposing his dad to a list of complaints. Before I would ask his dad to come in, Ed would have to be exactly sure what he wanted from him. Besides, complaining to his dad would only reinforce Ed's sense of being a helpless victim. Ed agreed to try to move beyond complaining into communication. He also agreed to come in for individual sessions between those father–son meetings.

At last, I had the opportunity to meet Dennis Paterson. Ed's father was a tall, handsome man who came to our appointment dressed in a tailored grey pin-striped business suit and iridescent orange silk tie. He shook my hand firmly and spoke to me in the bold, forthright manner of a man who is used to being in charge.

He started off by making it clear that he had canceled an important appointment in order to make time for our session.

Looking in comparison almost frail, Ed seated himself stiffly on a couch opposite his father. He seemed particularly childlike and uncertain.

Then I asked father and son to move to opposite ends of a large couch, facing each other. I wanted them to address each other. Both began laughing nervously, obviously uncomfortable. Ed hugged a couch pillow to his chest as if it were a shield.

As they began some superficial banter, I could see that both father and son truly desired closeness, but were afraid to show affection after so many years of frustration with each other. Dennis Paterson clearly wanted to improve the relationship, but his direct and forceful manner only seemed to inhibit Edward. Ed tended to be vague in his meaning and indirect in his expression of what he wanted. Uncomfortable with Dad's let's-get-to-the-point style, he was now totally flustered.

In my experience with father–son sessions, I have found that fathers typically get stuck on the content level, avoiding feelings. Unfortunately the sons, in attempting to maintain some form of communication, allow their fathers to stay on this superficial level. I could see that Ed would have liked more feeling exchange, more emotional expression from his father. Mr. Paterson often lapsed into lengthy lectures on life, career, and his favorite topic—self-discipline—during which Ed simply zoned out. Father seemed to be making closing arguments to the jury. Caught up in a lecture full of old clichés, Ed was clearly disappointed.

Attempting to break the deadlock, I broke in. "How do you think your father perceives you, Ed?"

Ed shrugged his shoulders, as if stuck between fear and hope. He could not answer.

Finally he spoke up in a boyish voice filled with emotion. "Sometimes I don't know where you're at, Dad . . . what you're getting at."

Defensively, Dennis Paterson responded, "Well, Eddie . . . what do you want from me?"

This is your chance, Ed! I thought. The perfect opening.

I knew what Ed wanted. We had literally rehearsed what he would say in our private sessions. Yet he could not answer.

There ensued a long lapse of silence, during which the clock ticked away while the pair sat there tensely.

In his own way, Mr. Paterson was trying to make contact with his son, but his lectures on self-discipline were obstacles to any real communication. Ed's defense against his father's lectures was to take the opposite position, saying that he wanted more freedom. Yet freedom had nothing to do with it. What Ed really wanted, what remained unspoken, was his father's love and acceptance.

For four sessions they arrived together. Each time father

and son would enter my office apparently unprepared, as if they had never given any thought to what they would talk about. Indeed, Ed told me they would ride to my office in silence, as if there were nothing to say to each other. Even at such brief times during the session when they emotionally touched each other, they did not stay there very long. Each quickly headed for the safe ground of futile debate over the issue of freedom versus self-discipline. I sensed a fear. Each knew that under the surface, there was hurt and anger. It was as if they both knew, "If we speak honestly, we'll be furious at each other."

Mother was always the phantom present during these sessions—both Ed and his dad would frequently report what "Mom" or "she" said. As is typical of the family that produces the homosexual son, she had been overinvolved as mother/ interpreter in the relationship between father and son. I decided it was best not even to try to conceal my impatience, and finally I simply set down the rule, "No more talk of Mom. We're here to deal with the two of you—directly."

I tried to reach under the surface, to get past the son's avoidance and the father's tendency to cross-examine. I did not dare bring up the subject of *The Big H* because they were obviously not ready to talk about it. Yet it was there nevertheless, weighing heavily on all of us.

I attempted to challenge Mr. Paterson to break through the speeches and talk about his relationship with Ed, but he constantly interrupted me. It seemed clear that he had no idea how to reach out to his son. As I listened to them speak, I felt so much of what was unspoken. For the first time, I could sense Dennis Paterson's hurt and sense of failure as a father.

I knew my days with Dennis Paterson were numbered. He would not continue to adjust his legal appointments much longer. Besides, I sensed his increasing frustration.

My past experience with fathers and their homosexual sons has taught me not to expect major, sustained break- through. So when Ed and his father arrived for their fifth session, I decided I had better push them with some strong intervention before Ed's father bowed out of therapy perma- nently. I wanted them to go away with something.

While Ed was clear and eloquent in our private sessions, he could not express himself effectively to his father. I decided to begin by voicing what each of them must surely have been feeling.

"I'm not sure how both of you are feeling, but I'm feeling bored and frustrated with what's been happening in these sessions. Let's get down to business. Mr. Paterson, what do you want from Ed?"

He answered, "I've told Ed what I expect. I want him to become a responsible adult."

"Fine," I responded. "But do you know what Ed wants?

"Quite frankly, no, I do not," he told me.

"Last week you started to connect with your son," I told Dennis Paterson. "When you connected with him, I could see him calm down. He became focused on you, because you were giving him what he wants. But you have to keep after him. Ed has trouble talking to you. He needs you to reach out to him, to connect with him. To *go get him*. I see you trying to do that, but it always seems to deteriorate into a lecture. Don't lecture. I want you to let your son know he's important to you. Ed wants to reach out to you, but he doesn't know how to do this."

Mr. Paterson listened thoughtfully. Then he turned to his son. "Well, Ed, I guess Dr. Joe is right. Last week I did a lot of talking and telling you, 'Hey this is what I need from you.' Maybe now it's time for you to speak up." Ed was quiet, looking down.

His father went on, now expressing a deeper need: "Maybe I should hear whether you have any long-term plans of how you want to relate to me."

Ed laughed nervously, still saying nothing.

"Do you want to speak up to your father?" I pushed.

He gave another nervous laugh, and still said nothing. His father continued, "Are you saying, at practically 18 years of age, 'Hey, Dad, good-bye, I'm going to do whatever I want to do?' Or do you plan for us to have a long-term relationship?"

"Yeah, I'm planning that." Another nervous laugh.

"Which one are you planning?"

"The long-term relationship."

"I'm asking this," his father continued, "because I've heard you say so often to your mother, 'When I graduate from high school I'm out the door for good. That's it.' "

It was clear to me now that Dennis Paterson felt he had been rejected by his son and treated as though he were unimportant. "The reason you're asking the question is that your son is very important to you," I prompted.

"Well, sure," the father replied. "He always has been."

I turned to Ed and asked, "What is your father saying to you?"

"That he wants us to have a good relationship," Ed said.

"That's right. But your dad doesn't know how to sustain it. He needs your help," I pointed out.

Then, turning to the father, I said, "Dennis, this is the first time you've truly reached out to your son in a session. See what happens when you express a feeling?"

Encouraged, he continued. "What I'm saying is, 'Hey, son, our relationship is in trouble. You're growing up and going to leave us, and we'd better make it better right now, before we lose you.' "

"Right," I said, nodding.

"A lot of things are going to happen soon," the father continued. "In a couple of weeks, Ed, you'll be leaving home and going to college. If we don't establish a more trusting faith between us, then I'm predicting that you're going to be gone forever. We ought to get down to exactly what is causing the problem. Why the alienation?"

Ed remained silent. I prompted softly, "Talk to your father."

"I don't know who I am, what I am . . . what my identity is," Ed said plaintively. "That's why I didn't want to bring anything up."

In a show of surprising sensitivity, Dennis seemed to rescue his son from the painful issue of his homosexuality. "Look son, anything you might have to say to me about yourself, your identity, is beside the point. If I have a good relationship with you, that's what's important."

"I don't really know what to say," Ed stammered, retreating further.

"You're fearful that your father will judge you?" I prompted.

"I'm not critical of *you*, Dad," Ed blurted. "I really don't know why you're so critical of me."

"Maybe I . . . ought to get to know you better," Dennis Paterson said.

I turned to Ed. "What things do you do that make you feel *good* about yourself? That build confidence inside you?"

"I feel confident when I'm into my acting, my drama classes. I've also been into writing poetry." Turning to look directly at his father for the first time in the session, he said, "There's lots of stuff I haven't told you about myself, Dad." His voice was reproachful yet his eyes were wide, even hopeful.

Dennis Paterson nodded. "I wrote some poetry too when I was your age, son."

"And I even wrote a poem that I'm trying to get published." Ed laughed.

"I'd like to hear about that. I want you to feel proud of yourself," his father said. "If you're going to be in the arts for a living then you're going to have to be very, very forceful about it because there's a lot of competition, just like in the law business."

He added, in a sympathetic tone, "You're not forceful enough in a lot of things, son." Teetering on the brink of lecture, he continued, "If you're not successful, you won't feel good about what you do. I want to help you be successful in something. I can't teach you poetry or acting. I can only teach you what I know."

I asked Ed, "What is it that you want from your father now?"

Ed shrugged his shoulders, as if this were the question of the ages.

Here I saw Ed locked in a see-saw pattern which is obvious in so many father–son sessions—when one extends, the other withdraws. Ed, who so desperately wanted his father's affirmation, now, in the face of it, seemed withdrawn, indifferent. Here were living remnants of boyhood defensive detachment. I could understand the frustration of fathers of homosexuals.

Seeing Ed's hesitation, his father turned to face him. "When you were 2 or 3 and your Mom was out of town, Ed, you got the chicken pox and we took you to the doctor. The waiting room was very crowded and noisy, and you were crying."

For the first time, Dennis Paterson's voice grew tremulous. "I held you in my arms and I rocked you, and I didn't care about everyone around us and what they were thinking of me, and I just sang lullabies to you. Even though you were crying, you smiled up at me . . . and for the first time, I really understood what it means to be a father. You taught me that then, son, just by letting me comfort you."

This time Ed's laugh was deep and genuine. He looked at his father with affection.

His father went on, "I thought, 'I love this kid. Nothing must ever separate us.' I was determined to keep that moment in my memory. I know I somehow forgot it through the years. But you taught me that, son, one day when you were little."

The next week Ed arrived by himself. As often happened, his father was out of town on business. Ed and I agreed to return to individual sessions; his father would come in only on an as-needed basis. Yet Ed was barely able to suppress a jubilant grin because his father had offered him a summer job in his law office. "We had a long talk in the car going home from the session," he said. "I asked him to show me as much as he could about legal work, in case a career in the arts doesn't turn out to be practical. He said there was a lot he could teach me." Ed's voice was full of pride and confidence.

We summed up how his parents' personalities had influenced him. "Your mother is very emotionally expressive, perhaps too much so with you. You always were overinvolved with her on an emotional level." Ed nodded. I continued, "Your father has generally been the opposite: strong, direct, and opinionated in business matters, but ineffectual emotionally within the family."

I pointed out Ed's obvious defensive detachment toward his father. I told him how I saw a style of turning off his dad, a behavioral pattern he would have to take responsibility for. It was clearly in opposition to the relationship Ed sought with his father.

Fathers of homosexuals tend to reveal a sense of helplessness, discomfort, and awkwardness when they are required to interact directly with their sons. They usually have few, if any, male friendships, and have often had poor relationships with their own fathers. They seem to be particularly dependent upon their wives as guides, interpreters, and spokespersons, especially in relating to their sons. In the course of treatment I typically see a mutual antipathy, a resistance and a deep grievance on both sides. Approximately half of these fathers say their sons seem to have rejected them from early childhood. Seeing Ed's own rebuff of his father's efforts at closeness, I could understand how these fathers—like their sons—felt rejected.

The single most common trait among such fathers is that they seem incapable of summoning the effort required to correct the relational problems with their sons. These fathers feel stuck and helpless in the face of their sons' indifference or hostility. Rather than confront the problems with their sons, they tend to retreat and avoid, protecting themselves from vulnerability. Their emotional availability is somehow blocked, and they are typically unable to take the lead in turning the relationship in a positive direction. Some are brittle and rigid, others severe and critical, still others are soft, weak, and passive. For this emotional unavailability their sons often call them "wimps," although they may in fact be quite strong and successful outside of the family.

Edward has made substantial progress as of this writing. He is in his second year of college, majoring in drama and working Saturdays in his father's law office. For the first time in years, he has made several straight male friends. Joining a fraternity, he underwent a contemporary male rite of passage—rush week—and found it to be a powerful experience. He found he could survive the risk of rejection to gain peer acceptance. Living with his fraternity brothers, he also found ample opportunity to practice the separation of sexuality from his authentic same-sex needs of attention, approval, and affection. He feels happy in college and believes his life is moving in the right direction.

Ed has distanced himself from his overly close relationship

with his mother, and he now gets along far better with his father. However, while some significant barriers were broken down between Ed and his dad, my experience suggests a limited capacity for long-term closeness between homosexual men and their fathers. The healing of the father-wound appears to be less the result of the father's own substantial change than of the son's growth in understanding and acceptance of his father's limitations.

It is too soon to be sure what direction Ed's life will follow. As a 20-year-old he will surely go through many changes, yet there are strong indications that this sincere and well-meaning young man will continue with his hard-earned progress toward heterosexuality.

8

Roger—"Do I Really Want to Be Here?"

The moment he entered my office, 27-year-old Roger Schulte made clear his ambivalence about starting therapy. A high school chemistry teacher, Roger told me over the phone as we arranged an appointment, "I usually like to figure things out for myself. I'm only seeing you because I'm at the end of my rope with this problem."

When he appeared at the door I saw a rather pale, serious-looking man with a thin face framed by a pair of oversize glasses. Roger's clothing style was unique, what might be called "studied outlandish." He sported an extra-wide, bright-patterned silk tie over a rumpled, khaki-colored cotton shirt. A well-worn pair of black cords was finished off with a pair of two-tone, lizard skin cowboy boots. Like his ensembles, Roger would prove to be a study in ambiguity.

Roger nervously seated himself in the chair, hands folded in his lap. As I looked at him, I was reminded of the stereotype of the absentminded professor. His longish, rather unruly brown hair had been drawn back off his face with a couple of rough strokes of a wet brush. His pointed-toed boots, once luxurious, were scuffed and dusty.

He soon plunged into the story of himself and his only long-term lover, a man named Perry. Both men had decided to go into psychotherapy in the hope of giving up their homosexuality. Now his ex-lover had changed his mind. "Perry has decided therapy doesn't work at all for him and now spends three or four nights a week trying to pick people up at The Rage," Roger said, his voice betraying hurt and anger.

I had heard of The Rage from my other clients. This bar was to gay nightclubs what Circus of Books was to pornography—the biggest, the best, and the most popular of its genre in Los Angeles.

Roger told me of his pain at watching Perry drink and flirt and dance with other men. While officially they had broken up after their nine months together, there remained a painful codependency.

"I decided I should find a male therapist to work on this problem," he then said with an awkward laugh. "But now that I'm here, I don't know what to talk about." He shrugged and looked away, suddenly overwhelmed by self-consciousness.

I realized that beneath the provocative clothing style was a shy man, fearful of expressing his true personality. "Perhaps you are not used to being encouraged to verbalize your feelings," I said. "Or perhaps, you're not accustomed to being taken seriously."

Roger nodded slowly. "That's true. I even wonder if my students take me seriously." From the start I was hearing a common therapeutic issue that could be traced back to childhood when the prehomosexual boy's parents failed to take him seriously.

Roger began to tell me about his early life with his parents, who had worked long hours as assistant managers of a large resort hotel in the Catskill Mountains of New York. "I never saw much of them except their one day off a week, when they were too tired to have any fun or talk to me. When we did go somewhere together, I felt like a prisoner."

He told me sadly, "I always felt paralyzed in my relationship with my father. All the time I was growing up, he would become devil's advocate against anything I wanted to do.

"I must admit, though, that I have my father to thank for my having become a teacher." He laughed ironically. "He came from a strict German family, every one of them a scholar. The written word was the way he communicated to me. He would hand me a newspaper and point to an editorial, saying, 'You really should read this, Roger.' We rarely spoke, though."

Roger was clearly very limited in his emotional expression. I could see the emotional deprivation of his family background. And like the teenagers he taught, Roger used clothing to express an identity he had no other way of asserting.

He looked at me and admitted, "I remember the jealousy I had toward my brother very early in life because I felt he was getting all the attention from my father. My brother was a tough character. He was the schoolyard bully, while I was the quiet kid with glasses who always had a backpack full of books. I always seemed different. I felt like an orphan kid that somehow got adopted by mistake into a household of Nazi storm troopers." He laughed at this, but his eyes were bitter.

Then he shook his head sadly. "A lot of memories of my relationships from childhood are coming up, and most of them are hurtful. It's scary. My instant reaction is to stuff them back down . . . forget about them."

Roger then told me about his attempts to deal with fear.

"I know I need desperately to reach out from myself and start trying to meet other people, but there's a fear of doing that. I'm afraid of people, afraid of facing them. I'm afraid of rejection." He laughed, shaking his head disgustedly. "I'm afraid of trying to make friendships because I don't even know what a good, close friendship really is!

"This is not just a recent fear. It's a fear that's always been with me, in fact as far as I can remember . . . maybe since birth. As I look back, most of my friendships were initiated by the other guy. Sometimes I meet somebody on a hike with the Sierra Club chapter I belong to, and we exchange phone numbers. I'll never be the one to call first. I wait for him to call me."

"Because of the fear of rejection," I said.

"Because of the fear of rejection," he repeated. "That's the fear I've always felt. At least that's part of it. There's also a fear that all of a sudden I'll think, 'Maybe I was mistaken to think the guy had a good time the last time we got together. Maybe he won't call me back again, after all.' I get scared of that.''

"You're afraid of your own success.''

"Yes,'' he admitted.

I explained, "This is a power issue. You're afraid of the responsibility of success. You can't believe you possess the strength to maintain the success you have already accomplished.''

"Right. And even worse, I can't control the homosexual desires when they come up. That's what really depresses me.''

"You don't have to control your homosexual feelings to work on outgrowing them,'' I said. Roger looked surprised. I continued, "Control is not where the healing lies.''

Roger was falling into the trap that often presents itself in the early stages of treatment—focusing on controlling surface symptoms rather than resolving deeper needs. In fact, to focus solely on controlling himself—a self-defeating battle, one he would no doubt lose—only serves as a way of avoiding the deeper challenge of establishing intimate, nonsexual male friendships.

"Your homosexual temptations should not distract or discourage you from the essential, underlying task. Your first task is to push through your fear and loneliness to develop close male relationships.

"Instead of looking at these guys sexually, you will need to face the feelings underneath the longing. Your sexual feelings camouflage a lot of real pain and alienation, and you will need to learn to deal with that pain in a more appropriate, more fulfilling manner.''

"You're right about the pain,'' he said.

"Tell me,'' I said, "exactly what the pain is.''

He sighed. "The pain of always being afraid. The pain of loneliness. The pain of feeling like I just don't belong anywhere.''

He shook his head dejectedly. Our time was up, and I asked Roger if he wanted to continue next week. He said he'd give it some thought. The following day, he left a message on my exchange—he'd changed his mind about therapy.

Three months later, Roger telephoned for another appointment. At the designated hour, he walked into my office looking sad and disgusted.

He spoke for awhile in generalities, giving only vague reasons for his return to treatment.

"But why are you coming back now, Roger? What made you change your mind?"

With some hesitancy and embarrassment, he began his story. "Last week I had a pretty unpleasant experience—in fact, it's humiliating even to talk about it . . ."

"Don't worry, Roger," I assured him. "I don't think there's much that can shock or surprise me any more."

"Well—I went to this older guy's house, a man I had never met before. Got his name from the back of a gay rag—you know, those free newspapers you find in gay bars. He was 'looking for a relationship.'"

I nodded.

"Anyway, I went to his place and he told me he liked younger guys to be 'top' and himself 'bottom.' So we did that. I was wearing a rubber—but then I noticed this odor and," his voice softened, "um . . . it was a turn-off, and it was tough for me to continue."

I interrupted, "What was it that you noticed?"

"Shit," he answered, looking away from me. There was a long pause before he was able to continue. "Uh . . . afterwards I went into the bathroom and there was . . . there was shit on the tip of my dick. It was a total gross-out. Thank God I had a rubber on. I got out of there pretty quick. It suddenly hit me how perverted the whole thing is. I thought, how low do I have to go? Is this what a gay man has to do for sexual gratification?

"I just believe sex between men is unnatural."

Roger committed himself to a schedule of weekly meetings. When a few weeks had passed, he seemed much more happy about being in therapy. One day he launched into a discussion about the day-to-day challenge of facing what he called his "little fears"—his self-consciousness and anxiety.

"I spend a lot of money on my clothes," Roger told me. "I can't resist a good sale when I see a nice pair of boots, or something else that grabs me. Yet when I have to go to the store, I'm afraid of the sales clerk. I can't look him in the eyes. I feel like a little kid wherever I go. A little kid in an adult world. Which is pretty ironic, when you consider that I'm a teacher.

"But lately I've been telling myself I've got to overcome this, so yesterday I went to the mall, and for awhile I just walked around. I tried to look people in the eye, not feel so self-conscious."

"Here again it's the little successes that make the difference," I pointed out. "You've got to continue making those little behavioral changes."

"And yet in spite of the fact that I've gotten better at putting myself out there socially, I still have a fear of people that is so intense. I still feel false when I'm facing social situations."

"You're overcoming your shyness behaviorally, but the fear remains," I agreed.

"I feel I always have to project myself, push myself out toward people or I'll never say a word to a soul." He sounded grim.

As Roger spoke of his self-conscious, self-protective isolationism, I could not help thinking, this must be how Roger felt as a child in the presence of a mother and father who never encouraged his spontaneous self.

Roger then spoke of his old lover, Perry. "Over the weekend I finally broke down and called him. 'Well, I'll just find out how he's doing,' I told myself. I couldn't reach him, I only got the answering machine. Then hearing his voice on the tape, I lost any desire to talk to him. I just felt this intense anger and sadness. And a deep sense of loss. I want to resolve this relationship—we never did that, we just left it hanging. I find myself making him into the bad guy and I know that's not real."

"It's not realistic," I agreed.

"I know it's not real. But it's what I've done with every other relationship. I always end up angry and disgusted with the men I thought I wanted. I decide they're bastards after all. It's the way I felt with my father."

"Exactly," I said.

"I 'know' all of this on one level, but it still doesn't take away the sadness. The moment when I'm the saddest comes when I picture Perry or hear his voice in my mind. I realize I'm not remembering him as he really was, but as an idealized image. I loved him because he was sort of free and crazy and outgoing—the image of the man I've always wanted and felt I needed."

The idealized self, I thought to myself. Exactly what Roger would want *to be,* if he could feel less inhibited.

"Yet there are aspects of that relationship I really do miss. Despite all the fighting and turmoil, there were moments when we were real for each other. I think that happens for any two people drawn together, even momentarily.

"I know there were good, healthy aspects of the relationship," he continued. "But on the other hand, there was this anger for having allowed myself to succumb to his blatant manipulation. There's this feeling of rage that I let myself be manipulated."

"Has this happened before?"

"After a demoralizing affair with a kid during my senior year in high school, I swore that I would never again let myself be manipulated by another guy. Then I ended up with Perry."

After a long silence, he said, "For many years I've been looking for Mr. Right, but each time, there have been terrible hurts and disappointments. Now I know that that perfect friend will never come along. And I understand *why.* Yet even now as I express this conviction to you, I feel a real sense of loss. I can't bear to face the fact that I was just chasing an illusion."

Roger had hit upon one of the most difficult steps in reparative therapy.

I said, "I think you have to feel the sadness of that loss. You have to give up the perennial gay dream that one guy is going to be your eternal friend, sex partner, faithful lover, buddy, brother, soulmate, all rolled into one. I think you've really got to mourn the loss of that dream," I said.

"At our final meeting at The Rage," Roger said, "I was upset at some of the insults Perry directed at me. I felt he was trying to get under my skin for a reason."

"To push you away, I suppose. He probably has the same ambivalence you have."

"What do you mean?" Roger asked me.

"He also dreamed that he could have something special with you, and when he was disappointed, he decided to destroy what was," I explained.

Roger said slowly, "It's the same feeling as 'I hate the thing I love, because I know I can't have it.' " He added, as though thinking it through, "Hmm. Hearing that makes me feel better."

"Because you now understand what's going on. Homosexual relationships are so characteristically volatile because the homosexual hates what he loves. He realizes on some level that no man can fulfill his unrealistic expectations."

Again Roger said, "Hmm." Then added sadly, "That shatters the romantic glow, I guess." Then, "It's not easy being a male couple, that I can tell you."

"Not unless you're willing to live with the inherent limitations of same-sex relationships."

The homosexual relationship is full of irreconcilable paradox: fear of, yet attraction toward men. Same-sex couplings usually begin with an unrealistic perception of the other person, an image. This image represents aspects of the man's own lost masculinity. Typically based upon shallow traits of the other's personality, these projections are destined to lead to disappointment. And because these relationships are based upon wishful projections, the couple has difficulty moving beyond the stage of romantic infatuation to the formation of long-term monogamous commitment.

When he seeks erotic contact with another man, the homosexual is trying to take in a lost part of himself. But because this attraction stems from personal deficit, he is not completely free to love the other.

Dr. Herman Nunberg (1938) spoke of the type of homosexual client who seemed to believe that "through mere contact with a man of strength, or through an embrace, or through a kiss, he would absorb this strength and become himself as strong as the man he desired" (p. 5). This search for the masculine ideal is characteristic of gay relationships. This is one reason why we see in gay relationships the frustrating cycle of attraction and sexual contact followed shortly afterward by disinterest. It is a cycle of often lifelong, frustrated desire for intimacy.

The straight man is not as psychologically dependent on finding the feminine ideal. The feminine ideal is less important because his partner will not be needed to fulfill a deficit in his original gender. Instead of finding a partner like himself, his partner will be complementary.

The gay man often places his hope in the dream of some future lover. Indeed, we see statistically that homosexual pairings almost never remain monogamous and faithful. Yet mature relationship means accepting the inevitable limitations imposed by the choice of one lifelong partner, and creating what can be created from the relationship.

Gay couplings often show an intensity of dependency, jealousy, and suspicion. The most volatile domestic relationships I have worked with have been those of male couples. There are typically complaints of intense ambivalence, sometimes violent conflicts, and even physical injuries. Because the relationship is forced to bear the excess baggage of unmet childhood love needs, there exists a great deal of hostile dependency.

I cannot believe any man was designed to live his life in a same-sex pairing. Without the feminine influence in a love relationship, an essential grounding force will always be missing.

A few months later, Roger walked into the room with an immediate question. "For a person to have good self-esteem, parents have to give the kid positive recognition, don't they?"

Before I could say a word, he added, "Because my parents never did."

"To answer your question, sure," I agreed. "But more important than positive recognition is accurate recognition. To develop a true self-identity, the child needs to have who he is as an individual accurately reflected."

"This is my problem," Roger somberly stated. "I was either ignored or manipulated." He thought for a minute, then corrected, "Actually—let me get this straight. I was ignored by my father, manipulated by my mother." A sense of satisfaction showed on his face.

Roger then shifted to the present. "Yesterday I was at my parents' house for Sunday dinner. Every time I'm there, I feel restless. Everything they say annoys me. After I got back home to my apartment I felt this tension and found myself needing to masturbate as soon as I got in the door."

There followed a long silence, as if he did not know where to go with that observation. Like so many homosexually oriented men, once Roger expressed a strongly felt complaint, he had a great deal of trouble moving forward in the discussion. Often he seemed satisfied simply to express the complaint, and lacked the motivation to move toward self-understanding.

"Why?" I pushed. "You've got to ask 'why?' "

He stared across the room, taking a deep breath. Then he looked straight at me and said, "Because I'm not listened to when I'm with my parents."

"O.K. So, what's the connection between the restlessness at your parents' and the masturbation?" I challenged.

He drew a blank.

I said. "Whenever we feel restless, bored, irritable, anxious, or depressed, these feelings are signals from our bodies that we're out of touch with ourselves." I continued, "You were out of touch with yourself and masturbation was a way of connecting with yourself again, a way of feeling your body again. The mind zones out while the entire body centers on the orgasm. Masturbation, like overeating and other addictive behaviors, has a unifying function."

I leaned forward and looked at him earnestly. "Remember to ask yourself, 'What am I feeling right now that I can't express?' Most of the time it's anger that you don't give yourself permission to express and—"

Roger interrupted impatiently. "How do I show my anger to my parents? Start screaming at them?"

I felt his frustration, but continued calmly. "Matching your feelings with your behavior doesn't mean you have to throw a temper tantrum. Try speaking more directly about what you're experiencing. Just being honest with yourself that you are angry will cause a shift in feeling. You will feel a sense of control just by labeling the feeling. You will suddenly feel more in possession of yourself. Then you can decide how to express the anger appropriately, which may simply be to get out of your parents' house."

"Which is what I did," Roger said, evidently hoping to get some credit.

"Yes," I said, giving it to him, "because you had no other choice. You weren't about to speak frankly with your parents. Instead you turned your anger into a sexual expression, The Big M. This is a common—I'd say characteristic—dynamic of the homosexual male. His intrinsic power is diverted into sexual behavior."

After some seconds of reflection, Roger laughed, then his voice turned serious as he said, "It sounds so sick." He mused, "A unifying function."

I added, "But after all, orgasm's ultimate unifying function is procreation."

Roger looked at me, shrugged his shoulders noncommittally, and then proceeded to tell me about his first sexual experience, a long-term situation of sexual abuse by an older neighbor.

"It started when I was 5 and he was 13. It was the Fourth of July, and Larry and I were playing hide and seek in the bedroom while our parents were outside at a hotel barbecue. I hid under the bed, and Larry found me there and asked me to give him a blow job.

"Back then, I had no idea this was what you would call sexual molestation. I enjoyed what we were doing, and I was really flattered at the special attention he was giving me. I'd always been insecure and shy, and to have this older, stronger boy take me under his wing . . . I guess you could say I soon got hooked. It was exciting. For many years, my masturbation fantasies centered around Larry."

"So you felt good about Larry?"

"I was special to him. He accepted me. I was getting approval from him that I wasn't getting anywhere else, from anyone. My father gave me nothing—I was a matter of complete indifference to him. And I got no encouragement from my big brother. He was a real jock and a personality boy, and next to him I felt wimpy."

"Do you think this experience had something to do with making you homosexual?"

"Oh . . ." Roger thought for a moment. "It was really more of a soup, I guess . . . throw in an overpossessive mother, a father who wasn't involved, and my relationship with Larry—all of those things just must have pushed me in this direction."

"When did the sexual relationship end?"

"The last time we did it I was 13, and by then, it felt awful because I was so confused about what was happening. I was having some heterosexual feelings too—I had a sort of crush on this girl at school—and I was confused whether what I did with Larry meant I was heterosexual or homosexual. From then on, I had no more sex with guys until my last year in high school."

As we ended our session, I suggested Roger keep a journal to record any thoughts, feelings, and experiences he might think important. Journal writing facilitates the conscious sorting-out of interior processes. Like most of my clients, Roger was too easily affected by external events. My hope was that through journaling, he would more routinely look within himself to find answers.

The following week Roger arrived in an animated mood. To describe his mood as happy would be too strong for Roger; he was always so emotionally unexpressive.

"Well . . . I did what you said, and it worked," he told me.

"Good! Wha'd I say?" I joked.

"I was walking in the mall last Saturday and feeling upset . . . again, the restlessness. I'm self-conscious about how I'm looking. 'Do I look gay?' I ask myself. Whatever . . . just stupid shit. Finally I say to myself, 'Hey, what's going on here? How am I really feeling?' Like you said I should do. I realize I'm irritated that my mother sends me on this errand to get a new band for my father's wristwatch. I'm not mad at my dad but that my mother sent me, like 'Oh, Roger, go take care of this, and while you're there, do this, too.' Like a schmuck, I go! She seems to think I'm 16 years old and I have nothing else to do. But if I speak up, we'll end up in an argument or I'll hurt her feelings."

I explained, "This sorting-out of your own feelings is the process that was stifled in childhood. You ended up in the role of the good little boy who had no clue as to what he was feeling."

Roger added, "Who was powerless."

"And who in turn came to admire other boys who were spontaneous, free, and self-confident," I said. "That's why you fell in love with the image projected by Perry—he was so outspoken and extroverted. But you have got to keep up the awareness of how you're feeling, and respond to those feelings of anxiety, boredom, and depression."

"Plus irritability and restlessness," he added.

Then Roger told me about an interesting impression he had had of a photograph he had seen last week. From this, he was able to learn something about the deeper needs that lay behind his erotic attraction to males.

"I was in a bookstore looking through the art section, and I saw this coffee table–type book of artistic shots of male nudes. Nothing pornographic or anything. Anyway, I felt myself drawn to this shot of three guys standing around in a swimming pool. You could only see their backs and they were waist-high in water, so there was nothing sexually explicit. Yet there was something terribly compelling about that picture."

I encouraged him, "Stay with that image. What exactly is so appealing about that picture?"

"Sort of like, I wish I was there with them. They were laughing, enjoying themselves, naked, free, outdoors. And I wish I was there with them." In a tone of sad reflection, Roger continued, "I never really had that sort of natural male experience. You know, like the local swimming hole where boys go skinny dipping. I never had that."

"You have identified the deeper longing for that natural, physical connectedness. As you grew older, it became eroticized."

"That's it! When I'm looking at a porn video of guys having sex, my fantasy is that I'm in that movie with them—I'm 13 years old again, sitting around in a jerk-off circle."

"You did that at 13?"

"No. In a funny way, I wish I had. Maybe I wouldn't need to be doing it now."

Roger's insight reminded me of the ideas of the well-known psychiatrist Harry Stack Sullivan, himself a homosexual. He had the odd idea—certainly not understood at the time—that homosexual behavior between young boys helps to establish the foundation for adult heterosexuality. I believe Sullivan was right about the basic principle: that the young boy needs male intimacy (though not of a sexual nature) in order to move on to opposite-sex attraction.

Roger then threw out a question. "Perry and his friends were at a Women's Rights rally recently, and it struck me that gay men are almost always feminists. Why?"

"Gay men and feminists share a distrust of male power. They don't trust that male power can be benevolent."

"Hmm. I think that's true," Roger nodded.

"It's a coalition the two groups have created against the establishment, which is basically a white male political structure."

Roger then brought up a problem that was bothering him. "Just last week I got back my annual employment evaluation. I was told by my supervisor that I'm too sensitive." He wrung his hands tensely. "It's true. When the kids make silly remarks behind my back, I pretend that I don't hear them, but their words echo in my head for days. 'Maybe I *am* this, or this, or this.' I've been sensitive like that all my life."

"You're vulnerable because the image you maintain is not real," I explained. "That's why you feel so fragile."

"Yet there are days that I feel so strong and positive. I feel like, 'There's nothing anybody's gonna say that will shake me.' "

"Good. So now you know the difference between the false self and your real self," I said. "You may notice that when you lose yourself into that false self, it may take half a day or more simply to identify that this happened. Now, the time it takes to get back to your true self—in other words, your recovery time—will become shorter and shorter as you practice coming back to it."

Roger demanded, "But what the hell does this have to do with homosexuality?"

"Everything," I said. "Homosexuality is just a symptom—only one manifestation of the lost masculine power you never actualized from boyhood."

As Roger took a few moments to absorb these new ideas, I thought of the philosopher Eli Siegel's understanding of homosexuality as essentially a problem in living. Siegel's Aesthetic Realism challenges the homosexual man to break out of his passivity to make authentic contact with opposing elements of the world, including the polarity of men and women.

Roger resumed, "I've lived in this passive mindset for so many years of my life, that it feels second nature. It's like . . ." he searched for a word, "normal."

I assured him, "But now, you know the difference. And you will be able to make the shift on the inside when you want to come back to your authentic identity."

The following week, Roger told me he had run into Perry while walking out of a movie.

"I went to see him last Saturday night at his apartment, and the old feelings were still with me. At the beginning of the evening, he told me all about his exploits, and I couldn't help but feel jealous. He told me about the new friend he met at the Bunkhouse. That's a new gay bar with a country-western motif."

"Where everybody's a cowboy."

"Right." He laughed. "So . . . this new guy is the perfect boyfriend, according to Perry. Anyway, Perry said he is now totally at peace with his homosexuality, giving me the it's-a-gift-from-God lecture.

"But then in the middle of it all Perry turns to me and asks, 'Have you ever come away from a sexual experience feeling fully satisfied?' I thought about it and said, 'No, never,' and he said, 'Neither have I.' Then he said, 'You know, I don't think it's homophobic to admit that.'

"He's still going to the bars, running around and distracting himself. I think he's actually very unhappy and torn with conflict, the same conflict I'm going through. That's why it hurts so much."

"Tell me why *his* pain hurts *you* so much."

"I feel so connected with him that it feels painful." Roger had identified a frequent problem in homosexual relationships—narcissistic mirroring.

I explained, "What you're feeling has to do with *twinning*. You become twins, feel the same things. This is a term coined by gay psychologists to describe what happens to gay men in the romantic phase of a relationship. It is a narcissistic identification with the other person. The other man becomes a projection of your ideal masculine self."

Roger said, "It's like our feelings match and that should feel good. But there's a pain to it that doesn't feel right." Struggling to express his binding attachment, he continued, "I don't know. There's something wrong—it's too painful to be real." And then he hit upon the essence of twinning: "It's too painful to be natural."

"Yes," I assured him.

Roger said, "It feels too desperate." He added, "The guy who wrote the book *Straight* said something I really identify with. He talked about 'endowing the anonymous partner with a personality he does not really have.' And I sense it's the same with this twinning thing. Even though Perry is hardly 'anonymous,' I see him as the wild and free image of the man I wish I could be."

I said, "Like Narcissus, you can drown while pursuing your ideal image."

"*Tell* me about it! I feel like I *am* drowning," Roger said. Then, calming down, he returned to Saturday night. "Then we did some more talking, and Perry was floored that I'd continued with therapy. I told him about this journal I've been keeping about my therapy. There was some competitiveness between us. We got into 'Well, let me tell you about *me*' sort of stuff."

He sighed, continuing, "Then we went back to my place. I should tell you, nothing happened. He said, 'Could I see your journal?' I was surprised he remembered. I took it out and he read whole pages of it in utter silence. He was shaking as he read it and he almost started to cry. There was a long moment of silence, then he looked at me and said, 'This journal has so much feeling. You have a lot of courage. You are doing the right thing.' He paid me a lot of compliments.

Roger stopped, then said to me, "But Joe, I don't think he was talking about *me*. It was about *him*. It was that narcissistic thing. What I was doing—going to therapy, trying to change— affected him not so much because he was happy for me, but because he wished *he* could be doing it."

After a long silence, I asked, "How did you feel after he left that night?"

"It was good to see him. The compliments he paid me on the journal were empowering. But seeing him drained me, saddened me, because I am still feeling the ambivalence of whether or not I should continue in this struggle to change my homosexuality.

"Perry and I stopped off at the bars for awhile. The guys in there seemed perfectly happy. They say they're happy, and I have no reason to doubt them. Then on the other hand, I look at the guys I met at the Exodus Conference who are coming out of homosexuality, and they also seem happy. They don't care if they ever completely change or not, they're moving toward a far-off goal and they're just at peace to be moving in a direction they believe is right. It's the right road for them whether or not they change completely. They are at peace with that."

Then he became agitated, "But the problem that keeps coming back is, why am I still caught in the middle? Other people seem to find this peace on one side or the other that I can't find."

I corrected, "That I haven't found."

"Right," he repeated. "That I haven't found."

"Not because you need to explore the options better, but because you need to know yourself better," I said.

"It's very difficult at times, isn't it?" He repeated, "It's very difficult. Sometimes I still ask myself, 'Why do I come here?' "

The next week, Roger walked in the room with a typically eccentric ensemble—this time a black leather vest over a white tee shirt, faded jeans with rips above each knee, and loafers (without the penny and without the socks). This was Roger— shy, but needing to express himself.

This week he had brought in a dream. This dream would lead us to an important discovery about how homosexually oriented men approach women.

Roger began, "I am naked. I look to my left and see a beautiful dark-skinned woman lying on the ground. I want to make love to her. Suddenly a very muscular man appears and I look at him. He looks good to me. Then, he has sex with this woman and I find myself wanting to lie on top of him. I change my mind and, instead, pull him off of her. I engage in inter- course with the woman, but have ambivalent feelings about it. Then I wake up."

"O.K.," I said. "Two rules in interpreting dreams. First, every part of the dream has a significance, whether or not we understand it. Second, every part of the dream represents an aspect of ourselves."

Roger offered cautiously, "Well . . . the man is me, and having sex with a woman is what I want to do, what I'm striving toward."

I clarified, "But you're not prepared to do so directly, so you do it through your ideal male. You say he is muscular and good-looking. He represents your lost masculinity. This dream has a reparative theme—approaching a woman by first cap- turing your masculinity through another male. And notice that you look to the left. The woman is approaching from the unconscious, the unactualized side."

Then I asked, "But tell me, why is the woman dark- skinned?"

"Well, let's see." He seemed embarrassed. "I find dark women attractive. Isn't it weird, I'm more attracted to dark women?"

"No, not weird at all," I said. "I've noticed a number of white men with a homosexual problem find African-American or Oriental women more attractive. Men who have had con- flicts with their mothers may only be attracted to women who are a type that is 'other than Mother.' "

He laughed. "Are you shitt'n' me?"

Roger was delighted and surprised to discover that what he feared to be weird about himself actually had meaning and was common in other men as well. Homosexually oriented men seem to be particularly reassured to discover qualities about themselves that are common in other men. It is as if the man needs to reassure himself, "Here is yet another way I am the same as other men."

"You know, that's what I suspected myself," Roger was saying. "Maybe, I thought, I like black women because they're so different."

After a pause, accompanied by a smile, he announced, "I am! I'm attracted to black women." Then he laughed loudly. "Great!"

Roger then spoke of his relationship with Jim, a straight friend and fellow teacher. He explained, "I've been playing racquetball on my lunch hour with him, and I always look forward to it. Last week these two secretaries from the administration office wanted to play doubles with us. Jim was willing but I felt uncomfortable."

"Why?" I challenged.

"I don't know," he told me, puzzled.

I offered, "Competition? Performance?"

After some reflection he said, "No. I don't think it was any of that. It sounds silly—I wanted Jim for myself." Uneasy laughter. "Not sexually, but I wanted just the two of us—this male thing together." His voice then sounded irritable. "I don't like women to get in the way. Those women put me on the spot when they asked me to play, and I didn't know how to get rid of them without hurting their feelings."

Roger was identifying an important dimension of his masculine identification—the need for full and complete involvement with men, without feminine intrusion.

"Sound familiar?" I asked.

Roger looked totally confused. I repeated, "Does it sound familiar? You feel intruded upon and taken advantage of by the feminine, but if you are frank, you fear you'll anger her or hurt her feelings."

He recognized what I was saying and instantly replied, "Mom! Her again."

"Yeah, 'Mom,' " I said. "You still don't know how to stand up to the intrusive feminine. You don't know how to speak up to a woman because it taps into that powerless enmeshment you felt with mother."

"I have no desire to be with the girls," he said angrily. "I didn't have many friends among the guys when I was growing up. Now, I want to play with them. The guys support me—they keep me going."

Our androgynous culture has lost appreciation for a boy's need to be supported by his own sex. Boys' clubs and teams are now obliged to integrate girls, neglecting the boy's authentic need to take in maleness. Boys have a natural need to reject girls—at least for a certain period of years during their development—in order to prepare themselves to approach women in maturity.

Roger looked animated, happy. "You know, I am really starting to see my sexual feelings as distorting what I really need from men." He paused for a moment, reflecting. "Like the other day . . . I was thinking about Mark, a guy I just met at my church group. I was having some vague sexual feelings around him and I had to stop and tell myself, 'This is a lie. This is not what's really going on. What's happening is that you're lonely and you're looking for that emotional charge instead of honest friendship. Sex is the immediate and convenient way you've satisfied that longing in the past, and now—you just can't do that any more.' "

He added quickly, "I'm not going to say some guy isn't going to walk across my path and tempt me at a weak moment. But most of the time when I see a guy who is my type walk by, I think, 'Well, he's good-looking, but I don't need him sexually.' Little by little, I've been feeling better about myself . . . stronger. For the first time in months, I can say I know why I'm coming here."

Roger now faced the anxieties and challenges of entering group therapy. As he walked into the room for a session with me one day, he seemed irritable and agitated. I could see that this upcoming challenge had created a temporary setback. Taking his place tensely in the chair, he blurted out his fears and apprehensions about revealing himself to the other men.

He began by describing a typical bind of gay men. This bind forces them to choose either loneliness, or a codependent relationship characterized by "crazy stuff." Roger confessed, "When I'm not in any close relationship I can function pretty well. I'm lonely, but at least I feel in control of my life. But as soon as I get really close to somebody, all the crazy stuff starts up again. Then I pull back, go forward, pull back, go forward, pull back." A painful, ironic laugh. "Then when the other guy pulls back, I find myself pursuing him."

After a pause he added slowly, "There's always that search for the close friend, but even when I'm in a relationship, I still feel isolated." He added thoughtfully, "It's nuts."

"But so typical of same-sex relationships," I said.

"Isn't this true of straight relationships?" Roger asked.

"Straight relationships are not typically as ambivalent or as frustrating. This is because the unmet identification needs of the homosexual create a codependency."

Roger went on, "I see gay men repeating this pattern without examining why their relationships don't work. They just learn to adapt to this pattern.

"Yet I know for myself," he continued, "trying to change seems scary . . . because I have no idea what I can change *to*! I know I just have to start taking the initiative to see where change leads me. Yeah . . . like I have to feel the fear and do it anyway."

Roger's concerns now shifted to the group and his plans to join their next meeting. "I've been thinking about next week, and meeting the guys for the first time." A long pause. "I know all the reasons why I should join the group . . ." he hesitated. "Yet, I wonder if it's right for me after all. I mean, what if I don't get along with them? If they don't understand me?"

Realizing Roger needed some reassurance, I said, "So entering the group is stirring up all the fears. Remember, as long as you stay honest with yourself, identify the feelings as they come up, and risk verbalizing them to me or the group, you'll be O.K."

Roger insisted, "It's a very scary thing."

"I know," I told him. "So be scared, but do it anyway."

"Well, I'm trying but it just doesn't feel right. There's something so . . ." he searched for a description, "so unsettling."

"You are doing something new, exposing yourself to possibly very intimate relationships with other men," I pointed out.

Then I saw in Roger a common, self-defeating reaction so often shown by clients who are faced with a personal challenge.

He said, "Thinking about what I have to do, I feel my self-esteem going down. I see myself almost collecting reasons to feel bad about myself. Even at school, if somebody says something slightly negative about my teaching—boom!—I use it against myself. My apartment manager acts cool to me—bam!—more evidence against me. A clerk says something sarcastic on the phone—bang!—add it to the collection."

"What's this about?" I asked.

"I don't know," he said. "I see what I'm doing—I'm making myself feel like shit—but I don't know why."

Trying to lighten his own harassment of himself, I suggested, "Take a wild guess."

Roger ran his fingers threw his shock of unruly brown hair before answering. "I suppose . . . I suppose I'm setting myself up so I won't be disappointed by the group." He nodded slowly to himself. "That's it . . . I know I do this to myself. I'll feel like a nothing by the time I walk into the group meeting."

"Why would you do that to yourself?"

"So it will have to be a complete disaster."

"Right. On the other hand, there may also be the distant fantasy that these new guys will be so terrific that they'll rescue you from yourself."

Roger tried not to laugh but admitted softly, "Maybe so."

"Anyway, this self-defeating dynamic is important for you to understand. The group offers both exciting hope for a new way of relating to men and the threat of rejection and disaster. Carlos Castaneda says, 'The warrior walks between terror and wonder'. You, too, feel both terror and wonder, but you don't allow yourself to savor that hope. And—"

"You're right," he interrupted. "I can't even feel the excitement and hope. Only the fear."

"Then why are you agreeing to be in group?" I asked.

"Because you're telling me it's time to pursue this, and I'm trusting you."

"Good enough," I said. There was a lesson here too. Roger was willing to trust a male authority figure to lead him into new challenges. Not out of intimidation or fear of disapproval, but simply through the blind trust established in the relationship with the mentor.

"The way you've dealt with the fear of failure is to fail yourself first. In a strange way, setting yourself up for one failure so as to avoid the other failure gives you a sense of control," I told Roger.

"Sounds weird." Roger laughed.

"Yes. But it's a mind game learned in childhood. 'I'll fail myself before someone else fails me.'"

With a look of relief as though he felt he understood what was happening, Roger continued. "Overcoming my fear is what joining the group represents for me. I'm seeing new ways in which this problem of fear has been paralyzing me. Like when some guy walks into the faculty lounge and we start talking.

"I see how I instantly shut off, and this is a pattern I can trace back to high school, even earlier.

"I always felt left out but always knew *I* was doing it—*I* isolated *myself*. The battle of getting friendships, doing the work, is frightening to me. I see it, go up to it, and then back off—see it, go up to it, and back off."

Then he said, without realizing the importance of his own insight, "But this time, I feel the fear. Even as I'm talking about it, I feel the fear. I feel 'just leave me alone.' With all the stress that relationships impose on me, I'd just rather be lonely. I don't know, Joe—maybe starting group is simply asking too much of myself."

Roger was participating in group sessions cautiously and self-protectively. While he was interested in what the other members said, he offered very little of himself. Yet his growing interest in the other men caused him to reevaluate his understanding of male relationships, particularly, what men could offer him.

He told me in our next session, "What scares me is that my concept of male friendship is totally askew. I don't know what real friendship is. I don't know what it's supposed to feel like, what it's supposed to look like. How can I have an intimate friendship with a guy who's not my lover?

"I see straight guys together and I think, 'How do they do that?' I don't know how two guys are supposed to *be* together." He laughed, as if this were an absurd idea, and continued, "I'm scared of getting involved with people—I mean guys— because I don't know what I should expect of myself. What should I be working toward? I mean—I can't imagine a close friendship without those intense in-love feelings. Without that crush. Like when you were 7 years old and you were crazy over your best buddy on the playground." Roger was expressing a common complaint.

Then he went on to tell me of his deepest fear, a fear shared by *all* homosexual men in reparative therapy. He said, "I'm afraid that the mature, mutually supportive nonsexual relationships you always talk about won't have any emotional fulfillment. I'm afraid of having those intense feelings and being unable to do anything about them."

Roger spoke of "being stuck between what feels like the meaninglessness of ordinary friendship and my typically intense, romantic crush." He confessed, "I'm afraid of those two extremes, either becoming dependent, or else just having a blah relationship—nothing." Then desperately, "I just don't know how to connect closely with a guy without those old, intense feelings."

I heard an anguished cry for practical direction. I assured him, "You will discover a balanced place between those two extremes. While you may sometimes slip into dependency or erotic attraction, we will monitor those feelings as they happen."

Roger shook his head. "Keeping that balance is like asking me to get into foreplay, but not go to bed. To develop a taste for what's dull. It doesn't sound like positive change, just arbitrary limits."

I said, "Like telling someone who's dieting, 'see the food, smell it, chew it . . . but spit it out instead of swallowing.'"

He laughed. "Exactly."

"I understand," I assured him. But could I really feel his experience? I felt the limits imposed by my own heterosexuality. At this point, only another ex-gay man could offer that special empathy to Roger. This was something I hoped the group would give him.

"If this is what homosexuality is all about," Roger continued, "I can see why gays get burned out before they're 40. They just get cynical about relationships. One crush after another, and after awhile it wears on you. You go through this cycle enough times and you just don't care any more. These guys know their relationships will end in a couple of years, and they'll be back on the roller coaster again. Or at least, if they stay together for friendship's sake, they know they won't be faithful. They know this without reading the sociological stuff. So they say, 'What the hell, I'll stay in 'til the two or three-year mark, then dump the guy before I get dumped.' "

He sighed, and then added, "I just don't know the answer, Joe."

Our hour was up, and on that unfinished thought we concluded our session. I knew Roger would benefit most at this point in therapy from relationships with other men who shared his struggle. I counted on Father John and Charlie to assist me.

The next week Roger walked in, sat down, and did not say a word. I asked, "How are things?"

He broke out in a smile. "Not bad. Last night's group wasn't half as painful as I thought it would be. Nobody pounced on me."

"Good. So, was I right?"

He grinned. "You were right. I'm surviving."

Then Roger's voice turned serious. "But otherwise, I've been struggling lately. Like Monday morning I got up and was feeling anxious and depressed. A couple of things were eating at me. One of them was that the bank made a mistake on my statement. I knew I was going to get upset getting it straight-ened out if the teller argued with me."

Suddenly he grew intense and asked, "And it's so weird. . . . Why do I get this big stressed-out attitude about my job? I guess I don't feel I'm up to being a teacher. I've always gotten decent reports and people tell me I'm doing a good job, but deep down I still feel like I'm just not good enough to do it.''

I have found that the inability to claim credit for personal achievement is a common problem of the homosexual man. Clients typically complain of feeling weak and inadequate, and this has led me to understand the homosexual condition as one of a deficit in personal power. Not only was the prehomosexual boy often unsupported in his male gender identity development, but he was often not bolstered in his sense of personal power. Developmentally, gender and power are related.

Reparative therapy is an initiatory-type treatment that challenges the client to integrate new behaviors and attitudes. Roger now needed to be challenged out of his self-pity. I asked, "So what are you doing to strengthen yourself?"

"Well, nothing much. But something will come up to do, I'm sure."

"That's passive—'something will come up.' You need to have a program."

As if anticipating another one of my previous lectures, he said, "Well, I've gotten together with my friend Jim a couple of times and we're planning on seeing each other once a week."

"Great!" I reinforced him.

Reparative therapy has been criticized for its use of techniques that are called manipulative, even coercive. If giving approval and making suggestions can be considered manipulation and coercion, then in my opinion, such techniques are justified.

Roger changed the subject. "I was in the food store the other day and it reminded me of when Perry and I used to do our shopping together. We'd always go to get our dinner at Gelson's deli and bakery. And I felt melancholy and sad, remembering how nice it was to have another guy to share the little chores of life with. As I started to leave the store, this good-looking guy walked in, and I found myself hoping he'd notice me.

"Then what hit me all of a sudden was that I still feel myself to be this little boy who, when he sees a 'man' ''—Roger made quotation marks in the air—''still needs to run to him and get his attention. I'm still that little kid. It's not even so much sexual, believe it or not. It's just the need for a *man's* recognition and attention."

"That's right," I said. "The need for attention, if it's not fulfilled in childhood, eventually leads to homoerotic feelings."

Roger continued, his tone becoming wistful, "And I still have a desire, a dream, of being embraced, nuzzling my head and face into the chest of a bigger, stronger man."

"Exactly, and it's not necessarily anything sexual either—just that warmth, that security, that relaxation," I assured him.

He nodded.

Hearing Roger's pain, I thought how many men had told me it was only the cuddling they wanted as a boy, but as they grew older and more exposed to the gay scene, this original search for nurturance and acceptance became buried under increasingly sexual and impersonal encounters.

Many studies document male homosexual promiscuity. In a very large study done in 1978, the Kinsey Institute reported that 43 percent of those surveyed had had sex with 500 or more partners, while 28 percent had had sex with more than 1,000 partners. While the AIDS epidemic has changed these figures somewhat today, I still think they reveal a lot about the nature of the homosexual condition.

I reminded Roger where this dream of his came from. "These feelings of warmth and acceptance were denied you by your father."

"Yeah, now when I see my father . . ."

"Hold it," I interrupted. "Before we go to father, let's go back to the grocery store. What emotional state were you in *before* you saw that attractive guy?"

"Feeling lonely," Roger answered. "Thinking of Perry and missing him."

"Yes. And I believe those feelings made you particularly susceptible to that stranger. I doubt you'd have been so drawn to him if you hadn't been feeling so lonely."

Roger paused, then said in a sing-song voice of doubt, "I'm not so sure it's that simple."

"O.K.," I continued, "how would you have felt about that

attractive guy if your straight friend Tim had been with you in the grocery store? If you and he were enjoying each other's company and you felt connected?''

Roger considered my question. "Well," he finally replied, "I would have still found him attractive. I mean, I would still have definitely noticed him."

"Right," I continued, "but would there have been those desperate feelings?"

"Well, I see what you mean," he conceded. "There wouldn't have been such a longing."

"There might still be the attraction, even a passing sexual feeling. But the neediness would be less intense with Tim next to you.

"The healing of that yearning," I continued, "comes through your relationships with male friends. When you internalize that male affection, you diminish the erotic compulsion. In this way, slowly, your homosexual attraction will lessen, become more manageable, less distressing."

"Yeah, I guess you're right," he repeated softly.

From experience, I understood the sadness that Roger was feeling. Already he felt a nostalgia for that surge of sexual and romantic excitement. He had felt that yearning since boyhood and it was a very deep part of him. Now he had glimpsed the price he must pay for growing out of homosexuality.

His tone abruptly changed. "I've been doing better about setting things up to do with Tim—playing racquetball, going hiking. But I have to sustain it."

"Exactly," I agreed. "That's what I mean when I say that 'you've got to keep a log burning on the fire.' When you experience a setback like that feeling of longing in the grocery store, don't stay stuck—keep moving, get going."

Roger laughed. "I know. At first impression, what you're saying just sounds like hype bullshit, but . . ." His tone turned sad and thoughtful. "Doing that just feels so unlike me." He laughed ironically. "When I used to play baseball as a kid, if I'd get hit with the ball or something I'd say, 'This sport is dumb. I'm quitting.' I'd see those Little League coaches screaming at those kids to get up and get back in the game. I hated those coaches. I thought they were bastards."

"You avoided them, and you ran away from their challenges. Now you have to pay a shrink to coach you."

Roger still sometimes shook his head at something I said, or expressed ambivalence about reparative therapy. Yet clearly, he was learning a lot and gaining more awareness of what he needed to do to diminish his homosexuality.

Growth through reparative therapy is an ongoing process. Usually some homosexual desires will recur during periods of stress or loneliness. Rather than *cure*, therefore, I speak of the goal of *change*, in which there is a shift in the identification of the self. While he may continue to have homosexual feelings, a man will usually no longer be identified with those feelings. Within that essential meaning transformation, the client gains new ways of understanding the nature of his same-sex yearnings. He begins to view his problem differently. As one ex-gay man described it, "For many years I thought I was gay. I finally realized I was not a homosexual but a heterosexual man with a homosexual problem."

If the use of the word *change* rather than *cure* sounds pessimistic, we should consider *cure* as it applies to other psychiatric conditions. No psychological treatment can be conceptualized in terms of absolute cure. Poor self-esteem is never completely overcome to produce a client free of insecurity. Alcoholics are never cured, but are referred to in the transitional state as *in recovery*. Rather than focusing on the idea of cure, we should think in terms of reduction of homoerotic needs through healthy, nonerotic male relationships. Healing will range from partial, to significant, to complete freedom from unwanted homosexual attractions. For some men, heterosexual marriage will be possible.

The validity of any therapy, no matter what the treatment method or goal, is found in its overall effect on the life of the client. Good therapy must do more than alleviate the specific symptom for which the client seeks treatment in the first place. Good therapy must have positive effects that radiate throughout every aspect of the client's personality, every aspect of his life situation. If the treatment is right for that person, it will bring a general sense of freedom and well-being.

Besides reducing distress, the move to health will bring greater awareness of intrinsic power.

The most critical and often the most painful part of the psychotherapy for the client is to look honestly at feelings he has transferred onto the therapist from previous relationships. This emotional displacement of feelings from the past is called *transference,* and is perhaps the most powerful factor in the healing of the psyche. The client sees the therapist through the eyes of the child he once was, and to some degree still is. The transferred feelings include fear, anger, aggressive-defensive reactions, and sexual desires.

For a long time, Roger reacted to me with suspicion and even hostility. While such reactions of transference can occur in any relationship, the therapist–client relationship stimulates particularly strong transference reactions because of its dependent, intense, and intimate nature.

The therapist should be able to tolerate these transferred feelings and should not prematurely cut off the client's expression of transference reaction because it makes him feel angry, uncomfortable, or embarrassed. I made sure not to do this with Roger. Through my gentle and tolerant interpretation of the transference, Roger dared separate himself from his long-term perceptual and behavioral patterns.

Fear and hostility are the other sides of the eroticized transference. Although Roger often scoffed at what I had to say, nevertheless he feared my criticism. He often tried to protect himself from the positive feelings he had for me by hiding behind sarcastic comments and expressions of skepticism.

Negative transferences should always be interpreted in therapy. From my experience, the more hostile and traumatic early relationships with the father produce the most intense repressed rage in psychotherapy. As a boy, Roger gained no satisfaction from his impersonal father. Like so many homosexually oriented men, he held on to the impression that "I can never win with that man," and he often played devil's advocate in our own relationship.

For this reason, homosexual clients never work well with distant and aloof therapists. Therapists trained in the traditional psychoanalytic method and taught to remain—as Freud advised—"opaque," are intolerable to the homosexual client.

The homosexual client desires and requires authentic personal contact with a man who is emotionally present. The therapist must never be austere, aloof, or authoritarian.

In my relationship with Roger, I had tried to be the good father—emotionally present, active, and challenging, but always accepting.

As the months went by, Roger went through a gradual pattern of changes. Like the swinging pendulum that slowly diminishes its arc and finally stops on center, Roger finally found his own perspective on the question of homosexuality. As he said, "I find myself giving up the gay identity not through some sort of moral conviction, but by experience. It doesn't work for me." After two years of group and individual treatment, he felt satisfied enough to terminate therapy.

During the following years he would return for occasional tune-ups. He now had a strong circle of straight and ex-gay friends, and had outgrown his old dependency on Perry. Homosexual behavior was rarely a problem. When he did have a fall, he understood the whys of his acting-out. He traced a fall to negative feelings about himself, and he increasingly felt that such behavior did not represent his true identity. As he told me, "Even when I do act out, I know exactly why I'm doing it. It's not about sex or love. It's really about forgetting to take care of my emotional needs properly."

9

Men Together— How Group Therapy Heals

Group sessions are a very important part of reparative therapy. Not only do they offer support and exchange of information, but most essentially, they provide a source of healthy male relationships. All of the eight men described in this book participated in group therapy during the time they were seeing me for individual sessions.

I urge them to take responsibility for their time in group. "Make something happen for *you*. Have one or two challenges in mind to work on. Put them out—let the group know where you are with them.

"Let the group know what the issues are that you're dealing with, and make yourself accountable!" I tell them. "These challenges are like the rungs on a ladder. Something to hold onto, something to pull yourselves up by. If you don't have any of these goals in mind, you're just going to float— you'll go nowhere.

"In our dialogues, let's remember to balance our need for male support with the need for therapeutic challenge. But while we're challenging each other," I warn them, "let there be no hostility for its own sake. We are here to share our feelings and experiences, and to support each other.''

I also tell them, ''Remember—we're responsible for ourselves, but we're also responsible for the other guy. One way we help each other is to be a little probing, a little assertive, to run the risk of somebody being annoyed at us. In spite of our wish to be the nice guy, at times we have to be provocative.''

''O.K., guys,'' I said. ''What's been bothering you?''

Steve was the first to talk. ''Last week, I had to run some errands over the hill in Hollywood. When I finished I went to a nearby porno bookstore.

''I told myself, 'I just *have* to see the latest issue of *Playgirl*!' '' Snickers from the group. ''Then as I walk in, some guys turn their heads and their young guy comes up and stands beside me.

''He glances down at my crotch and that really turns me on. I think, 'Hmm. He could be fun.' Then I think, 'Gee, if I do something, I'll have to tell Dr. Joe, and I don't want to do that.' Then I say to myself, '*So what* if I have to tell him!' ''

More laughter.

''Then another thought crossed my mind. 'If you're going to do it, at least be a little more picky.' He wasn't exactly my type. So I left the store after paying for *Playgirl* and drove back to the Valley.''

Everyone was quiet. I waited. Finally Charlie challenged him. ''*Playgirl* sounds a little . . . shall we say, *tame* for a porn shop. Are you sure that's all you went there for?''

Steve seemed put on the spot. ''I guess not. I was kinda confused. Maybe it was a compromise.''

''Games we play,'' muttered Dan.

Then, as if redeeming himself, Steve continued, ''But at least I turned the guy down. I feel good about that.''

Charlie persisted. ''Yeah, it's easy when they're not your type.'' (Group laughter.)

I said to Steve, ''You turned the guy down, but the arousal was already in your system. I want you to realize that once you go into a place like that, the cycle has begun. Even if you say no to a particular temptation, you have stimulated your system and you'll want to complete the addictive loop—rent a porno video, read a magazine, whatever, to follow through on that cycle.

"So . . ." I asked the inevitable question, "I've gotta ask you, did you just go home and go to sleep?"

Steve hesitated, then admitted, "No. I masturbated with the *Playgirl*."

"Of course. You had to complete the cycle, if not with a real guy, then with a magazine."

"Well, thank God for little miracles," Charlie introjected. The guys snickered.

I looked across the room at Ed. He seemed startled by the explicit disclosures. I thought: well, at least he's hearing it from *this* side of the ideology.

Steve seemed hurt, and Roger rescued him. "I think Steve accomplished something that we're not giving him credit for," Roger said. "I could spend five hours at The Rage saying 'no, no, no, no, no,' then leave the bar feeling good, get in the car and be compelled to act out sexually on the way home. To stop at some porno bookstore. As you say, Joe, I've got to close that loop."

Roger continued, "I used to travel along Santa Monica Boulevard a lot. You know, where the male hookers hang out. I could stop, pick out any guy, and have him for twenty dollars. For me, I think this is actually more than an addictive loop. It's about a little voice in my head that seemed to tell me that this kind of shit was what I really deserved."

Several men in the group nodded their heads in agreement, and for a moment there was silence.

"I'd like to discuss something that's been weighing on me, if you're finished, Roger," said Albert.

"O.K."

Many times in our private sessions, Albert had complained about his image of himself as weak and helpless. He had told me he hoped to get up the courage to tell the group of his frustrations and anxieties.

"Last week," Albert began, "somebody brought up something about his brother that struck a responsive chord inside me. I realized that the reason I've had such a horrible, horrible sense of who I am is that I've always played the victim in our family." His voice was now becoming high and anxious.

"I've felt since the day I was born that I was completely weak and out of control. I guess this should be no surprise. I mean, look at my original two role models. First, my step-brother David. My very first impression of him is of his fist jammed against my jaw, his kick in my shins, his elbow in my stomach. That's what I remember him giving me. He had to get out his aggression and act tough in some way, and his way was to beat me up."

As Albert spoke, we all felt a sense of his frustration. The group listened attentively, and Albert continued.

"The other role model I had to deal with was my dad. A dad who was emotionally not there. He did not affirm me in anything, period. I remember he took me swimming with him a few times at his country club. I could swim like a fish and I was thrilled to go, but afterward in the locker room I would suddenly feel bumbling and inadequate. So many naked men . . . should I undress in front of them? Should I take a shower? I didn't know what to do next. He would never take me under his wing, show me what to do. He just expected me to figure it out on my own." He sighed. "It would have meant so much to me if he had made me feel taken care of."

Albert sat up straight, his voice now taking on a tone of determination. "But recently I've been telling myself, 'No, this is the past and I'm sick of crying about it. It's got to stop. It's time I started to take control of things.' For the first time in my life, I can say I don't hate myself."

He paused, glancing up at everyone, then went on. "It's been hell, but I see myself beginning to come alive and I say, 'Thank God. It's about time.' Last month, an older man at an ex-gay conference came up to me and said, 'You are so lucky because you're starting to straighten out your life while you're still young. Go for it!' "

Sometimes the group is used not for dialogue, but simply for the opportunity to be listened to. At times there is the need to express feelings without input, feedback, or commentary— just for the sake of being heard. Albert felt such a need now.

Then he posed a difficult question. "But even though I feel

good about my progress, I'm scared that if I succeed in the direction I'm headed, I'm going to end up neutered. You know—never have a romantic relationship with any human being. Never be in love with any person, man or woman. Who will I love? This is my unanswered question."

The group remained quiet for awhile. Then Charlie spoke up. His slow but forceful rhythm contrasted sharply to Albert's nervous staccato. "I'd like to tell you where I am, personally, with that question, Albert."

We all waited as Charlie took a long pause, studying Albert thoughtfully through his wire-rimmed glasses. "I've had those same concerns myself. Am I going to be a neuter—a sexual nothing—if I erase my homosexual attractions? But as I see it, right now in my life there is nothing more important than lessening those attractions. Maybe someday I'll be receptive to a woman, maybe not. But for now, I'm just grateful to have some power over a part of my life that was out of control and terribly stressful. And I can say that by now, those attractions have become more *dis*tractions."

I broke in, "About half the men I've worked with do grow into an attraction toward women. Some have married. The other half aren't necessarily strongly heterosexually attracted, but they are relieved to have gained control over the feelings they've found disruptive and extremely distressing."

Albert said, "I guess for me it's one challenge at a time. I'd better trust my own happiness in the present and not get preoccupied with the future."

There was a thoughtful silence.

Then Edward, our youngest member, spoke up to change the subject. "I've been bothered about some gossip I heard recently from some gay stage people. They said I must be gay, and they thought I might be fooling around with one of the stagehands." He sounded indignant. "I may have some of these feelings, but I wouldn't label myself gay!"

"That's a very relevant question in terms of how we define the person," I said. "In fact, the sad truth is that in the gay world, one's sexual feelings are considered *the* stamp of one's essential identity. The whole lifestyle then usually revolves around this countercultural gay identity."

Charlie summarized my point. "Gay art is erotic art, and gay poetry is erotic poetry, and gay cinema is erotic cinema. It's a very sex-centered culture."

Steve added, "I remember when I was about Ed's age—actually, I had just started high school—when I met this old guy who owned an antique shop, and I let him do things to me. He had a ceramic penis on display and other sexy stuff all over the store. There was another old guy who was his roommate, and they showed me some pictures of naked guys with whips and chains in a gay magazine."

Ed spoke up emphatically. "You should see the "Personals" ads in the back of those gay magazines. They're a real eye-opener."

At the start of the following meeting, Father John began by expressing a lifelong frustration.

"I've been praying to God to let me know the man I truly am. Because I've come to realize that I've been hit with a double dose of the false self. First, I was the obedient son. Then, I found myself in the role of the obedient priest. For so many years, I've been buried under all this good boy bullshit. I don't even know any more if this is *me*.

"Now it seems I'm in trouble with the pastor. I have been learning to face conflicts more assertively. This means casting aside the false, compliant me, and the monsignor's not used to it. In fact, I don't think he likes '*me*.' Last night at dinner, I finally confronted him. I told him I was tired of always being the one who had to do the 6:00 A.M. mass. He stared at me, and almost dropped his wine glass."

The group snickered.

"Do you blame him?" I asked.

"Well, he really shouldn't drink so much." More snickering.

"Do you blame the guy for giving you the early mass if you never complained about it?"

"I guess not. Maybe he just assumed I was an early bird." He laughed. "Which I'm not. With my night life, it hasn't been easy getting out of bed that early."

"Tell me more about this true self you've been finding," I said.

"When I'm living from the true self . . . well, I'm honest with myself and others. I speak up directly—no more good boy role. I'm not afraid that people will call me a jerk—if I deserve it—because I still have an inner conviction that I'm O.K. . . . that I am still lovable."

"I think that's what everyone in this room wants," Dan said.

Angry Dan, I thought, of all people, understood the need to express anger and still feel lovable.

Father John studied Dan's face, then nodded. "For myself, I've always played the role of the good guy. I've always come across as smiling and gracious. I'm a pleaser most of the time, and this comes easy. But there are very few people with whom I'm honest."

Father John was describing a feature common to many homosexual clients—an overconcern with self-protection. "There are many things I'd like to express, but never do. I even know how much I'm going to say here in the group. I reveal things a little bit at a time and wonder whether people are turned off by this. Can they still say, 'I care about you?' "

Now Dan spoke up to describe his own experience. "I get paranoid making up stupid things in my mind about what the other person might think of me. Overdramatizing the situation."

He added, "I can call up other people from the studio when I'm concerned about them. But to make a call for myself, to say to someone, 'Hey, help me—I'm hurting'—that's almost impossible. I don't encourage friendships because I hate that feeling of vulnerability."

"It's the whole risk thing, not wanting to be hurt again," Father John said.

Dan challenged Father John. "You said 'again.' How were you hurt the first time?"

"The first real hurt I can remember was my father's obvious preference for my older brother," the priest said. "I was about 3 years old and I felt there must be something wrong with me. And I remember an intense relationship between my mother and me, but no physical affection. I don't recall my mother ever hugging me or my brothers and sisters."

He went on, "The only time I ever remember being touched was years later when I was sexually molested. I probably responded because . . . it was better than nothing. And—as I know to be common in those types of man–boy relationships—when the novelty wore off, I was tossed to the side. That's how I felt. I could never understand it."

As I listened, I found myself pleased to see these two men hearing and understanding each other. I knew it was hard for either one to engage in this kind of self-disclosing dialogue.

In these sessions I was privileged to see the evolution of each man's therapeutic process. This group continued for eight years, with some men leaving and others entering. Most men would stay a year or two; others, three or four years, depending upon their personal issues and rate of improvement. I felt proud to see each group member's progress, but I knew the work would continue long after each man left us.

Two months later, Steve described his slow disengagement from a painful relationship with Randy, his on-again, off-again lover. As he spoke, I heard the familiar gay issues of power struggles and narcissistic competitiveness.

"Our relationship has flip-flopped completely from the way it was the day we met," Steve told the group. "Then, I was on top of things and enjoyed meeting people. I had lots of friends. I was always out, always happy. If I had a fight with Randy, it didn't bother me. I wasted no energy on him. I was feeling strong, and this put me in control in our relationship.

"Now, Randy is the one who is on top of things. He's doing well at his job as half-owner of a restaurant. He's going places, meeting new people. He's the center of attention. Our positions have switched. Now he's treating me just the way I treated him—like dirt. And I can't say I blame him."

Then he asked plaintively, "Is there always one person who's on top in a relationship?"

I said, "There is a natural competitiveness between same-sex partners, especially males . . . so this situation is pretty common in male couples."

Steve added in a shaky voice, unusual for him, "Ever since we met, it was a competitive relationship—we beat the crap out of each other. I was supposedly the handsomer one. When we were out, I was the one people stared at. Then he started working out at the gym, like I used to do. It bothers me to turn into the feminine one in the relationship—the weaker one, the guy who has to come crawling. Now when people see the two of us walking down the street, it's gotten so they'll look at him first. It sounds egotistical, but it makes me feel lousy."

Steve paused. We all waited for him to go on, but he didn't say a word. We could hear the anxiety and sense of powerlessness as he spoke to us. Charlie finally said, "You were feeling out of control in this relationship."

Steve nodded.

"The point is, Steve, how did you want this relationship to be for you?"

This was a question I often asked the guys, and it was now being adopted by them to help each other.

"I'm sick of feeling sorry for myself in relationships." Steve said. "I wanted a relationship that felt good, but it was like an addiction. I couldn't break it. My biggest problem has always been my isolation. I've always had lots of friends, yet I can't seem to trust men. I can't accept kindness from them. I don't want anybody to invade my space, intrude into my life. Not on an intimate level, anyway. And when I'd fall in love with someone, I'd completely lose control and get walked on."

"You don't want to get close because it feels like entrapment," I said.

Steve admitted, "Last week, the thought came to me, 'I wish I had never started therapy with Joe. Ignorance was bliss.' Then it hit me—'Nah, that's not true. It wasn't bliss.' I would have kept on with the rat race of relationships I was into. I just wouldn't have understood why I was doing it."

Steve's description of his power struggle with his lover reminded me of the extensive literature that describes homosexual relationships as highly ambivalent. In my work with many couples, both homosexual and heterosexual, the most violent domestic arguments have occurred in male relationships.

As the months progressed, Steve was slowly and with much backsliding disengaging himself from his unhappy relationship with Randy. The group offered steady support and encouragement for the breakup. The intensity of Steve's ambivalence clearly showed me the lingering power of his and Randy's codependence.

One week, we opened our discussion with Roger's report of his recent trip to San Francisco. Mocking an announcer's voice, he said, "The latest word from the guys at the J.O. Club in San Francisco, for those of you not up on these things, is that instead of having their ears pierced, they are having their penises pierced."

Albert retorted in mock agony, "Ah-h-h! No details, please!"

"They really do that?" Father John whispered to Dan, wincing.

"They do! They do!" Roger replied animatedly. "They're basically into sexual mutilation. They have sexual intercourse with their pierced penises."

Albert repeated his mock agony. "Oh, no!"

"What is this about?" Ed asked.

Charlie shook his head. "The children of the night. Such insanity."

"But what's the J.O. Club?" Ed asked.

Roger explained, "The Jerk Off Club—there's one in every major city. Basically you pay an entrance fee, take off all your clothes and check them in a locker. You're only allowed footwear—that's the only way you can make a fashion statement. You're given a complimentary paper cup of I don't know what—Crisco—and guys walk around with hands on each other and get into circle jerks. It's a safe-sex orgy."

I asked the group, "But what about this pierced penises thing? Do you understand the sadomasochistic theme of self-mutilation? Do you know what it represents?"

"Yeah. It's the really dark side of homosexuality," Roger said.

"Remember what we've always said about same-sex ambivalence," I told them. "There's an inherent resentment in all homoerotic attraction, resentment rooted in the relationship toward the rejecting father. Homoerotic attraction begins with the resentment of the father and a sexualization of that rejection. Consequently, there is a built-in hostility toward all male love objects. This is why you see so much sadomasochism in homosexuality.''

"But how can there be both love and hostility?'' Ed asked.

"Well . . . you could say that the homosexual is in some ways a little boy trying to get daddy's attention, but he perceives himself as unworthy of it. At the same time he's angry at daddy for the fact that he's in this frustrating and unfair position of having to pursue him.''

I described a recent survey which showed that 20 percent of the Personals in a gay periodical, *The Advocate*, seek male-on-male violence—that is, whipping, spanking, urination on each other, bondage, fisting, rectal penetration with objects, verbal humiliation, and so forth.

Roger asked, "Yes, but don't we see this sadomasochism in heterosexual relationships?''

"Yes, but it's much less characteristic. On the other hand, gay magazines typically run porn photos with themes of control and domination.''

"Guys in cop uniforms and stuff, whips, leather boots—supertough masculine types,'' Roger added.

Tom spoke up. "I can relate to what you're saying, Joe. Sometimes when I look at men I can feel the anger within me, and I see how sex is a genital expression of that anger. Before Cynthia and I were married, I remember once I got into a bang-bang, hard-hitting, pain-inflicting act with a man who suddenly turned on me, demanding I pay him for what he was doing to me. It seemed that I was not worth his attention unless I paid in advance for it. All desire went out the window.''

Father John became agitated. "Then there's the whole fascination with youth and beauty. It's 'You're O.K. because you're young, attractive, well-built, well-hung,' whatever, but 'I am not O.K. because I'm older, not so attractive, balding, getting a pot belly.' And as soon as the orgasm ends, there follow the guilt, shame, fear, and self-loathing, and the desire to push the kid out the door before he sees me for what I really am. Then I go through the *meshuga* trip—''

Ed interrupted, "A what trip?'' He seemed to think he had heard of a new perversion.

Stopping in his tracks, Father John smiled and shifted to

the role of teacher. "*Meshuga* means a craziness, a neurotic quirk."

With an appreciative nod from Ed, Father John resumed his frantic pace. "So I push the kid out the door and I think 'Oh my God, I may get AIDS and I deserve it because I'm such a shit.' The whole trip is so self-defeating." He added, "It's good to be pulling away from all this craziness. It seems that all I saw in the gay world was craziness."

These three men—Charlie, Father John, and Tom—were the wisest and most articulate members of the group, though they did not always reveal the intimate details of their lives except in private sessions with me. They were leaders, in a sense, wishing to help out the younger members.

"In some ways, I think I've been attracted to that adventure, that craziness," Albert said.

Charlie agreed, "Sex brought us not just the feeling of acceptance, but that special kind of fun, excitement, and adventure that men have with each other. I think there's a male energy that the homosexual guy wants to share in."

"That's what so appealing about gay bars. There's a wildness we didn't get as boys," Albert admitted.

I said, "Homosexual men were often repressed, good little boys. In childhood they were inhibited, so in adulthood they make up for it by joining Act-Up."

Father John joked, "There's a new ex-gay organization now—they call it *Grow*-Up."

"But I think I'm learning about the price we pay for that wildness," Albert continued. "A few months ago I met this guy who started working at the nursery. He was real friendly. I thought, 'This guy could be the kind of friend we talk about in therapy. I could have a healthy, good male friendship without sex.' Then, after we saw each other a couple of times, we had a party with his girlfriend and I got kind of high. Somehow they got me involved in a *ménage à trois*. I was an emotional wreck. I immediately cut off my relationship with this guy. It brought back feelings of being used and totally out of control, like when I was a kid and was molested.

"I felt shaky. All the old hurt returned as I relived the experience with my cousin. I also felt totally ashamed. I was not a man, not respectable. I was this weak, helpless little creature who got himself dragged into something shameful. I lost my my self-respect, my identity."

He added, "It was then I started coming to group so I could have some real relationships."

For awhile, no one spoke.

"We're very glad you did, Albert." Father John interrupted the silence.

A few weeks later we started with a discussion of passivity, lack of assertion, and fear of "doing something wrong," all part of the male homosexual condition. The men talked of their fear of job change, along with their attempts to become more assertive.

Dan had recently been laid off from his job at the television station. To save money he returned home temporarily to live with his mother. It was obvious he had experienced a setback in his therapy, because his homosexual temptations had resurfaced with a vengeance.

"The past few weeks I've felt really disconnected with myself," Dan explained. "I just feel out of control again, like I always used to."

"What is the reason for feeling out of control?" I asked.

"I guess being dumped from my job at the studio," he said. "And being back in the house with my mom."

"Out of control"—how many times had I heard this complaint! It is a phrase used over and over by the men to describe the pervasive sense they have of their lives. They feel powerless and helpless. Gaining a sense of self-possession is essential to diminishing same-sex attractions.

Dan was saying, "I've been feeling that I'm just hurtling backwards. Giving up all my progress."

"Why do you think this is happening?" I asked.

"I guess it's because I have to live with my mom again. Here I am, almost 40 years old. I've been out of the house since I graduated from high school. Now I feel uncomfortable with my mom helping me out. I feel kind of drained . . . really helpless."

Taking a deep breath, he continued, "One of the goals I set

for myself in this group was to be more active and involved, but right now I feel weak and detached from everyone.''

"Tell us more about that," I challenged.

"I just feel detached. Even from the group. I don't believe I can express my thoughts any more. I feel like I'm curled up into a ball, smothering in my own emotions, and I don't know how to get out of myself.''

I recognized that Dan was in what I call *the black hole*, an emotional quagmire characterized by an inner deadness—an inability to feel or express feelings—and an overwhelming sense of powerlessness. It is a state that can last hours or days. This feeling first appears in early childhood, when parents give contradictory messages that confuse the boy to the point of emotional paralysis. When the early environment does not reflect and support the boy's expression of his true self, when parents all too often acknowledge false self-expression, the boy is taught not to trust authentic expression. Later, in adulthood, especially during times of stress and challenge, he is tempted to withdraw inward to passive disconnectedness from his emotional flow, while entertaining self-gratifying fantasies such as self-pity.

There is only one way out of the black hole, and that is through matching inner feelings with outer expression. When a man correctly matches feeling with behavior, he reconnects with his natural energy flow.

One *false* way to jump-start the feelings and connect with the masculine self is through homosexual behavior. For a brief time, the associated emotional excitement, or rush, seems to offer immediate connection with one's own unactualized maleness. But this fails to offer sustained connectedness. One *authentic* way to reconnect with the masculine would be to express feelings to a male friend. This option does not offer the addictive rush, but it does provide a sustained, more deeply gratifying, connectedness that is far more genuine.

To help Dan out of his black hole, I used Eugene Gendlin's therapeutic technique of focusing on matching word to feeling. I have found this method very useful for men who are stuck. In time, they learn to use the method on their own.

"What are you feeling right now?" I asked, as the group listened quietly.

In a flat monotone Dan said, "I'm not feeling anything."

"What does *not feeling anything* feel like?"

"What?" He sounded perplexed.

"What does *not feeling anything* feel like?" I repeated.

"Confusion," he answered.

"Good. Now stay with that feeling of confusion. Sit with that feeling. See if that feeling changes to another feeling. See if you come up with a better word than confusion."

He sat silently, glancing around him at the other group members. But eventually he looked downward toward his own body. That was a good sign. When people glance laterally at eye level they are thinking. When people look up, they are remembering. But when people glance down, as Dan was now doing, they are searching within for a feeling.

Finally, he said, "The feeling is that I'm frustrated, I guess."

I thought, "When they say 'frustrated' they usual mean 'angry.' " I encouraged him, "Fine. Stay with 'frustrated.' Does that word really describe how you feel now?"

He scowled. "I guess I'm angry. Angry at feeling so fuckin' out of control. I have to masturbate three times a day just to keep my spirits up."

Feelings were released now. We could all see that Dan was now authentically present. We waited for more.

"It's not about my mom," he said. "It's about *me*—even though she bugs the shit out of me." Heads nodded in sympathetic understanding. "It's all about getting my life in order. *Doing* something. Taking control of things."

Dan now fully felt his feelings; first anger at himself, then gradually, with the group's assistance, a clarity about what he must do to help himself. Seeing Dan's satisfaction, Roger now spoke up.

"I've been dealing with the same issues lately," he said. "I can also get stuck in passivity and a failure to do things. Like right now I have to face ten or fifteen of the little, unpleasant chores of life, like going to the dentist, renewing my driver's license, and getting a new prescription for my glasses. It seems the more I condemn myself for not doing these little things, the more passive I become. I can either get stuck in that black hole, or start making small decisions to start doing some of these things I need to tackle."

Edward said, "I've been stuck, too, over a decision. A friend of mine has been pressuring me to accept a waiter's job at Hamburger Hamlet to fill in the time when we don't have play rehearsals. But honestly I'm scared to death of waiting tables. It's funny that I can act in a play, but I'm afraid I'll make a fool of myself in a restaurant—drop plates, mess up orders . . . that I'll fail, or feel incompetent, or be laughed at. And I don't relish being yelled at by the manager."

He added, "But I also feel I have to do this in order to overcome my fear and passivity." Ed then managed to involve the group in a chatty but unproductive debate on the pro's and con's of waiting tables.

Finally Charlie broke in. "For Ed, the real issue is 'To be, or not to be a waiter: that is the question.' "

Steve whispered, "Don't you just love the way he introjects Shakespeare."

The group snickered. Tom looked at Steve. "So witty, so avoidant."

Now addressing the larger question, Charlie continued, "We all have to overcome the fear of making a decision. We all feel that any decision we make can be potentially devastating."

Ed said, "I really need the extra cash that job would pay. So if I *don't* take this opportunity, I'll feel like I've defeated myself. I should be able to do this. Get over the fear. Just go do it, even if I don't do the job perfectly.

"That's what this is about—perfectionism," Charlie continued. "Perfectionism is part of the false image. Breaking free of the defense of perfectionism stirs up all the old anxieties and feelings of inadequacy."

Ed admitted, "Growing up I was supposed to be perfect— never make a mistake. I was careful never to stand out, never to get criticized. On the other hand, I could get up on the stage and not feel uneasy. Isn't that strange?"

"Not strange at all," I said. "That's the false role. As soon as you get up on the stage, you're portraying someone who is not you. It's easier to step up in front of an impersonal audience than to be one-on-one with another guy."

Steve added, "Some of my own most painful memories are of failing in front of my peers and being laughed at. They are so painful I tend to avoid things that might cause anyone to laugh at me."

"All kids fear being laughed at by their peers," I told them. "But while most just bounce back, some kids feel so devastated, they detach from all future challenges. For the prehomosexual boy, the learned response is withdrawal. He retreats into his own little world of fantasy, occupying himself with solitary activities such as drawing or music. He consoles himself with the belief that somehow he is better than the other boys, special. Often, his mother supports him in this idea of his specialness."

At this point Father John commented, "I, myself, withdrew by getting into music and playing the piano."

Many studies show prehomosexual boys to be interested in theater and acting. Many of my clients also played piano from the time of early boyhood. I see this as one more retreat from life challenges into the safety of the false self.

Albert added, "My escape was through nature. I remember often running away from my house into a grove of tall trees. I climbed up into a tree and sat on a limb, imagining myself to be a little bird. I thought, 'No one will find me up here.' "

As is so often the case in reparative therapy, very few of our discussions were about sex. Mostly, the men talked about their struggle for their sense of identity.

Father John continued, "One thing I've learned here is to fight back against passivity and feelings of hopelessness. Before, I would just fall into my pornography addiction. Even now, while I'm watching a porno film in my room at the rectory, doors locked, shades down, I'm saying, 'I know what this compulsion is about. It's about wanting entry into the club of men.' I can really relate to that phrase, 'feeling excluded from the club of men.' All my life, that's how I've felt."

Charlie added, "I understand that temptation to fall back into those familiar doldrums—trapped in the darkness of the soul. It feels bleak, but at least it's familiar."

Father John looked pensive, seeming to muse about those last words, "in the darkness of the soul." "Those experiences that I used to consider downers," he continued, "I now see as opportunities for transformation. This is what my hero, Colin Cook, means by *failing successfully*."

Ed asked, "How can you fail successfully?"

"My failures are letting porno stuff and masturbation bum me out for days—it used to be weeks," Father John said. "But failing successfully means if I'm gonna fail, I'll turn those moments into occasions for praising God, in spite of all the ugliness."

Albert looked doubtful, suspicion in his eyes. "Sounds like gay spirituality," he said.

"Not at all," Father John assured him. "I still take responsibility for my sins. I don't want that shit in my life. But my mistake was pushing God out of my life at those sinful times. Colin Cook says, 'Keep God in the picture.' "

He added, "Early Christian theologians spoke of the *felix culpa* or 'happy sin,' which sounds like a contradiction, but failing can become an opportunity for transformation."

It was time for us to end our session. As the group adjourned, the men slowly left my office in groups of twos and threes, talking quietly.

Colin Cook, ex-gay counselor and author, had been a national figure in the ex-gay movement, with a well-funded ministry. Scandal broke when Colin became sexually involved with some of his counselees. The scandal sent shock waves throughout the then-fragile ex-gay movement. Gay spokesmen and critics of reparative therapy used Colin Cook's story as evidence that gays cannot change. Since then Colin has slowly reestablished himself, gradually building trust, and has gone on to make even greater contributions to the cause of men desiring to be free of homosexuality.

In our next session, Tom began with a discussion of his previous experiences in psychotherapy.

"The other therapists told me I must accept my sexual orientation. But where did that advice leave me? Outside affairs with men are incompatible with my marriage. For years I tried to live in two worlds. That therapist left me sitting on a picket fence—with the sharp end up my ass!"

Steve laughed loudly, then said apologetically, "I'm sorry, Tom. But what you just said tickled me."

"The devil owns that fence," Father John whispered.

Charlie added, "I had the same problem Tom did when I first saw a shrink. The guy told me, 'Live with it. Others have lived with it, and so can you.' I said to him, 'But I can't.' He said, 'You have to accept it, because you cannot change what you feel. This is *you*, and you have to be true to yourself.' "

I told them, "Many members of the profession have bought a politically convenient solution to an existential problem. They've bowed to pressure from gay psychologists who want their orientation viewed as equivalent to heterosexuality.

"This reminds me of an old joke," I said. "A man walks into the doctor's office and says, 'Doc, every time I bend my arm, I get a shooting pain.' The doctor says, 'Don't bend your arm.' This is how psychiatry responds to dissatisfied homosexuals. A man goes to the therapist because he is dissatisfied with his homosexuality. The therapist says, 'Don't be dissatisfied.' "

For many years, men such as my clients—whom I call nongay homosexuals—have been ignored by the mental health profession. They are victims of the politicization of psychiatry.

Charlie opened one session by returning to an old issue of problems with his father.

"When I didn't go out for football, this seemed like a personal rejection to my father. When I didn't want to play the game, he took it as my rejection of *him*, of *his* love for football. I got the same feeling when he wanted chores done at home a certain way. If I started to resist, I was rejecting him personally. He had a tremendous ego."

"As if you existed for him alone," I said.

At this point Dan, who usually did not talk much in group, offered, "That happened to me, too. I told my father I wasn't into team sports or guns. He was disgusted."

"Yeah. Like it was a personal affront," Charlie added.

Dan went on, "To my father, football was like his first love. Games came before his family—they were more important. Also guns. He had a three-thousand-dollar machine shop in his basement devoted to guns."

The men continued to share their memories of disappointing a father with stereotypic expectations, and their deep sense of failure at not having met these expectations.

Then Roger talked at length about his former lover Perry. Although the relationship had ended, clearly there continued to be a codependency with loss of personal boundaries between the men.

Throughout their tumultuous nine months together, Roger and Perry had both tried to go straight. While verbally committed to healing their homosexuality, they often backslid, which resulted in contradictory feelings about both their healing and each other. When their relationship ended, Perry had suddenly given up his commitment to change and found a new lover. From my clinical experience, nothing shakes a commitment to reparative therapy so much as when a former lover finds a new and seemingly successful love relationship. Glowing reports about the new relationship serve as a reminder of the client's own unfulfilled emotional needs.

Roger now mustered the courage to be more direct, telling us that he really had doubts about continuing in therapy. Yet his feelings were radically contradictory. He envied Perry's new love life, but he knew such relationships never worked for him. One minute he seemed to desire to return to the gay world. The next minute he turned around and criticized that choice as a cop-out. He said, "I'm in my car listening to the radio, one of these talk shows, and there's some guy saying how happy he is being gay, and how miserable he was the years he tried to change—you know, the generic coming out story. I know intellectually there has to be more to this guy's story, but I've got to admit it sounds real tempting. This is the kind of stuff I get hit with every time I read the newspaper or turn on the television."

I thought, Roger was right. The man trying to heal his homosexuality wages a war on two fronts—the internal one against his own feelings, and an external one against a society that neither values nor understands his struggle.

Then Roger said to the group, "Every time I feel attracted

to some guy now, my inner voice asks, 'Yeah, but how would it work out in the end? Wouldn't it just work out like all my other relationships?' I'm tired of trying to figure it out. I feel weak, weak and very tired.''

I could see that Roger was concerned that I would not understand or accept a decision to drop out of therapy. Turning to me, he demanded, "So what should I do?" His voice was now sharp and angry.

From years of experience I have learned not to get into an adversarial posture in defense of reparative therapy. Rather, I leave it to the client to determine if he will find personal value in treatment. In taking the neutral position, I disappoint his expectations that I will rescue him from the pain of determining his own direction.

Roger continued his anguished ambivalence, attempting to seduce me into deciding for him. Finally, I said, slightly irritated, "Look, Roger, you know my position. But you will have to decide for yourself if this is right for you. I'm here—we're all here—to help you do the work if you want it."

In a gentle voice, Father John said to him, "We don't grow just by resisting a negative, but rather, by moving toward a positive. The right way for all of us, Roger, is to find God in this."

"I don't know what I want, Father John. And I don't know where God is in all of this. It seems impossible for me to make decisions for myself. I always end up turning this over to other people. I ask for their opinion, I want them to tell me what to do."

Charlie mused, "Advice is what we ask for when we already know the answer, but wish we didn't." He continued, "I don't think your doubts came up just because your old boyfriend is now happily in love. I think that just stimulated your own ambivalence about healing."

Roger said, "I feel like a little white rat that's run through all the paths in the maze and found himself right back at the start. No matter how many sidetracks I take, I come right back to face all the things I've been avoiding."

As it became clear to Roger that we would not tell him

what decision to make, he could no longer be angry with us. He asked, "Do I want to do the work, face the issues? Do I really want to change?"

Charlie pushed further, "Whose 'should' is it? Make sure it's your 'should,' Roger. No one else's. Otherwise you will be setting yourself up to be resentful of this therapy."

Roger turned to me. "Do you have a sense of what I'm feeling?" Before I could answer, he added, "I've only done what I've been trained to do, which is be the obedient child. To take direction from others."

"Absolutely," I replied. "Some men in reparative therapy agonize more than others. For some guys, it's not a one-time decision. They go back and forth before they find the right direction."

Charlie said, "Ambivalence is the nature of the beast," adding, "homosexuality *is* the beast."

Tom turned to Roger, saying softly, "Don't resent being in the struggle. You don't have to be here."

"I know." Roger spoke slowly. Sadly.

Mutuality is an important concept in reparative therapy. Men with homosexual problems have difficulty establishing a sense of mutuality and equality in their male relationships. They tend to develop relationships with an imbalance of power, where they either devalue the other man or put him on a pedestal.

Unlike conventional psychotherapy, which prohibits outside meetings between group members, reparative therapy encourages friendships in order to counter the isolation characteristic of the condition. Albert and Steve had been meeting socially outside the group, and I had been supportive of their relationship because I saw it as an opportunity for a healthy mutuality.

At one session, Albert began his session complaining about Steve, who was absent. He said, "I find Steve very encouraging in so many ways, but there's a problem."

"What is it?" Charlie asked.

"I'm not sure," he said, haltingly.

Albert was clearly having difficulty identifying what was

wrong with this friendship. For homosexual men, the challenge is constantly to adjust the tendency to overvalue or undervalue other men. There may be an inclination to become passive in relationships, and to let power and boundary issues get out of control.

Albert went on, "Steve's been such a positive role model for me—he's where I want to be in my own development. He gives me a lot of assurance. But in the past few weeks he's made me feel uncomfortable." Eyes darted around the room inquiringly. Albert hastened to add, "There's nothing sexual between us." Then he continued, "We saw this movie where one of the guys was real cute and Steve made some jokes—he's always doing that."

"So, what about it?" I felt impatient at the hesitant and roundabout way Albert brought up his concerns.

"Steve often notices guys on the street, makes sexual references, and—" hesitantly, "I gotta be honest, it's a turn-on. He's got a wild sense of humor. We can easily get into teasing each other."

He stopped, then said, "I don't know what to do. Maybe I'm just being too sensitive. I want to be honest with Steve, but I don't want to lose his friendship."

Homosexual relationships are often characterized by codependence. The men's needs become entangled, those of the one superceding and disguising the other's. I decided that the unraveling of mutually overlapping needs must begin with Albert's feelings.

"O.K. Let's start with the simple question 'How do his comments make you feel?' " I said.

"Um . . . upset," he said.

"Stay with it. Give me more," I asked.

Then I heard the real conflict. "Um, I gotta admit I'm excited by his jokes and comments. He makes me start thinking about guys and I begin to regress." He laughed nervously.

We waited in silence.

"But that's not what I want in our relationship."

Tom said, "So Steve creates in you a conflict. You enjoy the feelings but you really don't want them."

Tom's reflection of Albert's feelings held an implicit validation which started the flow. Animatedly, with some self-righteousness, Albert retorted, "Yeah, like, I really don't need that from him. He doesn't help me by bringing my attention to those things. I want to substitute other pleasures in place of the ones I'm trying to give up. I don't feel he supports me in my goal."

"Great!" I said.

Albert now looked sure of himself. He had given himself permission to identify a grievance. This was not *complaining*, as van den Aardweg talks about it, but the expression of a valid need. On to the next step.

"O.K., what can you tell Steve?" I asked.

I saw a drop in posture. Long pause, blank gaze. Then Albert said, "I just don't want to hurt Steve. He doesn't mean to—"

Anticipating a new tangle, I interrupted, "Never mind his intent. Only Steve can talk about that. Right now, the question for you is 'What can I tell Steve?' "

"I suppose I could say, 'Look, I know you don't mean it but your sexual jokes and comments about other guys are not helping me. And not helping *us*!' "

"Right." I felt satisfied that Albert was able to take the two steps necessary for resolving the hostile dependency which is so characteristic of homosexual relationships: (1) identification of his needs, separate from the other man's; and (2) effective expression of these needs. These two steps seem simpler than they are, and they are necessary for reestablishing mutuality.

Albert asked, "But how do I *tell* him how I feel?"

A typical question the homosexually oriented man forgets to ask himself about another man's behavior is "How does this man make me feel?" The tendency instead is to focus on the other person—he cannot be queried or challenged for fear he will be lost as a friend.

"What stops you from talking to Steve? You're clear about what you want to say to him. So why is it difficult to establish mutuality?"

"Explain that."

"You and Steve are equals. You have established equality between you. Neither is better or lesser than the other."

"I guess I have been putting him on a pedestal," Albert admitted.

I explained, "Your challenge—which is the same challenge of all men with homosexual problems—is constantly to adjust the tendency to overvalue or undervalue other men. Don't be afraid of what Steve will think of you if you have something to tell him. Speak up about your feelings, and don't put him on a pedestal."

I thought, how strong is the wish of the homosexual man to be able to verbalize his needs, his wants, his fears. He tends to let the other man lead, and to let power and boundary issues get out of control.

"You're right!" Albert said. "I'm really scared to tell anyone what I think."

Tom pointed out, "I notice that you bring this problem up when Steve's not in group. I can see that it's much easier for you to express your feelings because he's not here tonight. I think it would be better for you to address your feelings to Steve directly."

The group sessions were bringing about slow but steady progress. The men were slowly assimilating communication techniques that would help them relate to other men more effectively.

Two weeks later, the group dealt with a seemingly insignificant event involving Steve—the act of reserving a seat for a friend.

More than any other group member, Steve was able to provoke intense feelings in the other men. His extroverted, outgoing style drew attention, including some negative reactions.

At this group meeting, Dan was, as usual, very quiet. Then during the last twenty minutes, he spoke up more frankly than he ever had before.

Turning to Steve, he said, "I don't know where this is going, but I want to talk to you, Steve." He then turned to the group. "Last Saturday, I made plans to meet Steve and his friends at a concert. I walked in late, and there was Steve with an empty seat next to him. I wasn't sure if it was reserved for me. So I asked him if someone was sitting there. He said, 'Yes. It's taken,' which really hurt me because I thought we'd be together.

"When I heard that, I just stood there. Then I stepped back, totally surprised. Steve didn't say anything for a long time. As I turned to go, he said, 'Just kidding.' By that point I was really hurt and angry.''

Dan turned to Steve and said very softly, very seriously, "The way you said that to me, Steve, seemed hurtful, spiteful.''

The nature of practical jokes among friends—what is funny and what is hurtful—becomes a painful issue for our men. A simple incident, easily dismissable, may provoke a struggle for understanding. "Am I too sensitive? If they are laughing, why does it hurt? What is it about me that provokes hostile humor?''

Due to early injury from the father's neglect or hostility, the homosexually oriented man is sensitive to any hint of male rejection. The double message of the practical joke—is this fun or hostility?—stirs up the old theme that began with Dad: "I can't win with him." Then the question arises: "If I stay true to my feelings and defend myself against injustice, will I risk being found unacceptable by men?'' There are deep issues here of belonging and acceptance.

Dan fell silent a moment, as the group watched him. Then he went on, "The reason I bring this up is that—'' very softly, with determination, "*I don't want to be treated like that*. This is all I have to say.''

No one spoke up in the group. Then Steve finally said, "I agree. Nobody wants to be hurt and I apologize. I'm very sorry that you took it that way.'' Then, defensively, "If you asked people about me, you'd find out that I'm a practical jokester. But you said you expected a seat to be saved for you—and I did.'' Then, in an argumentative tone, "I'm glad you expected it, so why didn't you trust I would do it for you?''

"I wasn't sure. I wanted to feel part of your group of friends. I was hoping a seat would be saved.''

Roger then broke in, "All night, you looked like something was bothering you, Dan. Why didn't you say something earlier?''

"When I get hurt, I just shut up," he answered.

"I won't joke with you any more, Dan," Steve said. "It sounds like that's what you're asking of me."

"Let me clarify. Don't joke with me *in that way*." A very serious tone.

"So you dictate how I'm gonna joke around." There was irritation in Steve's voice.

"Well—"

Steve broke in. "So I need to ask permission? Like, 'Dan, can I joke now?' "

Returning to how he felt, Dan asked, "Can't you see how what you did was hurtful?"

"Sure! Absolutely! I've been in that place." Pleading his case, he continued, "But any practical joke can backfire, be misinterpreted."

"If you believe every joke has a hurtful interpretation, then I don't want your brand of humor."

"That's just the nature of a practical joke," Steve insisted. "Playing on someone's weakness but making light of it. It's just—"

Dan interrupted angrily, "Oh, so you're saying that the purpose of a practical joke is to play on a person's weakness. Were you making fun of a weakness you see in me?"

"No, I wouldn't do that," Steve said defensively.

Tom inserted, "Hey, lighten up, Dan."

Dan kept his eyes on Steve. "No. You found it exceptionally funny to play on my weakness."

Steve sighed, looking frustrated. "Part of the joke was to keep quiet for a while, let it sink in. If I had—" then interrupting himself, "See, it took a long time for it to work. If I had laughed right away, it wouldn't have worked." He added, sounding desperate now, "It took an element of time to be funny."

"Yes, and you found that funny? You found that whole experience funny?" Dan looked at him almost with contempt.

Albert spoke up in a soft voice. "He was just kidding, Dan."

"I found it awkward, once I saw it hurt you," Steve said. "But once you said—"

Dan interrupted, "Did you know that it hurt me? Did you see that it hurt me?"

"Not initially. No. Not until you brought it up now." Steve sounded sincere.

"And then, did you still find it funny?"

Steve seemed confused. "That it hurt you? No. Anyway, I apologize."

Dan pressed on, "And then? When you saw it hurt me, did you still find it funny?"

"Then?" Steve was puzzled. "No. It would have been funny if you had laughed. I would have found it funny if you had found it funny."

The other men remained silent, feeling helpless as they witnessed this harassment.

Dan went on unrelentingly. "Oh, so a practical joke is only funny if I laugh."

"That's right," Steve said. "Only when the other guy laughs, is it really funny."

The silence went on.

Steve sounded desperate as he tried one more time to call a truce. "So, you didn't laugh. So flop, it failed. It wasn't funny. I'm sorry."

He waited for a reply. We all waited. Including Dan.

Finally Steve took a deep breath, trying again. "I did not know you had these insecurities. Now I can understand how a joke about a saved seat would stir up those feelings. But I don't want to think I can't have a laugh when I'm with you. But if that's the way it is, I'll respect that."

Pausing a moment, Steve continued, "You know, I've got to admit I'm tempted to back off from you entirely, but I really don't want to do that. Maybe I need to understand your insecurities." He sighed heavily, then looked at Dan directly. "In fact, I'm glad—very glad—you brought this up."

Dan said in a slow, deliberate tone, "But you *knew* what you were doing."

"That I would hurt you?" Steve sounded incredulous. "That I would want to hurt you?"

Dan slowly nodded, "Yes."

"That hurts, if you really believe that," Steve said. "That

I would purposely hurt you. You believe that I would purposely hurt you?" He sighed, "Boy do I have my work cut out with you."

Charlie cut in. "I don't think so." Turning to Dan, "I think you'd better start taking responsibility for your own hurt. You can put some blame on him, and he can apologize—but you have to take some responsibility and not dump it all on Steve."

Dan said softly, "What does that mean?"

Charlie explained, "I mean that you have to trust Steve. You've got to get to know him, what his personality is like. You have to take these things on the shoulder—just brush them off. When Steve said the seat was taken, you could say, 'You knew I wanted to sit with you guys, why did you give the seat away?' Instead, you got quiet and stayed hurt."

"Because it did hurt me," Dan said plaintively.

Charlie's voice was forceful. "Take some responsibility for that hurt and shoot back at him."

"I don't appreciate your coming down on me too, Charlie, I really don't," Dan said softly but firmly.

"Tough!" Charlie answered abruptly.

Dan said, "O.K. I'm just telling you."

"I know you don't like hearing this," Charlie said. "You'd rather just dump it all on Steve."

"Bullshit!" Dan now sounded angry. "I'm not saying I don't want to accept responsibility. I'm saying how it hurt me."

"You're asking all of us to be careful with you," Charlie said.

"Don't make a judgment on me," Dan shot back.

"I'm making an observation."

"Well, I don't like the way you're coming on. Like I'm doing something wrong."

Charlie said calmly, "I know the struggle. I'm just asking you to take more responsibility."

Charlie was getting to the heart of the issue.

"We can't take the responsibility for always being careful about how we behave around you," Charlie told him. "You simply have to let us be ourselves, then decide you're not going to get hurt any more when we are just being ourselves."

Dan said calmly, "Now, I could have heard that if you had said it that way in the beginning."

Charlie replied in a loud voice, "Fine! I'm not perfect, Dan." Then, more gently, "We have to work toward these things. It took us all a long time to get to this point.

"You've got to trust Steve, trust me, trust us, that we are struggling through this and are getting there. You can't just get caught up in your hurt and blame, because then you're pushing yourself away from us."

Everyone sat in silence. Then Dan said, "Well, I don't trust Steve. I just don't."

Charlie said, "Well, that is a serious, serious weakness for you. If you can't trust the men in this room, you can't trust any man."

Dan said quietly, "I trust Steve enough to tell him what I told him."

"I don't think so, or you would have brought it up individually with him," Charlie replied. "You only brought it up because everyone was here. It's safer."

"Uh-huh." Then a long pause from Dan.

"Be a little less uptight, more accepting of the way we are with you. Otherwise you're not gonna contribute very much to us, or get very much for yourself," Charlie said, this time more gently.

"Is that totally my responsibility?" Dan asked.

"The world won't bend to you, Dan," Tom put in. "We may bend somewhat to you, but the other guys out there are not going to. If you can't make it here, you'll never make it out there."

Roger spoke up. "Dan, I do the same thing. If I get too sensitive, I expect the other person to change. That never works. Instead, I've had to change my perception.

"But I've got to tell you, our motivation to change other men comes from our lack of identification with them," Roger continued. "We want to change them because we don't understand men as they are."

Father John now put in a word. "That kind of joke pushes the big red button: HURT AGAIN BY ANOTHER MAN! You would think that, of all places, that wouldn't happen here, between us."

Steve turned to Dan, then said in a sincere tone, "I'm sorry you were hurt. If I do something that hurts you, maybe you could bring it up sooner next time."

This session had opened up an issue fundamental to reparative therapy—namely, the need to work through anger and distrust to develop a sense of acceptance by other men. As each of the men spoke to Dan, reassuring him, they were also solidifying this essential lesson for themselves.

Problems with anger inevitably come up in the course of group therapy. Feeling the anger of another man is particularly hurtful, as it stimulates old narcissistic wounds originally inflicted by the father.

As boys, many of these men were not permitted any expression of hostility; their only defense was to retreat and sulk. When anger was directed toward them, it was experienced as a deep hurt, an emotional devastation of their fragile self-image. Therefore two boyhood lessons were deeply ingrained: (1) I am not entitled to express my anger—it is unworthy of expression, and (2) male anger directed at me equals annihilation.

The long-lasting effects of these two lessons become obvious in a group session when two members are locked in conflict. Expression of anger is as challenging for the one expressing it as for the recipient. The man giving vent to his anger may need this new opportunity to experience his anger as heard and respected. On the other hand, the one on the receiving end may feel assaulted and rejected as a person. He may have great difficulty regaining his self-possession and the trust that the other man will still be there for him in friendship.

Trust in the group process is the essential issue. The men must learn there is an innate sense of fairness in a group that comes together in benevolence. They must learn to trust the ability of the men to reconcile their individual differences. In their hypersensitivity, their vulnerability and defensiveness, they must remember that they are united in a common struggle.

Gradually the client outgrows the old sense of being left out, slighted, and unappreciated. Rather than passively waiting, or manipulating, for attention, he begins to assert himself and reach out to other men. Through reaching out to others and challenging himself, he will gradually outgrow the old assumption that he is hurt and helpless.

I now turned to Roger. "Not so long ago, you were having serious doubts about your commitment to staying in therapy. What happened to those doubts?"

"Now that I understand much better what I've been looking for in men, I feel a lot of the anxiety diminishing," he told me. "At the time I began therapy I was in a crazy state, and I knew I had to get control of myself. My relationships—like the one I had with Perry—were full of crazy stuff, and I was an emotional basket case. Here I was with these painful desires, these longings. They still are there to some degree, but I now have some control over them. Because I see them for what they are, and they're in better perspective. Now I know I can never fulfill them. They're unfulfillable."

"You've got it," Father John said, his tone congratulatory.

Roger smiled, saying, "I'm beginning to understand that such a realization is part of my self-acceptance."

"It *is* self-acceptance," I said. "The rejection of this unwanted homosexual part is paradoxically a self-acceptance."

"What do you mean?" Edward intervened, sounding puzzled.

"By saying no to the homosexuality, you're saying yes to something deeper. Your choice to be here is saying yes to something that is more *who you are* than your homosexuality."

Roger nodded thoughtfully. "I'm beginning to understand something you said about me once—'You know too much to go back, Roger.'"

"You *do* know too much. You can't have it both ways," I reminded him.

As if speaking to himself, Roger said, "This struggle is tough, but I have to remind myself that I'm the one who chose it. I'm doing this for me."

" 'I'm doing this for me,' " I repeated. "That's an empowering statement. It's about personal power, getting control of your life, feeling strong. What happens to you when you say, 'I'm doing this for me'?"

Roger said slowly, "There's a completely different feeling. A feeling of taking charge."

"That's what therapy is all about—experiencing a stronger sense of yourself, taking charge of your life."

I was glad Roger had made up his mind to persevere with therapy. For many months, he had openly doubted its worth. Then he had found a good supportive friendship with Charlie, whom he met once a week at a coffee shop at Venice Beach. Charlie led Roger to examine more closely his fear of male intimacy, and encouraged him to analyze what had gone wrong in his relationship with Perry.

I was pleased with the progress the members made in these sessions. All of the men grew through this dimension of therapy, through sharing their struggles with one another. Group therapy was offering them an opportunity for support and self-comparison and identification that individual sessions, for all their value, could not offer.

10

How Reparative Therapy Works

Frequently I am asked the question "How does reparative therapy work?" Like all forms of treatment rooted in psychoanalysis, reparative therapy proceeds from the assumption that some childhood developmental tasks were not completed. It is understood that when the client was a child, he experienced his parents as failing to assist him through these developmental phases.

One of the best definitions of psychotherapy is "the opportunity to give to ourselves what our parents did not give us." Nevertheless we still need help from others. Reparative therapy requires the active involvement of male therapists, male friends, and male psychotherapy group members.

The basic premise of reparative therapy is that the majority of homosexual clients suffer from a syndrome of male gender-identity deficit. It is this internal sense of incompleteness of one's own maleness that is the essential foundation for homoerotic attraction. The causal rule of reparative therapy is: "gender identity determines sexual orientation." We eroticize what we are not identified with. The focus of treatment therefore is the full development of the client's masculine gender identity.

Reparative therapy works on issues from both the *past* and the *present*. Work on the past involves understanding early relationships with parents. The client often realizes that while his mother may have been very loving, she probably failed to reflect his authentic masculine identity accurately. Mother has often fostered in her son a false identity, namely that of the good little boy, and developed a relationship with him characterized by an unrealistic overintimacy in which mother is confidante, soulmate, or best friend. The client may also have had an overidentification with grandmother, aunts, or older sisters.

While usually the mother has been overinvolved, the father is more often underinvolved and emotionally withholding. Typically, he has failed to recognize the boy both as an autonomous individual and a masculine child. Emotionally unable to reach out to the son to get the relationship on its proper course, the father was either unaware of what was happening in the relationship or incapable of doing anything to rectify it. He was most likely what I call *the acquiescent father*. Emotional neglect by the father is a particularly painful memory to be dealt with in treatment.

Other work on the past includes understanding hurtful childhood relationships with male peers, and often a hurtful relationship with a domineering older brother. Any early homosexual experiences with peers or older men need examination and interpretation. It is not unusual to uncover a history of victimization through sexual molestation in the client's childhood.

Work on the present includes understanding how the client has given up his sense of intrinsic power. Intrinsic power is one's view of self as separate and independent. Failure fully to claim one's gender identity always results in a loss of intrinsic power. This is how one client put it:

"As a kid, I didn't go out and ask for what I wanted . . . I expected others to know what I wanted, so I just waited."

"And if you didn't get it?" I asked.

"I've held secrets all my life. I kept my power secret."

"What power?"

"My power of getting what I wanted indirectly . . . you know, manipulatively."

Central to reparative therapy is the client's understanding of how his masculine deficit becomes projected onto idealized males—"The other man has something I lack, therefore I need to be close to him [sexually]."

Reparative therapy is initiatory in nature. It requires not just a passive musing over insights into the self, but an active initiation of new behaviors. The client must struggle to break down old patterns of avoidance and defensive detachment from males in order to form close, intimate, *non*sexual male friendships.

Therapy challenges the client to master gender-related tasks missed in early boyhood. His developmental path requires mastering of these tasks during adulthood. He is called upon to catch up, to conquer what the heterosexual man achieved years before. Thus he may eventually arrive at a heterosexual place, but from a different direction.

Many early feelings toward the father and other significant male figures will be transferred onto the male therapist. Therapy will offer a valuable opportunity to work through these reactions. Feelings for the male therapist may include anticipation of rejection and criticism, a tendency toward dependency—including hostile dependency—and also sexual feelings and anger.

Like all psychotherapies, reparative therapy creates a *meaning transformation*. This meaning transformation is the result of the client's gains in insight. When he comes to see the true needs that lie behind his unwanted behavior, he gains a new understanding of this behavior. His unwanted romantic attractions are demystified. He begins to perceive them as expressions of legitimate love needs—needs for attention, affection, and approval from men—which were unmet in childhood. He learns that such needs indeed *can* be satisfied, but not erotically.

When this is understood, there is a meaning transformation—"I do not really want to have sex with a man. Rather, what I really desire is to heal my masculinity." This healing will occur when the legitimate love needs of male attention, affection, and approval are satisfied.

Meaning transformation includes not just intellectual understanding (insight), but also the experience of *doing* new behaviors. Embodied experience—that is, the experience of the body *being* in the world in a new way—transforms personal identity. Transformation in personal identity occurs through repeatedly feeling different about oneself in relationship to others. In the case of gender deficit and homosexuality, increased ownership of one's maleness diminishes erotic attraction toward other men. The gradual internalization of the sense of masculinity distances previously distressing temptations.

In recent years, Gay Affirmative Therapy (GAT) has emerged to help homosexuals accept and affirm their sexual orientation. GAT presumes that dissatisfied homosexuals would be satisfied if they could only be free of the internalized prejudices of society. GAT sees reparative therapy as playing on a man's self-deception, guilt, and low self-esteem. It makes the arbitrary assumption that coming out is the answer to every homosexual client's problems.

Reparative therapy, on the other hand, sees homosexuality as a developmental deficit. According to reparative theory, Gay Affirmative Therapy is expecting the client to identify with his pathology and call this "health."

William Aaron (1972), in his biographical book *Straight*, says: "To persuade someone that he will make a workable adjustment to society and himself by lowering his sights and settling for something that he inwardly despises [homosexuality] is not the answer" (p. 26).

GAT presumes that homosexuality is a natural and healthy sexual variation. It then proceeds to attribute every personal and interpersonal problem of the gay man to societal or internalized homophobia. Its theoretical model frames the life experiences of the client in the context of victimization, inevitably setting him against conventional society.

One cannot help but wonder how GAT would explain the obvious benefits of reparative therapy—increased self-esteem and a diminishing of distress, anxiety, and depression. Better relationships with others and freedom from distressing distractions are typically reported by men in reparative therapy.

Interestingly, GAT and reparative therapy agree on what the homosexual man needs and desires: to give himself permission to love other men. But GAT works within the gay ideology of eroticization of these relationships, while reparative therapy sees sex between men as sabotaging the mutuality necessary for growth toward maturity. Reparative therapy frees the homosexual man to love other men not as sex partners, but as equals and as brothers.

Group therapy poses a special challenge to each man. The group must decide who will speak, for how long, about what, and for what purpose. Each man must decide for himself how he will use the group's assistance. Every member is expected to take responsibility for speaking up and making a place for himself in the flow of verbal expression.

Group therapy challenges the men to give up the old habit of passive listening. This is a removed, self-centered way of hearing, which stimulates private associations rather than an active response to the speaker. The habit of passive listening—a consequence of defensive detachment—perpetuates emotional isolationism.

Active listening, in contrast, means forgetting oneself in order to maintain a felt connection with the speaker. The active listener feels an internal response to what the other says. He can then choose to express his response in the form of questions, comments, or advice.

Group therapy offers the men the opportunity to relate to other males—a lesson never completely learned in boyhood. As one new client told me, "As a kid, I didn't know how to be a friend. If I liked a boy, I'd come on too strong, too intense, too possessive. Today, if I meet a potential friend, I still end up doing the same thing. I start with 'Let's go to dinner, let's go to a movie, [laughs] what are you doing for breakfast?' "

Most clients have never spoken openly about their sexuality with other men who share the struggle. This is a frightening but exciting new adventure, and every client is cautious, even fearful, at his first group meeting. Perhaps he even fantasizes meeting an attractive man with whom he might develop a particularly close, even sexual relationship.

Although the first group sessions are characterized by an intense curiosity about one another, there is also great anxiety about disclosing personal issues. These men are not proud of their sexual orientation, and there is some sense of shame they must face. There is the thought, "God forbid I should meet someone I know!" But eventually, these concerns recede to the background as friendships begin to form.

Once a part of the group, each man discovers that this is a place to feel accepted and understood. The group is a place where men share common problems, hard-won insights, and inspiration.

As one man explained, "For me, the group has been like putting on a pair of glasses when you're nearsighted. Before, I could only see vague images and patterns."

Another client said, "I figured out that I suffered this male deficit before I came here. I came because I knew I needed help in figuring out what to do about it. The reason I never made much progress before was that I was working in a vacuum; I was all alone, not talking to anybody."

Communication in our weekly group discussions proceeds on three levels: Without, Within, and Between.

Level One, "Without," is typical of the first part of each group session. Both in individual and group therapy, it serves as safe warm-up talk. Typically, it involves conversation about what has happened during the week, and is a reporting of external events with no consideration of interior motivations.

Level Two, "Within," occurs when two or more people begin to investigate and clarify a member's motivations behind the events he reports. There is a shared attempt to understand how he participated in causing the events to happen.

Level Three, "Between," is the most therapeutic level. It is the most personally challenging and risky, but offers the greatest opportunity for building trust. It occurs when at least two members of the group talk about their relationship with each other while it is happening. Timing is central to this third level and members must speak in the present. When expressing both their positive and negative feelings for each other at the moment, they describe what they are experiencing.

Considerable time may be required to break through to Level Three of direct dialogue. Group members may be easily hurt at this level and there is much approach–avoidance and fault finding. When a member feels hurt, he often makes veiled references to his doubts about whether the group is really of benefit to him. He may threaten not to return the next week. But for all groups, Level Three is the most rewarding. It affords the opportunity to experience mutuality, with its balance of challenge ("kick in the pants") and support ("pat on the back.")

In the first few sessions of a newly forming group, there is an initial phase of blemish-finding. There is resistance to identifying with the group, as complaints fly. "They're not my type": "they're too old" or "too young," "too promiscuous" or "too inexperienced," "too religious" or "not religious enough." This blemish-finding is a symptom of defensive detachment, perpetuating what Brad Sargent (1990) calls *terminal uniqueness*—in other words, the idea that "my specialness makes it impossible for other men to understand me." This fantasy keeps each man emotionally isolated as he is locked into the frustrating pattern of creating two kinds of men from all significant male relationships. He either devaluates, minimizes, dismisses, and delegates other men to an inferior position, or he elevates, admires, and places them on a pedestal.

Where one man places other men on this scale is determined by *type*, the symbolic representation of valued masculine attributes he unconsciously feels he lacks, and which the other man supposedly possesses. These qualities usually have little to do with the character of the person. Once a realistic familiarity develops, the person eventually loses his erotic appeal.

In our group process we frequently return to the distinction made between two kinds of males by our clients: ordinary and mysterious. Mysterious men are those who possess enigmatic masculine qualities that both perplex and allure the client. Such men are overvalued and even idealized, for they are the embodiment of qualities the client wishes he had attained.

This emotionally crippling pattern of scaled importance is always reenacted in the group process. Obsession with type is the source of much of the anger and disappointment in homosexual relationships and accounts for much of the gay relationship's volatility and instability.

Besides devaluing or overvaluing other men, there is a third possible mode of response: mutuality. This is the one toward which we strive. A relationship characterized by mutuality has the qualities of honesty, disclosure, and equality. Even where there is an imbalance of age, status, or life experience, deep sharing with another man serves as an equalizer. Mutuality in relationships is the goal of group psychotherapy, for it is on this level of human interaction that healing occurs. Mutuality creates the opening through which passes masculine identification. It is the passage through which each man enters into healing.

One group member said, "If I came to therapy with the thought that I just had to abstain from sex without any positive new direction toward intimacy with other men, I don't think I would be hopeful for real change. Now I have accepted my need for real intimacy, not the sexual expression of it."

Another group member described his experience this way: "My group is the masculine energy I need every day. It has been a powerful, intense, and enriching experience. Our group has become the father we all need and missed in our early years. There is a power, a presence among us that keeps us giving, healing, and caring."

All treatment must overcome some form of resistance against growth. We may say very simply that the treatment of homosexuality is the undoing of the resistance of defensive detachment from males. Group therapy is a powerful opportunity to work through this detachment, which is a refusal to identify with masculinity.

At times it seems as if all our group members are negatively charged magnets repelling each other. While there is a sensitivity and genuine concern for each other, there is also a guardedness and criticalness, which can paralyze the entire group process.

Defensive detachment was described earlier as the blocking process that prevents male bonding and identification. Originally a protection against childhood hurt from males, in adulthood it is a barrier to honest intimacy and mutuality with men. The homosexual is torn between two competing drives: the natural need to satisfy his affectional needs with men, and his defensive detachment, which perpetuates fear and anger in male relationships.

Manifestations of defensive detachment in group appear as hostility, competitiveness, distrust, and anxiety about acceptance. Group members are highly sensitive to issues of betrayal and deception. We see fearfulness, vulnerability, and defensiveness, as well as fragility of relationships and slow and tentative trust easily shattered by the slightest misunderstanding.

On the other hand, there is a resistance to developing friendships with familiar, nonmysterious males—those who do not possess these qualities. Ordinary men are devalued, sometimes contemptuously dismissed. One client described his perception of men as follows: "Unless I was attracted to a particular guy, I perceived men as these insensitive, Neanderthal types, these monolithic macho things I couldn't relate to, and had contempt for." As a result of this sort of misperception, most clients have had few or no male relationships characterized by mutuality. By placing other men in one of these two categories, a client justifies his detachment. He either feels too inferior or too superior to establish the mutuality necessary for friendship.

This resistance to friendships with nonmysterious males is one reason why, after an initial interest and excitement about meeting other group members, a client's feelings often turn to disillusionment. He sees the other members in the group as "just as weak as I am," and becomes contemptuous of them. He may be particularly disgusted by the "weaker" group members, those who are more effeminate, more emotional, and who display personality traits of vulnerability. It is important that this resistance be dealt with in individual therapy.

The essential therapeutic experience is the demystification of men from sex object to real person (eros to agape). Sorting out his experience of these two distinct perceptions, one 28-year-old client said: "Immediately after every homosexual experience, it feels like something is missing. The closeness I wanted with another man just didn't happen. I'm left with the feeling that sex is just not what I wanted. This is in contrast to my relationship with my straight friend, Bob. I don't feel the need to be sexual with him.

"To be so close to him, getting everything I want from our friendship, but not even thinking about sex—when I allow myself to be really *in* those friendships, that's very empowering."

When group members meet socially, there is always the possibility that they will fall into a sexual relationship. On rare occasions, there has been such a fall. Sexual contact unavoidably damages the friendship, but although it can destroy it completely, it can also furnish the opportunity for further growth through deeper honesty. The implications of such a fall are great, both for the individuals involved and for the group as a whole. Therefore I challenge the men involved to engage in self-reflection and dialogue.

"After the fall," the men are asked to speak to each other in response to the following questions:

1. When did the possibility of a sexual experience first occur to me?
2. What things did I do to set you up for the situation?
3. What emotional effect did this sexual incident have on both of us? Did I violate your personal boundary?
4. Do I feel any anger toward you?
5. Was I manipulative? Was I selfish? Did I put my needs before yours?
6. What were the authentic emotional needs I wanted gratified by you? Comfort, attention, security, affection, power, sexual release?
7. Did I get what I wanted? If not, what did I get instead? Did we impede our progress?

8. How has sexual behavior changed the quality of our relationship?

I also ask them questions regarding the future:

1. What authentic emotional needs do I have in relation to you now?
2. What do you want from *me* now?
3. How can I facilitate your development?
4. What lessons about male friendship do you want to learn from me?
5. What kinds of experiences do you still need from our friendship?
6. Do I need to ask your forgiveness?
7. Now, how are we to be for each other?

If these questions are answered in all honesty, however painful, then these two men will find new, nonerotic ways of helping themselves and each other.

The perennial gay fantasy is that sex is possible within a male friendship. But the group becomes aware of one inescapable fact—that a sexual encounter between two men permanently alters the quality of their relationship. Those engaged in a sexual encounter may deny that anything destructive happened. Or, they may admit that "something" did happen, but insist that it is of no consequence. But we must bring into focus the fact that sex is never a part of healthy male friendships.

Over the months, the group addresses many issues. Many of these are related to self-assertion. Often the men report a tendency to "lose" or compromise themselves for male approval. There is a sense of victimization, and anger at what they had to do to gain the other's acceptance. The men see how quickly they can get caught up in hostile dependencies.

Psychotherapy is a process that allows us to grow toward wholeness. I tell the group that although supposedly the subject matter is homosexuality, the underlying process, in fact, is really the universal one of initiation, growth, and change.

The men realize that every one is challenged to move forward into fullest adulthood, and each one—heterosexual and homosexual, client and therapist—has his own personal obstacles to overcome, based on past failures in emotional development. The distinctly human abilities to self-reflect and choose positive change are true miracles of human nature.

I am often asked the question, can a homosexual ever really become heterosexual?

Discussing his own healing, Alan Medinger (1992), a prominent leader in the ex-gay movement, described the following concern: "Years after I had left behind virtually all homosexual attractions, and years after a blessed and pleasurable sexual relationship in my marriage, one factor continued to disturb me. If an attractive man and an attractive woman enter a room, it is the man I will look at first" (pp. 1–2).

Indeed, critics of reparative therapy believe fantasy determines a man's sexual orientation. Yet if a straight man has a homosexual fantasy, does that make him homosexual? If someone has a fantasy of stealing something, does that make him a thief?

We might find an answer to this question of healing in Dr. Salman Akhtar's book, *Broken Structures*, where he tells "The Parable of Two Flower Vases."

Dr. Akhtar describes teaching a course on character pathology to a class of clinical psychology interns. Asked by one student if a severely disturbed client could ever be so completely healed by psychotherapy that he would be indistinguishable from a person who had always been well-adjusted, he replied:

> I thought for a moment. Then, prompted by an inner voice, I spontaneously came up with the following answer. "Well, let us suppose that there are two flower vases made of fine china. Both are intricately carved and of comparable value, elegance, and beauty. Then a wind blows and one of them falls from its stand, and is broken into pieces. An expert from a distant land is called. Painstakingly, step by step, the expert

glues the pieces back together. Soon the broken vase is intact again, can hold water without leaking, is unblemished to all who see it. Yet this vase is now different from the other one. The lines along which it had broken, a subtle reminder of yesterday, will always remain discernible to an experienced eye. However, it will have a certain wisdom since it knows something that the vase that has never been broken does not: it knows what it is to break and what it is to come together." [p. 375]

In my final meeting with the great researcher Dr. Irving Bieber, a few months before his death at 82, I asked him, "Did the homosexual clients you treated *really* change internally, or simply gain control of their behavior?"

Quickly, assuredly, he answered, "Of course! Many of my patients became completely heterosexual."

I continued, "But there often seem to be some remaining homoerotic thoughts and feelings."

With the same instant certainty he said, "Sure there are. There may always be some," and he shrugged.

Wishing not to argue with an old sage, I kept quiet but afterward thought, how could Irving Bieber so confidently describe an obvious contradiction?

Akhtar's metaphor offers an answer: the broken vase is now intact, can hold water without leaking, and is beautiful to all who see it. Only the very fine lines along which it had been broken remain a subtle reminder of the trauma of yesterday.

Straight men, vases formed of smooth clay, do not know the trauma of falling and breaking, nor the wisdom of what it is to come together. For many homosexual men, reparative therapy is a way of coming together.

References

Aaron, W. (1972). *Straight*. New York: Bantam.

Akhtar, S. (1992). *Broken Structures*. Northvale, NJ: Jason Aronson.

Bieber, I., Dain, H., Dince, P., et al. (1993). *Homosexuality: A Psychoanalytic Study of Male Homosexuals*. New York: Basic Books.

Castaneda, C. (1968). *The Teachings of Don Juan: A Yaqui Way of Knowledge*. New York: Ballantine Books.

Jacobi, J. (1969). A case of homosexuality. *Journal of Analytic Psychology* 14:48–64.

Medinger, A. (1992). Stimulation and healing. *Regeneration News*, February.

Miller, A. (1987). *The Drama of Being a Child*. London: Virago Press.

Nunberg, H. (1938). Homosexuality, magic and aggression. *International Journal of Psycho-Analysis* 14:1–16.

Sargent, B. (1990). Speech at Exodus International Conference, San Antonio, TX, July 8–14.

Index

Aardweg, G. van den, 97
Aaron, W., 214
Active listening, 215
Adolescence (*See* Edward)
Aesthetic Realism, 159
Affection, 4, 27, 99, 117
Akhtar, S., 222
Albert, 1–21 (*See also*
    Reparative group
    therapy)
  alienation from body, 2
  detached defensiveness, 19
  false self/false identity, 7, 21
  gender identity phase, 12
  pee shyness, 5
  reparative drive, 4
Alienation from body, 2, 81
Anger, in reparative group
    therapy, 201–208

Approval, 4, 27, 99, 117
Attention, 4, 27, 99, 117, 171

Betrayal/disappointment, in
    childhood, 28
Bieber, I., 80, 95, 223
Bisexuality, 36
Boredom, 32, 39
Bowlby, J., 19

Castaneda, C., 166
Charlie, 65–87 (*See also*
    Reparative group
    therapy)
  alienation from body,
    81–82
  gender identity deficit,
    66–69

Charlie (*continued*)
  reparative drive, 69
  self-disparagement, 73
Codependency, 199
  and loneliness, 165
Cook, C., 61, 74, 194

Dan, 89–103 (*See also*
    Reparative group
    therapy)
  defensive detachment,
    90–91
  false self/false identity, 96,
    97
  identification needs,
    99–100
Defensive detachment, 19,
    55, 134, 217
  anger as form of, 90–91
  in reparative group
    therapy, 218–219

Edward, 119–143 (*See also*
    Reparative group
    therapy)
  friendships, 131–132
  theatrical interest as
    defense, 122

False self/false identity, 7, 21,
    28, 80, 82, 193
  foundation for, 96
Fathers, 14, 48–49, 56–57,
    78–80, 119–120, 130,
    195–196 (*See also*
    specific cases)
  acceptance and, 102
  anger and, 102
  emotional unavailability of,
    142–143

forgiveness and, 103
  male rejection and, 202
  punitive, 95
  reality principle and, 12
  transference and, 174
Father–son therapy sessions,
    136 (*See also* Edward)
Fellatio, 78, 108
Fetishism, 112–116
Friendships, 131–132
  in reparative therapy, 198

Gay Affirmative Therapy
    (GAT), 214–215
Gender identity deficit(s),
    19–20, 26, 52, 53,
    66–69
  interpersonal boundary
    problems and, 100
  reparative therapy and,
    211–212
Gender identity phase, 12,
    129
Gendlin, E., 190
Gershman, H., 32
Group therapy (*See*
    Reparative group
    therapy)

Homosexuality, innate vs.
    developmental
    controversy, 32, 70–72,
    78, 86–87, 103,
    214–215
Horner, A., 18

Intrinsic power, 18
  deficit in, 170
  reparative therapy and,
    212–213

Jacobi, J., 78
John, Father, 45–64 (*See also*
     Reparative group
     therapy)
  pee shyness, 61
  penis preoccupation,
     47–48
  pornography, 45–46
  sadomasochism, 58–59
Jung, C., 78

Listening
  active, 215
  passive, 215
Loneliness/codependency
     bind, 165

Male friendships (*See*
     Nonsexual male
     relationships)
Married men, homosexuality
     and (*See* Tom)
Masturbation, 5–6
  unifying function of, 154
Meaning transformation,
     reparative therapy and,
     213–214
Medinger, A., 222
Miller, A., 78
Moberly, E., 19
Mothers, 7, 14, 78–80, 119
     (*See also* specific cases)
Mutuality, in reparative
     therapy, 198–201, 218

Narcissism, 106–107
Narcissistic mirroring, 160
Nonsexual male relationships
  fear of, 168–169

therapeutic aspects of, 19,
     27, 42, 55, 100,
     103–104, 108–109,
     148, 172, 215
Nunberg, H., 152

Overdramatization, 97

Passive listening, 215
Payne, L., 74
Pee shyness, 5, 61, 81
Penis
  alienation from, 81
  masturbation and, 6
  preoccupation with, 47–48
Pornography, 45–46
  sadomasochism and, 58–60
Promiscuity, 19, 171
Psychotherapy, contrast with
     reparative therapy,
     71–72, 194–195, 198

Relational immaturity, 30
Reparative drive, 4, 27, 69
Reparative group therapy,
     177–209 (*See also*
     specific cases)
  sexual relationships in,
     220–221
Reparative therapy, 4, 27,
     50–51
  anger in, 201–207
  basic premise of, 211
  challenges of, 75–76, 170,
     215–216
  change vs. cure in, 173
  criticism of, 25, 32, 50
  fear in, 168–169
  GAT and, 214–215

Reparative therapy
    (*continued*)
  group therapy and,
    177–223
  initiatory nature of, 170,
    213
  levels of communication
    in, 216–217
  loss of illusion in, 151
  masculine deficit and,
    212–213
  meaning transformation
    and, 213–214
  motivation for, 28
  mutuality in, 198–201, 218
  past and present in,
    212–213
  psychotherapy contrasted
    with, 71–72, 194–195,
    198
  self-mentor talk in, 83
  therapist's role in,
    174–175
  transference in, 174
Resistance, in reparative
    group therapy, 218–219
Responsibility, flight from,
    30, 35
Roger, 145–175 (*See also*
    Reparative group
    therapy)
  approach to women,
    162–164
  codependency, 146
  false self, 158–159
  loss of illusion, 151
  narcissistic mirroring, 160
  paradox of homosexual
    relationships, 152–153

Sadomasochism, 58–59, 101,
    186–187
Same-sex ambivalence, 12,
    19, 100
Sargent, B., 217
Self-mentor talk, 83
Siegel, E., 159
Society
  homosexual relationships
    and, 28–29, 32
Steve, 105–118 (*See also*
    Reparative group
    therapy)
  fetishism, 112–116
  narcissism, 106
Sullivan, H. S., 158

Terminal uniqueness, 217
Three A's, 4, 27, 99, 117
Tom, 23–44 (*See also*
    Reparative group
    therapy)
  childhood betrayal, 28
  flight from responsibility,
    30, 35
  motivation for reparative
    therapy, 28
  need for Three A's, 27
  relational immaturity, 30
Transference, in reparative
    therapy, 51, 174
Triadic relationship, 80
Twinning, 160
Type, obsession with,
    217–218

Women, homosexually-
    oriented approach to,
    20, 162–164